Wittgenstein

Key Concepts

Key Concepts

Published

Theodor Adorno: Key Concepts
Edited by Deborah Cook

Pierre Bourdieu: Key Concepts
Edited by Michael Grenfell

Gilles Deleuze: Key Concepts
Edited by Charles J. Stivale

Martin Heidegger: Key Concepts
Edited by Bret W. Davis

Merleau-Ponty: Key Concepts
Edited by Rosalyn Diprose and
Jack Reynolds

Wittgenstein: Key Concepts
Edited by Kelly Dean Jolley

Forthcoming

Alain Badiou: Key Concepts
Edited by A. J. Bartlett and
Justin Clemens

Michel Foucault: Key Concepts
Edited by Dianna Taylor

Jürgen Habermas: Key Concepts
Edited by Barbara Fultner

Immanuel Kant: Key Concepts
Edited by Will Dudley and
Kristina Engelhard

Jacques Rancière: Key Concepts
Edited by Jean-Philippe Deranty

Wittgenstein

Key Concepts

Edited by Kelly Dean Jolley

ACUMEN

First published in 2010 by Acumen

Acumen Publishing Limited
4 Saddler Street
Durham
DH1 3NP
www.acumenpublishing.co.uk

ISBN: 978-1-84465-188-7 (hardcover)
ISBN: 978-1-84465-189-4 (paperback)

British Library Cataloguing-in-Publication Data
A catalogue record for this book is available
from the British Library.

Designed and typeset in Classical Garamond and Myriad.
Printed and bound in the UK by MPG Books Group.

Contents

Contributors

Avner Baz is Associate Professor of Philosophy at Tufts University, Medford, MA.

David H. Finkelstein is Associate Professor of Philosophy at the University of Chicago.

Craig Fox is Assistant Professor of Philosophy at California University of Pennsylvania.

Heather Gert is Associate Professor of Philosophy at the University of North Carolina at Greensboro.

Arata Hamawaki is Assistant Professor of Philosophy at Auburn University, AL.

Lars Hertzberg is Professor Emeritus of Philosophy at Åbo Akademi University, Turku, Finland.

Phil Hutchinson is Senior Lecturer in Philosophy at Manchester Metropolitan University, UK.

Kelly Dean Jolley is Professor of Philosophy at Auburn University, AL.

Roderick T. Long is Professor of Philosophy at Auburn University, AL.

Eric Loomis is Associate Professor of Philosophy at the University of South Alabama, Mobile, AL.

Rupert Read is Reader in Philosophy at the University of East Anglia, Norwich, UK.

Avrum Stroll is Research Professor of Philosophy at the University of California, San Diego.

Abbreviations

BB	*The Blue and Brown Books* (1958a; 1960; 1965)
BT	*The Big Typescript* (2005)
CV	*Culture and Value* (1980d)
LC	*Lectures and Conversations on Aesthetics, Psychology and Religious Belief* (1966; 1970)
L: C 1930–32	*Wittgenstein's Lectures, Cambridge, 1930–32* (1989)
L: C 1932–35	*Wittgenstein's Lectures: Cambridge, 1932–1935* (1980e; 2001b)
LWPP I	*Last Writings on the Philosophy of Psychology, Volume I* (1982)
LWPP II	*Last Writings on the Philosophy of Psychology, Volume II* (1992)
OC	*On Certainty* (1969)
PG	*Philosophical Grammar* (1978a)
PI	*Philosophical Investigations* (1953; 1958b; 2001a)
PO	*Philosophical Occasions* (1958c; 1993)
PR	*Philosophical Remarks* (1980a)
RFM	*Remarks on the Foundations of Mathematics* (1978b)
RPP I	*Remarks on the Philosophy of Psychology, Volume I* (1980b)
RPP II	*Remarks on the Philosophy of Psychology, Volume II* (1980c)
TLP	*Tractatus Logico-Philosophicus* ([1921] 1974)
Z	*Zettel* (1967; 1988)

Introduction

Kelly Dean Jolley

Biographical sketch

Ludwig Wittgenstein was born in 1889 to a wealthy and cultured Viennese family. He decided to study aeronautical engineering, and so went to Manchester University (England) in 1908. There, he became deeply interested in the philosophy of mathematics, and eventually in the works of Gottlob Frege. He met Frege, who advised him to go to Cambridge to study with Bertrand Russell. He did so in 1911. Wittgenstein studied in Cambridge from 1911 to 1913. When the First World War began, he joined the Austrian army, fought, and was taken captive in 1917. The war ended while he was interned. During the war years he drafted the *Tractatus Logico-Philosophicus*, and after the war the book was published in German and translated into English.

Around 1920, believing that he had in the *Tractatus* solved the problems of philosophy, he tried a variety of jobs – gardener, teacher and architect. Finally, in 1929, he found himself again entangled in philosophical problems and he returned to Cambridge to work as a philosopher. Wittgenstein was dissatisfied in various ways with the *Tractatus*; the problems he had treated in it he was again puzzling over. For several years in Cambridge he worked feverishly to find new and better ways of thinking through those problems. He conducted famous and darkling seminars in which he worked out many of the ideas that would compose the *Philosophical Investigations*. He worked on that book for roughly twenty years, drafting and redrafting the remarks in it, as well as organizing and reorganizing them. He prepared to publish the book in 1945, but then withdrew the manuscript. The book was published posthumously in 1953. During his final years, Wittgenstein continued working in new ways on the problems that had gripped him from early in his career. He travelled to the United States and to Ireland, but returned to Cambridge, where he died of cancer in 1951.

The *Tractatus* (and the Continuity Thesis)

Most, but not all, of the contributors to this volume would agree to a version of the Continuity Thesis,[1] meaning that most, but not all, would accept the claim that Wittgenstein's late philosophical work continues his early philosophical work. Most of the contributors have their own stories to tell about the degree of the continuity and about its specific details. But most would dismiss the view that Wittgenstein performed a particularly violent volte-face between the early and later work, that he produced two different philosophies, and especially the view that he produced two radically different philosophies, each the antithesis of the other.

As mentioned above, Wittgenstein's two major works are his *Tractatus Logico-Philosophicus* and his *Philosophical Investigations*.[2] For many years, the accepted view about these books was that the second was written (in part) to contest the first. Wittgenstein was regarded as having produced not just two different books, but two different philosophies. Regarded in this light, he was sawn in two: he became the *early* Wittgenstein and the *late* Wittgenstein. The early Wittgenstein was some kind of positivist or at any rate largely responsible for positivism; the late Wittgenstein was some kind of ordinary-language philosopher or at any rate largely responsible for ordinary-language philosophy. Positivism was anathema to ordinary-language philosophy, and vice versa.

Let me say more about how the *Tractatus* was read. (I shall call this the Discontinuity Reading.) As I said, Wittgenstein's *Tractatus* was commonly seen as positivist or as ushering in positivism. On this reading, Wittgenstein's overarching concern was to erect a theory of sense, a set of considerations that would suffice to determine whether a particular form of words said something (whether true or false) or said nothing at all (nonsense). The celebrated central column of the erected theory of sense is the Picture Theory. According to the Picture Theory, a sentence makes sense when it pictures (i.e. does what pictures do in picturing), and is true if what it pictures obtains. If not, not. This theory of sense was supposed to enable readers of the *Tractatus* to divvy up putative sentences into the well formed, the sheep, and the ill formed, the goats.

The ill-formed goats turned out not to be sentences at all, despite being sentence-like. When their logical grammar was exposed, it became clear that the parts of the putative sentence failed to hang together in a way that was properly pictorial.

The putative sentences that turned out often, if not always, to be ill-formed goats were the putative sentences of philosophy. These sentences failed, when the theory was applied to them, to be properly pictorial. They tried grandly to picture picturing itself, instead of humbly picturing something other than picturing, the way the well-formed sheepish sentences of the natural sciences did.

Still, the ill-formed putative sentences of philosophy were not to be easily discarded. Given the theory of sense that was supposed to be developed in the *Tractatus*, it turned out that those ill-formed sentences of philosophy showed something even while they said nothing.

How could that be? The answer is that the theory crucially constructed a distinction between what can be said and what can be shown. Typically, that distinction was taken to stretch across both well-formed genuine sentences and ill-formed putative sentences. And, typically, that distinction was taken to be truly interesting only when considering ill-formed putative sentences. Well-formed sentences both said and showed; but ill-formed ones showed without saying. Showing without saying came to seem the truly interesting kind of showing – a pure kind of showing unsullied by saying. Ill-formed putative sentences that showed but did not say managed, in what they showed, to "say" something that cannot be said (at least not by any well-formed sentence that both shows and says). Although the ill-formed putative sentences said nothing about picturing, they "said" something about picturing. In their failure to say, they showed, as it were *disclosed*, the logical superstructure of saying. What they showed was taken to be saying-like but unsayable. That is why the best that could be done was to "say" it. So some of the nonsense (as rated by the theory) turned out to reveal super sense, the very superstructure of sense. If the philosopher was properly taught by the *Tractatus*, his/her job turned out to be deliberately producing, or at any rate noticing and learning from, revelatory nonsense, ill-formed but showy "sentences". It looked as if the *Tractatus* not so much shut metaphysicians down as shut them up. But, shut up, they could still do metaphysics, or something very much like it, by an unsaying but still knowing ostension – where "sentences" performed the job of "pointing", where "sentences" constituted the body of the theory "about" sentences.

Thus the early Wittgenstein. The late Wittgenstein was taken to have turned against the theory, indeed against all theories, of sense.

His earlier work he treated as paradigmatic of the confusions that his later work combated. His later work is to replace (in some complicated way) the earlier notion of meaning with the notion of *use*. Instead of teaching his readers to care about theories of sense along with the positivists, as he did in the *Tractatus*, in *Philosophical Investigations* he teaches his readers to care about use along with the ordinary-language philosophers.

But there is another way of reading the *Tractatus*, as I have already suggested, one that sees continuity rather than discontinuity. On this alternative reading (the Continuity Reading), the central problematic of the book is not the construction of a theory of sense, and in particular of the Picture Theory. Rather, the central problematic is our hunger for a theory of sense, and our willingness to swallow the Picture Theory. On this reading, crucially, the distinction between sense and nonsense is prior to the theory, not constructed in constructing the theory. In fact, the distinction between sense and nonsense is meant to be a distinction of colloquial language, the distinction we might draw when faced with Carroll's "Jabberwocky" and some stretch of newsprint, but still innocent of the *Tractatus*. This distinction does not theorize either sense or nonsense – in particular, it does not treat nonsense as showing while failing to say.

So, on this reading, Wittgenstein's interest is not in "sentences" that show but fail to say, but rather his interest is in our interest in such "sentences", in our desire to see something in such "sentences" instead of merely disregarding them as gobbledygook. We desire to see something in such "sentences" because we want to be able to construct a theory of sense, because we want something like the Picture Theory. Wittgenstein's apparent attempts to satisfy our desires are not finally to be taken as having that aim. He instead constructs the theory so as to get us to see that we cannot finally make any sense of the theory. We are supposed to learn, not something about sense, but about our desire to be able to transcend the sense we make, to see the sense we make from above, from the coign of vantage enjoyed by a Recording Angel. What we should learn is not that we desire something we cannot have, but that we finally cannot make any sense of our putative desire – it, too, is gobbledygook. We take ourselves to desire to make sense of the sense we make, but where that making sense differs from the sense we make (we do not want just more of *that*). Thus making sense has to be, so to speak, other than the sense we make. But the only sense we can make of any making sense is to see it as like the sense we make. (As Wittgenstein puts the point in *Philosophical Investigations*, "[O]ne feature of our concept of a proposition is, *sounding like a proposition*" (§134) – or, I might add, *looking like a proposition*.) So we seem to desire a making sense that both (somehow) differs from and is (somehow) like the sense we make.[3] Our putative desire is not (yet) coherent.

Let me now provide a bit more detail. On the first reading, the Discontinuity Reading, the sense/nonsense distinction is constructed in the constructing of the Picture Theory. Internal to the constructed distinction is the distinction between saying and showing. Some sentences say and show, some "sentences" show but do not say, and some do neither. The philosophically interesting "sentences" are those that show but do not say. On the second reading, the Continuity Reading, the sense/ nonsense distinction is prior to the construction of the Picture Theory. When we consider what we can say of those sentences that we have untheoretically categorized as sense, we shall see that we can say of them that they both say and show: what this means is that the sentences are not only sense, but that they are symbolizable sense – we can represent them in a symbolic language. Those "sentences" that we categorize as nonsense neither say nor show: they are unsymbolizable goobledygook. And, on the Continuity Reading, there are no sentences that show but do not say. Our desire to find such sentences is itself a function of our ambitions for the Picture Theory, our ambition to discover a limit to thought (as Wittgenstein puts it in the "Preface"). The fact that the theory falls apart is meant to teach us something deep – not about the theory, but about ourselves and our theoretical ambitions. In other words, on the Continuity Reading, we can regard the saying/showing distinction as a way of highlighting features of our commitments when we commit ourselves to a sentence's making sense. The distinction cannot aid us in making the distinction between sense and nonsense, since the deployment of such a distinction is prior to the deployment of the saying/showing distinction.

As should now be reasonably clear, on the Continuity Reading, Wittgenstein's aim both early and late is to wean us off theories of sense. Of course, the Continuity Reading does not deny that there are differences, some quite important differences, between the *Tractatus* and *Philosophical Investigations*. For example, one immediately striking difference is the omnipresence of symbolism in the former and its all-but-complete absence in the latter. In the *Tractatus*, an adequate symbolism was taken to be a necessary tool for elucidation, for rendering perspicuous the symbols in the signs of our colloquial language. In particular, an adequate symbolism is necessary to reveal when there are different symbols in the same sign, a problem Wittgenstein took to dog the efforts of philosophers (*TLP* 3.32–3.325). And, although Wittgenstein remains concerned about this problem or a related problem in

Philosophical Investigations – consider his distinction between surface and depth grammar at §664 – he no longer sees an adequate symbolism as necessary to its exposure or its avoidance. I take it that one reason for this is that Wittgenstein came to see that he had become prey to a mythology of adequate symbolism in the *Tractatus*. He saw an adequate symbolism as "divine" – as the language revelatory of the symbols in the signs and as the language exempt from the symbol/sign distinction. He venerated an adequate symbolism as a language of pure symbols. He later came to see clearly that no language, whether natural or symbolic, is exempt from the symbol/sign distinction. In even an adequate symbolism Wittgenstein saw that we recognize the symbols in the (symbolic) signs in "the context of significant use" (the phrase comes from *TLP* 3.326, but I take Wittgenstein not to have realized the full applicability of *TLP* 3.326 to what he is treating as an adequate symbolism). Since an adequate symbolism is not "divine", its role diminishes dramatically in *Philosophical Investigations*. There, Wittgenstein clarifies differences between surface and depth grammar by asking us to consider the word or phrase or sentence as it moves in a language-game or among language-games. He uses hardly any symbolism at all. This is an important difference between the *Tractatus* and *Philosophical Investigations*. But it is not a difference in aim between the books, but rather a difference in methods (and the understanding of methods, and the technologies of method) meant to achieve the books' shared aim.

For those who hold the Continuity Thesis, Wittgenstein's comment in the "Preface" to *Philosophical Investigations* is right: "It suddenly seemed to me that I should publish those old thoughts [the *Tractatus*] and these new ones together: that the latter could be seen in the right light only by contrast with and against the background of my old way of thinking." But so, too, is the reverse: only by contrast with and against the background of his new way of thinking can his old way of thinking be seen in the right light. As Augustine said of the Old and New Testaments: "In Vetere Novum latet est in Novo Vetus patet" (The New Testament is hidden in the Old; the Old is made accessible by the New). Because of this relationship, the present collection's firm emphasis on *Philosophical Investigations* should not be taken as slighting the *Tractatus*. Rather, what these essays intend to do is simultaneously to make *Philosophical Investigations* clear and to do so in a way that makes the *Tractatus* accessible.

Philosophical Investigations

By almost any standard of reckoning, *Philosophical Investigations* is a difficult book. But its difficulty is unusual. Its difficulty is not mainly a matter of the complexity of its arguments. It contains relatively little argumentation, and little of that is complicated. Its difficulty is not a matter of an alien lexicon. *Philosophical Investigations* contains few technical terms and few unusual uses of familiar terms. It is neither architectonically complicated nor given to detailed anatomizing: if it has a structure, its structure is nothing like that of Kant's *Critique of Pure Reason*; it does not produce lists, classifications or diagrams: there is no Table of Categories. Finally, although it is a writerly book, with exact attention paid to its composing, to its rhetorical figures, to its accumulating and dispersing of force of expression, it is not written in any particularly syntactically challenging way. There are no Henry James paragraphs, no megatherian sentences inching their way ponderously across the page. While it is true that Wittgenstein writes so as to keep what he is writing from turning dull under the mind, he does not try to animate dullness by embellishment. The book's sentences are mostly short, the syntax of the sentences rarely strenuous, mostly snappy.

Perhaps the most difficult feature of the book is the fact that few of the remarks in it are philosophically difficult: what is difficult is understanding why Wittgenstein chooses to make the remarks he makes. Take the following as an example: "And hence 'obeying a rule' is a practice. And to *think* one is obeying a rule is not to obey a rule. Hence it is not possible to obey a rule 'privately': otherwise thinking one was obeying a rule would be the same thing as obeying it" (§202). Take the second sentence: to think (believe) that you are obeying a rule is not to obey the rule. As claims go, this is obvious. I can believe I am obeying a rule, say, in a game like chess or tic-tac-toe, and fail to obey the rule. A football player, a cornerback, can be flagged for pass interference, and flagged rightly, even if he sincerely protests the call, even if he believes he obeyed the rule. Penalties do not require any intention to break the rule. So far, so easy. But now look where this easy piece takes Wittgenstein: since to believe that you are obeying a rule is not the same as obeying it, Wittgenstein concludes that no rule can be obeyed "privately". Why? Because if I could obey a rule "privately", my obedience would be settled by my sincere recounting of whether I believed I obeyed it or not. No checks on obedience other than sincerity would be possible. I could only flag myself, but could never penalize myself for intending to obey the rule but failing: so long as I believed I succeeded in obedience, I did. It is important to keep in mind that Wittgenstein does not mean that I cannot obey a rule while I am alone, in the privacy of my own room. That is not the privacy he has in mind. I could, for instance, sit alone in my room writing poetry. Imagine I intend to write a sonnet and, when I cap my fountain pen, I believe I have done so. Did I? Well, what if, a moment later, I count my lines and find that I have 13 or 15, not 14? Or what if I notice that I slipped out of the iambic pentameter in line 8? I would have to judge that I have failed to write a sonnet. I thought I obeyed the rule, "Write a sonnet, a 14-line poem in iambic pentameter", but I did not do so. As I hope is now clear, the point here is that my poetic disobedience is not something that I alone could recognize. If I had taken the poem from my room and shared it with a poetical friend, he could have noticed that I had too few lines or that I had otherwise failed to obey the rule. But where there is no possible check on my obedience except my own check, then it becomes difficult to see how to cleave obedience from believed obedience; they instead cleave to each other. (And do not forget that Wittgenstein is not impugning my honesty; he is assuming it.) So much further, still pretty easy. The difficulty is figuring out why this matters. What does it teach me philosophically?

"Obeying a rule" is a practice: so what? Let me try to answer by sketching out the way our thinking might move from here, how this easy point opens out onto a philosophical problem.

Talking is a practice; using language is a practice. I can talk to myself, of course, and even do so, silently. But in so doing I am not obeying a rule "privately". Whether, when I talk to myself silently, I am making sense or not is not to be determined by whether I believe that I am making sense. Here someone might say: "Right. Fine. Now what you are saying sounds like philosophy. But no philosopher would ever make such a mistake. No philosopher would say that whether I am making sense is determined by whether I believe I am making sense." But what if a philosopher said that a person can understand a proposition only if she is acquainted with each of its constituents? By "acquainted" I mean that she knows the constituents of the proposition as she might know her neighbour, with whom she is acquainted. But what if, further, the philosopher treats acquaintance as "private"? (And so as both like and *unlike* acquaintance with her neighbour.) Imagine such a philosopher. Imagine that she says that whether or not a person is acquainted with a constituent of a proposition is something that the person not only can, but must, determine "privately". So, if some person believes he is acquainted with a constituent of a proposition, then, the philosopher will say, he is. At least, that is how things will go if Wittgenstein is right about what he says in §202, and if being acquainted with a constituent counts as a practice. (I shall suppose Wittgenstein is right.) But why is it that the person cannot believe falsely that he is acquainted with a constituent when he is not? Why is it that he cannot believe falsely that he is unacquainted with a constituent when he is? In the first case he would take himself to understand when he does not; in the second, to fail to understand when he does. If these cases are ruled out, then it looks as if being acquainted with a constituent does not count as a practice. Maybe the philosopher will say that a person either is or is not acquainted with the constituents of a proposition, and that that fact – the bare presence or absence of the constituents – settles whether the person understands or does not understand the proposition. But this would mean that understanding language seems not to count as a practice, at least not intrapersonally – in what the philosopher treats as the "heart" of language. Or maybe the philosopher will say that being acquainted with a constituent does count as a practice, but that it is a practice that somehow cannot go wrong: whatever a person believes about being acquainted with a constituent of a proposition settles the question about whether he is acquainted with the constituent. Either understanding seems, we might say, immune to error due to *malpractice*, since no practice is involved – or it is immune to *error* due to malpractice, since malpractice is impossible.

My point is not to try to resolve this worry or to pin it to any actual philosopher, however much my imaginary philosopher sounds like an actual philosopher, say Bertrand Russell. (Something of his that resembles what I have been discussing is to be found early in his *The Problems of Philosophy*.) I do not claim that I have shown that the way I am pressing the worry is by any means unavoidable. (I do claim that I have pressed the worry in a way that is meant to show why Wittgenstein's comments might matter philosophically, and in a way that is meant to be suggestive about how to understand the other things Wittgenstein goes on to say about obeying rules and about privacy.) What I am trying to show is that and how something as easy to understand as §202 opens out onto worries that are difficult.[4] That what Wittgenstein says is not difficult makes it hard to see why he is saying it, since it can seem that no worthwhile philosopher could possibly be vulnerable to something easy to understand. Wittgenstein, however, thinks that a philosopher can be vulnerable to something easy to understand. But the vulnerability is not the result of the philosopher being witless or careless: rather the problem is that the philosopher thematizes the difficulty of philosophy as a difficulty of subtlety: "Here it is difficult as it were to keep our heads up, – to see that we must stick to the subjects of our everyday thinking, and not go astray and imagine that we have to describe extreme subtleties, which in turn we are quite unable to describe with the means at our disposal. We feel as if we had to repair a torn spider's web with our fingers" (§106). If a difficulty does not feel like a web-repair difficulty, we do not take the difficulty to be philosophical. And if we do take it to be philosophical, it will feel like a web-repair difficulty. If it feels that way, then being handed something easy is going to feel like being handed something hopeless: like being handed a shovel when trying to thread a needle. If Wittgenstein is right about the way that philosophical difficulty is thematized, then we can understand why it is hard to understand why he makes the easy-to-understand remarks he does: it is because we are convinced that they cannot help us, bent double and intent upon the torn web as we are. So Wittgenstein faces two formidable obstacles: (i) figuring out what easy-to-understand remark to make and (ii) how to get the philosopher to pay attention to the remark he makes. Wittgenstein does not exempt himself from the scope of §106 – notice the first-person plural, "we". That is, Wittgenstein has to overcome the obstacles *in himself* before he can strategize overcoming them in anyone else. He must brave his way to confronting a philosophical problem with a remark easy to understand and he must, as it were, resolve to pay attention to the remark, to take it fully seriously as a contribution to philosophy. I stress this because I reckon it is common for readers of Wittgenstein to estimate that his remarks and the seriousness with which he takes them are just natural to him, no achievement, but only the exercise of gift. But I doubt this estimate: thinking as he thinks costs Wittgenstein a great deal, he perseveres in thinking against the grain (his own as much as anyone else's), and the urges to misunderstand, the resistances, the foot-draggings, the doubts expressed by the interlocutory voices in the text are Wittgenstein's own. He is not merely forecasting the difficulties of others. He himself travels "the bloody hard way". He undergoes those difficulties, obstacles, himself. Overcoming the obstacles in himself will tutor his strategizing: what succeeds with him bears a good chance of succeeding with others.

Why do we thematize the difficulty of philosophy as a difficulty of subtlety? In part because of the way we are introduced to and trained in philosophy. Philosophical problems are presented to us as responsive only to subtleties. And our introduction and subsequent training render us comfortable with the thematization. But another more important answer lies in the features of philosophical problems themselves. Philosophical problems seem to call for subtlety, just on their own, as it were. A philosophical problem puzzles us, but it does not seem to present itself to us as revealing a lack of information. That is, it does not seem that we need to learn something new in order to respond to the puzzle.

Still, even though we do not seem to lack information, the problem does present itself as revealing a lack – we seem to know all that we need to know while still not knowing how to respond to the problem (§§89–90). It is as though we need to know something, and that we know it, but that it eludes our being able to access it so as to put it properly to use in responding to the problem – as if it were a detail of what we know but a detail that eludes effectual description, or a detail so small as to be ungraspable by our thick, clumsy fingers. Wittgenstein does not deny that philosophical problems present themselves as revealing a lack – in fact, he insists that they do. But he does deny that what the lack calls for is subtlety. As he says, we need to keep our heads up. What we need is not a detail, something found with our heads down, but rather is a perspicuous presentation of the "landscape" ("Preface") within which the problem is located: we need to command a clear view (§121). "A philosophical problem has the form: 'I don't know my way about'." The lack is a lack of a clear view, of perspicuity. It is not a lack of subtlety. What we need to see is not, as it were, nearly invisible because of its subtlety; it is nearly invisible because of its homeliness, its ordinariness. What we need to see is hidden from view because it is not philosophically striking – it presents itself as beneath philosophical notice, as undeserving of attention – not as too small to see or to pick up, but as too common, too base, too low to count philosophically. We should be reminded that what we need to see is not philosophically contemptible, but that what we need to see, these homely and ordinary things, constitute the common ground on which we live our common lives, the ground on which and the lives in which philosophical problems present themselves. They are not beamed in from outer space, in some alien "tongue" of metallic whirrs and clicks: philosophical problems are framed in our common language, and have to be, if there is anything for them to ask; so, too, responses to them will have to be framed in our common language (§120). That common language, and the common ground on which it is spoken and the common lives from which it is spoken, count, count even philosophically. It is because philosophical problems are framed in our common language and because responses to them must be, too (although the problems seem to require responses too subtle for our common language), that what Wittgenstein says in *Philosophical Investigations* is not hard to understand, and yet that it is hard to understand why he says what he says.

Philosophical Investigations demands of its attentive readers more than acquiring a method or methods that anyone of sufficient intellectual acuity, of sufficient subtlety, can apply. It requires of its attentive readers a practised discipline of response, a mastered openness to aspects of things that seem to fall beneath notice, gray, ragged and dusty (§52); it requires a refusal to set limits in advance to what will count in, or even as, philosophy; and it requires whatever intellectual and moral attitudes and habits are needful to practise such responsiveness, to master such openness.

Wittgenstein says that he does not want *Philosophical Investigations* to spare anyone the trouble of thinking; he wants to spur his readers to thoughts of their own. This contrasts with the *Tractatus*: there, Wittgenstein says that what he has written may be understood only by those who had the thoughts expressed in it, or similar thoughts. In *Philosophical Investigations* his aim is to initiate a process of (contemporary and subsequent) thinking; in the *Tractatus* it is to record the product of (previous) thinking. The aim of this collection is of the same sort as the aim of *Philosophical Investigations*: to initiate a process of thinking – about Wittgenstein's writings. It is not to record the products of thinking about Wittgenstein's writing. The essays are "undefined in front", to borrow a phrase from Henry David Thoreau. They are greenwood sites for growth in understanding Wittgenstein, not a greenhouse exhibit of fully ripened understandings of Wittgenstein.

Brief chapter descriptions

In Chapter 1, "Wittgenstein's Philosophical Remarks", I provide a way of understanding Wittgenstein's purpose in writing the sorts of remarks that compose *Philosophical Investigations*. I contrast my understanding with an understanding once offered by Gilbert Ryle. In Chapter 2, "Wittgenstein on Meaning and Meaning-Blindness", Craig Fox looks carefully at Wittgenstein's treatment of meaning, and provides a close reading of sections of *Philosophical Investigations*, particularly §43, the "meaning is use" remark. In Chapter 3, "Language-Games and Private Language", Lars Hertzberg investigates language-games and provides a discussion of the dialectical significance of the notion of "private language" in Wittgenstein's thinking. Craig Fox develops a strategy for reading the famous and difficult sections on family resemblance in Chapter 4, "Wittgenstein on Family Resemblance". In Chapter 5, "Ordinary/Everyday Language", Rupert Read offers a way of understanding the significance of the idea of "ordinary language" in *Philosophical Investigations* and explains the way in which ordinary language is to be understood to contrast, if it does, with other, extra-ordinary language.

Roderick T. Long elucidates Wittgenstein's discussion of rule-following and explains how that discussion is related to psychology and to metaphysics in Chapter 6, "Wittgenstein on Rule-Following", and in Chapter 7, "Thinking and Understanding", Phil Hutchinson explores the complications of thinking and understanding. In Chapter 8, "Psychologism and *Philosophical Investigations*", I discuss what psychologism is and why Wittgenstein is doggedly opposed to it, and in Chapter 9, "Moore's Paradox Revisited", Avrum Stroll takes a fresh look at Moore's Paradox as it figures in Wittgesntein's work. Avner Baz examines Wittgenstein's discussion of aspect perception and clarifies the function of aspect perception in Wittgenstein's thinking in Chapter 10, "Aspect Perception". In Chapter 11, "Knowing that the Standard Metre is One Metre Long", Heather Gert offers an unusual reading of the infamous metre-stick passage (*PI* §51). She claims that Wittgenstein does believe that the metre-stick is one metre long.

In Chapter 12, "Therapy", Rupert Read and Phil Hutchinson take up Wittgenstein's discussions of therapy in relation to philosophical method. In Chapter 13, "Criteria", Eric Loomis investigates Wittgenstein's much-contested discussions of criteria. Roderick T. Long and I discuss grammatical investigations generally, then offer a (bit of a) specific grammatical investigation as an example in Chapter 14, "Grammatical Investigations", and in Chapter 15, "Teaching and Learning", Arata Hamawaki tells the story of scenes of teaching and learning in Wittgenstein. He explains why such scenes count in Wittgenstein's philosophizing. Finally, in Chapter 16, "Expression and Avowal", David H. Finkelstein provides a clear and detailed introduction to Wittgenstein's treatment of expressions and avowals. Many of the chapters include suggested reading from the *Tractatus* as "Further reading".

Notes

1. Here and in what follows I shall employ (or suggest the employment of) the terminology of "Continuity Thesis", "Discontinuity Thesis", "Continuity Reading" and "Discontinuity Reading". The Theses are ways of understanding the relationship between Wittgenstein's early and late work; the Readings are ways of understanding the *Tractatus* according to one or the other of the Theses. (Of course, someone could proffer what I call the Discontinuity Reading of the *Tractatus* without proffering any reading of *Philosophical Investigations* – perhaps because the reader had never read the latter. But this sort of Discontinuity Reading is not my interest; I am interested in Readings of the two books in relation.)
2. The editions referred to in this chapter is *Philosophical Investigations* (2001a).
3. This provides a diagnosis of the interest in putative sentences that show but do not say. Unlike straightforward sense, that is, like the sense we make, such "sentences" do not *say*; but unlike the sense we make, such "sentences" do

show. And so they seem at once to differ from and to be like the sense we make. The problem with this interest is the instability of its use of *showing*. As I shall note, the showing done by the sense we make is not the sort of showing that discontinuity readers want. They want *showing* that does not require *saying* – in fact, showing that can occur only when *saying* fails. But, to the extent that the "sentences" of interest both show and say, they fail to be what readers want. (They are just more of the sense we make.) To the extent that the sentences do not say but only show, they fail to be like the sense we make.

4. I am not trying to account for the desire of the philosopher to treat acquaintance as "private". This desire is certainly of interest to Wittgenstein, and it is not unconnected to what I go on to discuss, namely the thematizing of philosophy as requiring subtlety. But I here offer no direct or detailed account of the desire. I shall say that a reason for the desire, as I suggest, is a conviction that ultimately the use of language should involve no obedience on the part of the language-user or should involve a form of "obedience" that is, somehow, compelled. We want our public use, practice, of language ultimately to be the outflowering of a private endowment that involves no rules and so no obedience. Whatever corrigibility we are vulnerable to in our public use of language should be the result only of the "distance" at which that public use stands from our private and thus incorrigible linguistic endowment. For discussion of related issues, see Chapter 3, "Language-Games and Private Language" (Hertzberg).

Further reading

Tractatus, Preface and 1–3.144.

ONE

Wittgenstein's philosophical remarks

Kelly Dean Jolley

Philosophical remarks and *Philosophical Investigations*

In his always instructive essay, "The Philosophy of Wittgenstein", Rush Rhees underscores that "If you do not see how style or force of expression are important you cannot see how Wittgenstein thought of philosophical difficulties or philosophical method" (Rhees 1970a: 38). Notice that Rhees binds together Wittgenstein's understanding of style or force of expression, and his understanding of philosophical problems and methods. In doing so, Rhees properly follows Wittgenstein. In the "Preface" of *Philosophical Investigations*, Wittgenstein confesses that "the best [he] could write would never be more than philosophical remarks; [his] thoughts were soon crippled if [he] tried to force them on in any single direction against their inclination".[1] But, after a long pause (embodied in one of his everlastingly elongated dashes), he redirects the force of his confession by binding his need to write remarks and to follow the inclination of his thoughts to the nature of his philosophical work: "And this was, of course, connected with the very nature of the investigation." I shall return to this binding of philosophical remarks to the nature of the investigation – but first I want to consider philosophical remarks themselves. What are they?

Philosophical remarks: a first look

Wittgenstein offers a couple of very brief characterizations of philosophical remarks. He calls them "short paragraphs". He adds that the short paragraphs sometimes form a fairly long chain about the same subject but that they sometimes jump from one topic to another. He also calls them "sketches of landscapes" – sketches made "in the course of ... long and involved journeyings" criss-cross in every direction a wide field of thought. The sketches together provide a picture of the landscape. The collection of them is, he says, "really only an album".

Philosophical remarks are short paragraphs: this may seem hardly informative, if it seems informative at all. But it is informative, even if it informs negatively. As short paragraphs, Wittgenstein's philosophical remarks are not aphorisms, at least not generally. Understanding the philosophical remarks as aphorisms has been common among commentators. There are good reasons for understanding them this way: first, some of the short paragraphs are aphorisms and some contain sentences that are aphoristic; second, Wittgenstein's palpable concern for style and for achieving a peculiar force of expression finds natural expression in aphorisms. (Compare, as commentators have done, Wittgenstein's short paragraphs to the aphorisms of Lichtenberg.) But many, and perhaps most, of the short paragraphs neither are aphorisms nor contain aphoristic sentences.

I need to clarify my point. An aphorism is a short, pithy, pointed sentence: "Life is short, and art is long" (Hippocrates). As I have said, some of Wittgenstein's philosophical remarks are philosophical aphorisms or closely akin to them:

> A philosophical problem has the form: "I don't know my way about." (§123)

> It is in language that an expectation and its fulfillment make contact. (§445)

And certainly many of the philosophical remarks contain sentences that are aphoristic (especially concluding sentences). For example:

> Philosophy is a battle against the bewitchment of our intelligence by means of language. (§109)

But Wittgenstein's philosophical remarks are not generally, as such, aphorisms. The most accurate thing to say is that aphoristic sentences sometimes punctuate the philosophical remarks. But if Wittgenstein is not generally writing philosophical aphorisms, what is he writing when he writes his philosophical remarks? Is he writing philosophical maxims, precepts, dicta, apothegms, adages, proverbs, epigrams or truisms?

I take it that the answer in each of these cases is negative, although, as was true of philosophical aphorisms, some of Wittgenstein's remarks are or contain philosophical maxims, precepts, dicta, apothegms, adages, proverbs, epigrams or truisms. To answer the question of what Wittgenstein is writing, I need to explore some of the dimensions of the remarks. As I do so, I hope to body forth their complicated nature.

Wittgenstein's governessy accents

Gilbert Ryle once complained about the "governessy" accents of Wittgenstein's philosophical remarks and about the "solicitous shepherdings" that characterize him as mentor of his reader (Ryle 1979: 131). Ryle's complaints are worth noting because they direct attention to a crucial dimension of Wittgenstein's philosophical remarks. Wittgenstein's philosophical remarks *teach* – and do so in a very specific way. They are the remarks of a master to an apprentice, the teacherly remarks that a master makes *while observing the actions of an apprentice*, actions performed as the apprentice struggles towards mastery of particular arts. The arts Wittgenstein is teaching are, to borrow another phrase of Ryle's, the "arts of conceptual disentanglement" (*ibid.*). When they are thus described, it may seem to some that Wittgenstein arrogates a role to himself that he ought not, in the interest of good manners, to arrogate to himself: the role of master. Even if he is a master of these arts, we might ask, need he take on the role of master? Of course, asking this, while it may express a genuine reservation about Wittgenstein's taking on the role of master, more probably expresses our disrelish for taking on the role of apprentice. Ryle complains about Wittgenstein's governessy accents and solicitous shepherdings on behalf of "undocile souls", especially including his own; Ryle has no taste for apprenticeship. But Ryle confuses apprenticeship and docility. While an apprentice is docile relative to the master during the apprenticeship, the purpose of the docility, because it is the purpose of the apprenticeship, is to acquire mastery. The master or the apprentice or both fail if the apprentice does not himself become a master. The purpose of Wittgenstein's teaching is not to make the apprentice perpetually docile, forever an apprentice. Far from it: Wittgenstein's purpose is for the apprentice to join him in mastery. Ryle, we might say, reacts to Wittgenstein's teaching as if it were to have no end, as if *Philosophical Investigations* had no final page, as if there were no graduation day. Another problem with Ryle's complaints is that they ignore the important fact that Wittgenstein is Wittgenstein's own (first) apprentice. Stanley Cavell has convincingly described the alternating voices that occur in Wittgenstein's philosophical remarks as the voice of temptation and the voice of correction. I would add that the apprentice's is the voice of temptation and the master's the voice of correction. But each of the voices is (first) Wittgenstein's. Wittgenstein views philosophy as a way of working on himself. He never so completely identifies with the role of master that he loses his active, inward sense of what it is to be in the role of apprentice. The temptations he corrects are temptations he (still) feels. Wittgenstein is concerned not just with the subject he is thinking about, but also with the subjectivity of the person whom he is training in the arts of conceptual disentanglement – about his own and his apprentice's subjectivity.

The source of Ryle's complaints is his misunderstanding of the form of *Philosophical Investigations*. Ryle believes that behind the mentor there is a philosopher: "The knots which Wittgenstein shows us how to untie are the knots which he himself had first to find out how to untie" (*ibid.*). And Ryle is right. But Ryle seems to think that the mentoring is simply an add-on to the philosophizing. He seems to think that the real content of the book is the philosophizing; the mentoring is a perhaps useful but finally mildly embarrassing way of presenting the real content, call it a rhetorical error. We might put what Ryle seems to think this way: *Philosophical Investigations'* expositing of its content can be separated, and really should have been separated, from its modulating of its content. But this way of thinking mistreats Wittgenstein in two ways: it treats his modulation of the book as external to its exposition; and it treats a putative error of modulation as if it were a merely rhetorical and not a philosophical error. Wittgenstein does not think that the modulation of the book is external to its exposition: what he has to teach has to be taught in a certain way. And Wittgenstein does not think that an error of modulation is merely a rhetorical error; it is a philosophical error.

Style and force of expression

Here is the place to return to Rhees's remark binding Wittgenstein's understanding of style or force of expression to his understanding of philosophical problems and method. In the "Preface" Wittgenstein writes that "I should not like my writing to spare other people the trouble of thinking. But, if possible, to stimulate someone to thoughts of his own." Notice how this comment looks in light of the master/apprentice distinction we have been exploring. The remark does not mean that Wittgenstein wants to stimulate others into thinking about what he is thinking. No, the object of the others' thoughts *is whatever Wittgenstein is thinking about*. As I said above, Wittgenstein's remarks are the teacherly remarks made by a master as he observes an apprentice struggling towards mastery, employing the arts to be mastered. In such a setting, the remarks of the master are not the sole object of the apprentice's attention. In such a setting, the remarks of the master are not the sole object of the master's attention. The master focuses on what he says in so far as he works to say whatever will best guide the apprentice's action. So the master is focused simultaneously on what the apprentice is focused on and on the remarks he makes in guiding the apprentice's actions. We might say that, for the master, the actions of the apprentice guide his offering of guiding remarks. The apprentice focuses on what the master says in so far as he needs guidance, in so far as his actions threaten to fall into incoherence. So the apprentice is focused simultaneously on what he is doing and on the remarks the master makes in guiding his actions. We might say that, for the apprentice, his actions guide his appropriation of the master's guiding remarks. Wittgenstein does not want to spare his reader the trouble of thinking, because only in so far as his reader is actively thinking, acting so as to acquire mastery of the arts of conceptual disentanglement, will Wittgenstein's remarks work as they are intended to work. His remarks are intended to teach by guiding a particular activity of philosophy. If the reader stops doing philosophy in that way, stops attempting conceptual disentanglement, and makes Wittgenstein's remarks the sole object of his thinking, then the reader is in the unteachable (because unguideable) position of an apprentice who stops acting so as to focus solely on remarks intended to guide his action. Consider the following from Martin Heidegger:

> A cabinetmaker's apprentice, someone who is learning to build cabinets and the like, will serve as an example. His learning is not merely practice, to gain facility in the use of tools. Nor does he merely gather knowledge about the customary forms of the things he is to build. If he is to become a true cabinetmaker, he makes himself answer and respond above all to the different kinds of wood and to the shapes slumbering within wood ... In fact, this relatedness to wood is what maintains the whole craft. Without that relatedness, the craft will never be anything but empty busywork ... Whether or not a cabinetmaker's apprentice, while he is learning, will come to respond to wood and wooden things, depends obviously on the presence of some teacher who can make the apprentice comprehend.   (Heidegger 1968: 14–15)

The arts Wittgenstein teaches can be taught only where the apprentice maintains a relatedness to what is being thought about, and never allows himself to become related only to the teaching. Wittgenstein's concern with style or force of expression in part measures his devotion to writing in such a way as to maintain the reader's relatedness to whatever is being thought about. If we take a moment to look over just a few pages of *Philosophical Investigations* we see sentence after sentence that begins "Look", "Think", "Conceive", "Ask yourself" and so on. The entreative/ imperative force of such beginnings maintains the reader's relatedness to what is being thought about and prevents the reader from thinking solely about the remarks themselves. That the remarks are expressed with a certain style or force of expression is the result of Wittgenstein's intentness on guiding the thinking of the reader, and on guiding it in a way that is memorable, in a way that can be internalized. The decisive activity of his reader, of the apprentice, is crucial. Were Wittgenstein's remarks to spare others the trouble of thinking thoughts of their own, the remarks could not teach what they are to teach. Although docility is involved, in no way is the docility of the reader the aim of the mentoring in *Philosophical Investigations*. "What is your aim in philosophy? – To shew the fly the way out of the fly-bottle" (§309). The aim of the mentoring in *Philosophical Investigations* is freedom, not docility. But the freedom to which Wittgenstein shows the way is a freedom obtained by disciplined mastery – and docility is required to acquire that disciplined mastery.[2]

So what is Wittgenstein thinking about?

In *Philosophical Investigations*, Wittgenstein is thinking about philosophical problems. Now, this might be taken to be ambiguous: it might be taken to mean (i) that he is thinking about the philosophical problem of, say, meaning, the philosophical problem itself, or (ii) that he is thinking about the concept of meaning. If we look at the opening remarks, we may say that Wittgenstein is thinking about the philosophical concept of meaning. Does that mean that he is thinking about (i) or about (ii)? It means that he is talking about both: the ambiguity is deliberate. That he is talking about both is one reason why he chooses to begin his remarks by quoting from St Augustine. Augustine, as Wittgenstein notes, works with "a particular picture of the essence of human language". As Wittgenstein thinks outwards from the quotation, he is thinking about Augustine's picture of meaning as well as about meaning. To think as Wittgenstein does about the philosophical concept of meaning is to think about the ways philosophers have thought about the concept of meaning, the philosophical problems they take to be grouped around the concept of meaning, the ways they have responded to those problems, and – it is to think about the concept of meaning. Someone might complain that all the philosopher needs to think about is – the concept of meaning. Thinking about the concept of meaning should not be mediated so complicatedly. But, first, it is worth noting that such mediation is constant in Wittgenstein (even if it is not always so complicated). He begins *The Blue Book* (a preliminary study for *Philosophical Investigations*) by asking: "What is the meaning of a word?" And then, instead of answering, he advises his reader: "Let us attack this question" (*BB* 1). Well, attacking the question requires thinking about the meaning of a word, to be sure; but it also requires thinking about the question, too. Thinking about the meaning of a word is mediated by thinking about the question "What is the meaning of a word?" It is mediated by thinking, among other things, about all the different questions that that interrogative form of words might express, and the ways the different questions (and answers) might become entangled, especially since they may be expressed by the same interrogative form of words.[3]

Second, given that Wittgenstein is teaching the arts of conceptual disentanglement, his insisting on mediation should not really surprise us. When we begin to philosophize about the concept of meaning, our thinking will be shaped by our preliminary sense of the shape of the concept. This is the product of two factors: our grasp on what Wittgenstein calls the "surface grammar" of the relevant word or words ("mean", "means", "meaning") and our conception of what correctly philosophizing about the concept of meaning requires of us. The second factor is one that we overlook as we begin to philosophize, since our conception of what correctly philosophizing requires of us is at this moment typically diaphanous.

I need to stress this. An uncanny feature of philosophizing is the way in which our conception of philosophical method seems available to us (to the extent that it is), seems something we can articulate (to the extent we can), only when we are not engaged in philosophizing about something, like the concept of meaning. When we begin to philosophize about the concept of meaning, our conception of method seems unavailable, inarticulable. And yet such a conception is *there*, guiding what we are doing. It may not seem as if such a conception is guiding what we are doing because we tend to reduce being guided to an experience, to an occurrent, datable feeling of being tugged, urged, led, repositioned, cautioned, slowed, stopped; and we ransack our experience and find no such feeling. But being guided is not an experience, a feeling. So, not finding such a feeling is no proof that we are unguided.

That our conception of philosophical method is diaphanous, opaque and thus available (to the extent that it is) only when it is not actively guiding us is why an articulated philosophical method seems often so distant from the philosophizing that it was supposed to guide. The method we articulate sometimes is not the one that actually guides our philosophizing; it may not be our method, or not all of it, or may miss what is central to it. Actually understanding the method that guides our or others' philosophizing itself requires philosophizing. We cannot take philosophical methodological comments automatically at face value – not even our own. Each philosopher's work contains – to borrow an expression from Heidegger – "un-thought-of element[s]", elements that emerge in and through the work of the philosopher but that he cannot (fully) articulate. The un-thought-of elements enter into relations with the thought-of elements, thus affecting the meaning and significance of the thought-of elements. Not all the un-thought-of elements are methodological, of course, but many are.

Wittgenstein's remarks aim at increasing his reader's awareness of un-thought-of elements in the reader's own thinking, especially the un-thought-of methodological elements. His remarks urge us to ask why it is that a certain form of explanation or answer seems fated, why certain pictures captivate us, why some words, but not others, stir us to reflection – especially when those stirring words, like unstirring words, have unexotic, everyday uses. Making progress through Wittgenstein's remarks requires achieving clarity not only about the concept of meaning but about all the things that shape our philosophical questions about meaning. Alexander Bryant Johnson once pointed out that

> Questions have interrogated everything but themselves. No subject is less understood than questions. They constitute a field not ungleaned merely, but unreaped. Everything pertaining to them is unmarked by the feet of curiosity, and untrained by the hand of cultivation. As the eye sees everything but itself, so questions have interrogated everything but themselves.
>
> (Johnson 1959: 241)

Wittgenstein interrogates questions; his feet mark the field; he not only gleans, but reaps; he cultivates questions:

What is the meaning of a word?
    Let us attack this question by asking, first, what is an explanation of the meaning of a word; what does the explanation of a word look like?

22

The way this question helps us is analogous to the way the question "how do we measure a length?" helps us to understand the problem "what is length?"

The questions "What is length?", "What is meaning?", "What is the number one?" etc., produce in us a mental cramp. We feel that we can't point to anything in reply to them and yet ought to point to something. (We are up against one of the great sources of philosophical bewilderment: a substantive makes us look for a thing that corresponds to it.)   (*BB* 1)

Mastery and freedom

Wittgenstein's philosophical remarks are the remarks of a teacher; they are a dialogue between master and apprentice. The remarks are riddled with question marks; they are to inculcate not only the habit of questioning, but the habit of questioning questioning. The reader of the remarks, the apprentice, must manage simultaneously to keep one eye on the philosophical problem at hand and the other eye on his hand, his method of handling the problem. Stereoscopy is necessary. And to keep the other eye on his hand, he must keep both ears open to Wittgenstein's remarks, to the guidance Wittgenstein is giving.

Understanding Wittgenstein's remarks in this way means that the remarks forecast their own eventual inutility. As I said, Wittgenstein's teaching is to come to an end at some time, as all teaching does. There is a graduation day. We may find that going back to the book from time to time is a good idea – we may need a refresher, or we may feel that we missed something in some part of the teaching. We may just think that we would benefit from reviewing the fundamentals. But an unending apprenticeship is a misunderstanding; devotion to the book for its own sake is a misunderstanding. Eventually, the good reader, the apt apprentice, acquires the arts of conceptual disentanglement, acquires the practised readiness of response to philosophical problems that Wittgenstein teaches. On that day, the reader's relationship to the book changes. And that day has been prefigured in little ways on many earlier days. *Philosophical Investigations*' remarks require activity on the part of the reader. This means that the reader has to act on what he understands. The reader has to *do* something. When he can do it reliably and correctly, his relationship to the remark that taught him to do it changes. And so it goes serially throughout the remarks of the book. Eventual mastery enables the good reader to add his voice to the voices of the remarks, as another voice of correction to help the new reader, the new apprentice. Understanding Wittgenstein's book means being able to do (and to teach others to do) what Wittgenstein is teaching in the book. Understanding the book does not mean being able to taxonomize the arguments presented in the book or to tally up the conclusions taught in it, then arguing for them or against them. Of course there are arguments and conclusions in the book, but they subserve the teaching of the arts of conceptual disentanglement. They are not self-standing achievements of the book. The same is true, *mutatis mutandis*, of the technical terms of the book. Like the book's proffered descriptions (descriptions proffered instead of explanations), the technical terms "get [their] light, that is to say [their] purpose, from the philosophical problems" (*PI* §109). Without the problems, the terms "go dark", become purposeless. So, a term like "language-games" is not a term meant to play a role in a philosophical theory of language, say, a "use-theory", but is instead meant to play a role in an investigation aimed at making clear what a philosophical problem is. Outside that investigation, the term goes dark.

I have taken up, without much ceremony, the form of words Ryle used to describe the aim of *Philosophical Investigations* as the arts of conceptual disentanglement. Ryle understands that form of words differently than I do. For Ryle, the arts of conceptual disentanglement are the arts of disentangling concepts *from one another*. That is right as far as it goes: Wittgenstein does teach how to disentangle concepts from each other. But more than that, Wittgenstein also teaches the philosophically puzzled person how to disentangle himself from concepts. In fact, when in the grip of a philosophical problem, the puzzled person is entangled in the concepts involved. To think of philosophical problems as structures solely of entangled concepts, as Ryle does, is to think that the structure is one that does not also entangle the puzzled person. To think as Ryle does is to think of philosophical problems as having no subjective dimension. It is to think that there is only the *what* of the entangled concepts. It is to think that philosophical problems are such that there need be no concern with the *how* of the puzzled person's relation to the entangled concepts. But the *how* of the puzzled person's relationship to the problem concerns Wittgenstein deeply, as deeply as anything does.

His concern comes out in a variety of ways, some explicit (like his likening of philosophy to therapy), some implicit. But none is more important to note than the family of concepts that characterize what has to occur to the person who is disentangling himself and concepts from one another: it is the family we might call "the family of *recollecting*" – realizing, recognizing, appreciating, seeing-as and remembering. Each of these concepts is, although in different ways, related to knowledge. Crucially, each is something that happens in relationship to what is already known. None requires "new" knowledge, knowledge from elsewhere; and so no question as to the sources or methods of acquiring the "new" knowledge arises. When we realize, recognize, appreciate, see *x* as *y*, or remember, what is presented at these moments is something already known to us. Something about what is known dawns on the person, flashes before him, strikes him, sinks in; or something already known suddenly comes back to him, recurs. There is no method that guarantees realizing, recognizing, appreciating, seeing-as or remembering. At the crucial moment, they either happen or they do not. But whether or not they happen is in part a function of preparation, of proper education or attunement. So although Wittgenstein cannot teach his reader to realize, and so on, he can work to ensure that the reader is properly oriented toward philosophical problems, oriented in such a way as to maximize the potential for realizing, and so on. The *how* is the reader's orientation, the puzzled person's orientation. Wittgenstein teaches a new way of hearkening, a new kind of receptivity (*PI* §232).

The need to affect the *how* of the puzzled person, the need to properly orient him, requires Wittgenstein to be keenly attentive to style and force of expression. He writes, trying to find *the liberating word*, the word that affects the *how* of the puzzled person. The liberating word is no fixed thing, however, no "Open Sesame!" that operates a host of mystical doors. The liberating word may vary across puzzled persons and even across the duration of the puzzlement of one person. A word that liberates one person by orienting him so that he realizes something, something that frees him from puzzlement, may be a word that does nothing for, or even further binds, another person. Wittgenstein stresses that his work is an album and that each piece of the landscape is sketched from a number of different vantage points. Wittgenstein proliferates sketches in the hope of hitting upon the liberating word for his reader.

I began by denying that Wittgenstein's philosophical remarks generally are aphorisms, maxims, precepts and so on. I admitted, however, that such occur in his remarks. So what are Wittgenstein's philosophical remarks generally if they are not aphorisms, maxims, precepts and so on? Well, they are *sui generis*: they are Wittgensteinian philosophical remarks. Their relationship to established, familiar literary forms for short paragraphs is a relationship across an unlikeness. To lose sight of the unlikeness while focusing on the relationship is to lose sight of the way in which Wittgenstein's philosophical remarks are, stylistically and in their force of expression, not only a philosophical but also a literary achievement.

Notes

1. Editions referred to in this chapter are *Philosophical Investigations* (2001a) and *The Blue and Brown Books* (1965).
2. "Docile" is Ryle's word, chosen with Ryle's characteristic pugnacity. "Docile" sounds (as Ryle intends) *sheepish*, sunned and woolly and drowsy. But the docility that Wittgenstein wants (as I have stressed) is a docility of full attentiveness, the docility of circumspectly measured, properly responsive action. I stick with Ryle's word since it is not wholly wide of the mark. But much better to have in mind here than an image of sheepish docility is a Kantian image – the image of perception as a synergy of receptiveness (docility) and spontaneity (freedom). Learning conceptual disentanglement is a synergy of receptiveness and spontaneity, of learning from others and of teaching oneself – a synergy of receptiveness that grows into spontaneity and is again grown into by that spontaneity.
3. J. L. Austin amply illustrates the variety of questions that may be asked in the same interrogatory form of words at the beginning of his essay, "The Meaning of a Word" (1961): "What-is-the-meaning-of (the word) 'x'? What-is-the-meaning-of a word? What-is-the-meaning-of any word? What-is-the-meaning-of a word in general? What-is-the-meaning-of-a-word? What-is-the-meaning-of-the-word-'x'? What is the 'meaning' of a word? What is the 'meaning' of (the word) 'x'?, ...". Note that I am not claiming, and that Austin is not claiming, that we should judge all of these to be worthwhile questions.

Further reading

Tractatus, Preface, 4.003–4.0031, 6.53–6.54.

TWO

Wittgenstein on meaning and meaning-blindness

Craig Fox

Introduction

It is at least plausible to assert that Wittgenstein's philosophical legacy lies with his discussions of meaning in the *Philosophical Investigations*. It does not follow from this, of course, that these discussions are well understood. One often sees allusions to them in the form of a single phrase such as "Wittgenstein's definition of meaning as use" or "Wittgenstein's use-theory of meaning".[1] A typical citation is the following, from a text on philosophy of language: "In according the concept of truth pivotal status, we are moving beyond the original Wittgensteinian doctrine that equates meaning with use" (Collin & Guldmann 2005: 35). This is then taken to be Wittgenstein's contribution: his theory of meaning as use. The idea is that he has told us how our words come to mean what they do (namely, by our use of them). This way of understanding what Wittgenstein says is tempting but wrong, in my view. Such a reading fails to capture what is truly philosophically radical in his work.

In this chapter I shall exhibit some of the various things Wittgenstein has to say about meaning in the *Investigations* as well as what we are to take away from them. First, I shall examine the early part of the *Investigations*, §§1–43.[2] I shall spend most of my time on this material, as I believe the main points to be laid out here. Second, I shall examine an often-overlooked part of the book, the mid-§§500s. Finally I shall turn to some relevant discussions in Part II of *Investigations*. It will become clear that Wittgenstein does not have a "doctrine" (in any interesting sense) that "equates" meaning with use. His discussions of meaning are important for a number of reasons. First, they establish important characteristics of Wittgenstein's way of doing philosophy. Second, they serve to undermine philosophical attempts to provide an account of what meaning is. Third, they prepare the way for other discussions of Wittgenstein's (e.g. those of rule-following and private language).

Although I maintain that Wittgenstein's work stands in opposition to providing an account of the nature of meaning, I do not mean to suggest that his work is somehow in opposition to meaning itself. We ought not to conclude that – absent a theory of meaning – our words do not have meaning or that talk of meanings is unjustified. That is exactly the opposite conclusion we should draw, in fact. Wittgenstein never suggests that "there is no such thing as meaning anything by any word" (Kripke 1982: 55). He has not given up on (what one might be tempted to call) "the normativity of our meaning-talk" – that is, what we say about meanings can indeed be right or wrong. We evaluate particular instances as they arise.

It would be misleading to say that Wittgenstein's account of meaning stays the same throughout the *Investigations*. His "account of meaning" does not stay the same throughout the book simply for the reason that he is not providing any such account. His way of discussing the topic of meaning, though, does remain basically the same. It is best exhibited by the opening sections of the book, which culminate in the notorious §43, where Wittgenstein links meaning and use explicitly.

Meaning in *Philosophical Investigations* §§1–43

The topic of meaning arises right away in §1.[3] Wittgenstein begins the book with a passage from Augustine, from which he extracts "a particular picture of the essence of human language".[4] This then naturally gives rise to "the roots of the following idea: Every word has a meaning. This meaning is correlated with the word. It is the object for which the word stands." Wittgenstein undertakes to criticize both the picture of the essence of language and the idea about meaning. He does so in a series of displayed questions and responses, effectively imitating a discussion that has originated with Augustine's passage.

Wittgenstein has, at the very beginning, already laid out a number of themes that will figure prominently in our investigation of meaning and of §43 (where "meaning" and "use" appear together). It will be useful to make these explicit, so that we may trace their recurrence more easily. There are four, and they persist throughout §§1–43 (and indeed the rest of the *Investigations*):

1. Attention to uses of language;
2. Appreciation of the temptation to provide explanations;
3. Naturalness of the desire to ask questions about meaning; and
4. Superfluity of talk about meaning.

Let me say a bit about each of these themes.

1. §1 begins with an example of a use of language: we get the example via the description of the initiation of a child into language. He then talks about an idea that he sees arising out of this example. Next he plants the seeds of a criticism of this idea, although he does not yet bring them to maturity. Before doing that, he gives us another example of a use of language. The shopkeeper is given a slip marked "five red apples", and Wittgenstein describes how he might use each of the three words to retrieve five red apples. He searches for a drawer marked "apples", he consults a chart for the appropriately labelled colour, and he recites the cardinal numbers in order while retrieving them. This example highlights features of the first example, while adding some complexity as well. Thus the two uses of language that he portrays play the roles of starting the conversation (literally "giving us something to talk about") and of starting us towards a criticism of an idea. This is an important illustration of Wittgenstein's way of working in the *Investigations*.

   An aspect of the second example that Wittgenstein emphasizes is that the shopkeeper *acts* [*handelt*] in the way that he does. That is, part of what is important about the description of language use is that the person behaves in a certain way, that he does something. Thus, when he is considering how language is used, he does not simply pay attention to words in isolation from the activity that accompanies them.

2. Following the description of language use that opens the section, Wittgenstein himself offers an explanation of the activity recounted. Based upon the description, he explains how it might be that language "works". This requires, first, some articulated idea of what language comprises. The explanation of how language works, then, takes the form of an idea about the meanings of our words.

3. Thus it is natural for us to want to give an explanation of how language works – to give an explanation of how it is that our words come to have meanings, which they clearly do. It should be noted that the impulse to say something about meaning in general comes after the description of language use. Given that description and

a little reflection, talking about meaning is natural. Following the second example of language use, again the topic of meaning is raised: "But what is the meaning of the word 'five'?" Wittgenstein's very placement of this question in the conversation shows his appreciation for the impulse to ask it.[5]

4. And yet, after each time he raises the topic of meaning here, he works to undercut it.[6] In the first instance, immediately following the suggested idea of what meaning is ("It is the object for which the word stands"), Wittgenstein suggests that Augustine's description may have been defective, thereby implying a problem with the idea of what meaning is. The suggestion here is that maybe we shall need to think more about our description of language use. In the second instance, when one asks about the meaning of "five", Wittgenstein's response is to stop the line of questioning altogether. He says, "no such thing was in question here". We might characterize his responses in the following ways: the first is more traditional, while the second is more radical.[7] What becomes apparent, especially following the second example, is that we do not need to discuss meaning to make sense of the talk: sometimes discussing meaning is out of place.[8] This gives us the suggestion of a motivation for the more radical response, namely, that talk about meaning can be superfluous or beside the point.[9]

To be sure, there are times when talk about meaning is not beside the point. Consider discussions of "marriage", for instance, beginning in the late 1990s. In these cultural exchanges, though, appeal to a philosophical account of meaning would be of no help. The question "what is the meaning of X?" could lead one in various directions. What Wittgenstein is working against from the beginning is that a philosophical account will somehow solve our troubles.

In full, §43 reads as follows: "For a *large* class of cases – though not for all – in which we employ the word 'meaning' [*Bedeutung*] it can be explained [*erklären*] thus: the meaning of a word is its use in the language. And the *meaning* of a name is sometimes explained [*erklärt*] by pointing to its *bearer*."[10]

A number of initial observations are worthwhile at this point. First, Wittgenstein says that this explanation of "meaning" will work for a large number of cases. All this means is that there are contexts in which the word "meaning" might occur in which this explanation will not help us.[11] Second, when *erklären* first occurs in this section, Anscombe renders it as "defines". It seems to me that "explains" is the best rendering in both contexts. Up until this point, Wittgenstein has generally avoided giving definitions of terms under discussion. The only time he does specifically address definitions (in the ostensive definition discussions, §§27–34), it is to show how the purported definition does not do all that one might naively expect it to do. There are a number of reasons, then, to avoid using "defines" in this section.

A third point to observe is that Wittgenstein does allow, in the last sentence of the section, that the meaning of a name can be explained by pointing to the thing named (although he does not say that sometimes the meaning is the thing named).[12] Presumably, it is the existence of such kinds of cases that may lead one to think that this phenomenon (in general) tells us what the meaning of a name is. One distills out the essence of these cases (or, "sublimes the logic of our language" (§38)). One should not, however, for at least two reasons. First, not all words are names (echoing §1). Second, names' meanings cannot always be explained in this way. Note, finally, that this last sentence bears a similarity to what he describes in the first part of the section – which is to say, it is an instance of an explanation of meaning, but one in which the advice (roughly: "look to the use of a word, if you want to say something about its meaning") of this section is not immediately helpful,[13] for here, Wittgenstein calls our attention to the fact that sometimes we can simply point, that *that* can count as an explanation of meaning.[14]

When Wittgenstein explains "meaning" by telling us that the meaning of a word is its use in the language, there is a sense in which he has told us nothing yet.[15] What we know is simply this: that if we are given some word, we shall often need to think about how that word is used in order to try to figure out what it means.[16] "How that word is used" is not something mysterious.[17] It is meant to be as simple, as commonsensical, as it sounds. But this point is also relevant: "how that word is used" ("its use") is not a *thing*; it is more like a loose description of what we take ourselves to know about the word, as competent language-users, upon reflection.

Another way of stating all this is to say that nothing tells us what some word's meaning is in advance of thinking about or knowing what we do with the word. Questions that it will be informative to know the answers to, for instance, might be: "When do we say the word?" "When do we not say it?" "How do others react when we say it?" and "What can I accomplish by saying it?" But these are all questions that one implicitly knows the answers to when one is a competent language-user (with respect to some given word, at least). An assumption here – if it is actually an assumption – is that since we use some word X competently, we know what X means.[18] (There is also the suggestion that its uses come prior to meaning. This can be seen going back to §1 and the shopkeeper example. However, this does not mean that ontologically, as it were, uses are prior to meaning – but rather that for us, practically, uses come before meanings.)

It is the employment of such advice that clears up, in §40 and following (consider especially §42), the misconception that a word is meaningless if nothing corresponds to it. We simply recall that we can talk about things that no longer exist – and that such talk is just as meaningful as any of our talk is – and we have cleared up something having to do with words' meanings.[19] What is offered in this section is offered in the context of that discussion, after a misconception has been revealed. We have no reason to believe that what §43 says will prevent us from falling prey to other misconceptions (although it might), and thus we have no reason to believe that §43 should in any way stand on it own, as it were, preventing all other misconceptions.[20] Other misconceptions about meaning may require other advice.[21]

Another remark here will be worthwhile. From §40 until this one, we have seen explicit discussion of words' meanings and of the word "meaning". The connection here is the following basic (yet significant) point: we talk about meanings, sometimes, when we use the word "meaning".[22] This keeps what he has to say grounded, as it were, and answerable to something (namely, to the use we make of this or that word). This is an important aspect of Wittgenstein's philosophical approach.

What we do not get in this section is a definition of "meaning", nor a general theory or account of what meaning consists in.[23] It is important to realize that Wittgenstein has not offered a theory of what meaning consists in; that is, a word's meaning does not *consist in* a word's use. Rather, it is the word's use that will often lead us to see what the meaning is. His having given a theory or some definition would be highly inconsistent with the tone and spirit of the work up until this point.[24] Both would eliminate the work that Wittgenstein wants to require of the reader – that of *our* reflection upon our own language. We are told, rather, a fact that we all know at some level, a fact that, when explicitly pointed out to us, can guide us towards figuring out what a word's meaning is; the work is still left to us to do, *if we are still inclined to do it*. I say this because there is an important sense that one is left with, after reading §43 as I am here, that "figuring out what a word's meaning is" is unnecessary or beside the point. What more do we get out of returning to a question about meaning, after all?[25]

Meaning in *Philosophical Investigations* §§500s

The §§500s are often overlooked, perhaps simply because they come so late in the book. They should not be overlooked, however – they comprise a very rich group of remarks. I shall focus here on §§560–68. This block of sections begins with: "'The meaning of a word is what is explained by the explanation of the meaning.' I.e.: if you want to understand the use of the word 'meaning', look for what are called 'explanations of meaning'". Surely this is not the statement of some theory of meaning that has – by this point in the *Investigations* – been established. Rather, this is a statement based on our ordinary usage of "meaning". It is also entirely consistent with how I presented §43: if we are interested in saying something about the meaning of a word, we should pay attention to uses of "meaning" (in particular, utterances we call "explanations of meaning").

Now, one such "explanation of meaning" is given by Wittgenstein himself: he says that "is" is used with two different meanings – "as the copula and as the sign of equality" (§561). That he would assert this about "is" is taken as the basis for the discussion in subsequent sections. Wittgenstein comments, though: "isn't it queer that I say that the word 'is' is used with two different meanings ... and should not care to say that its meaning is its use; its use, that is, as the copula and the sign of equality?" This shows us how we are to understand what he has told us in §43. When Wittgenstein said there that "meaning" could be explained with "the meaning of a word is its use in the language", he did not mean that we should simply take a word's use(s) and identify it (them) with its meaning. What he does in §561, rather, coincides with my explanation of §43: he considers the use of "is" and he concludes that it has two meanings. This is because, in his judgement (which is that of any competent language-user), we can distinguish two significantly different meanings.

Wittgenstein says that "one would like to say that these two kinds of use" falling under one word is *accidental* (not etymologically, but from "the standpoint of meaning", as it were). He then goes on to talk about the distinction between what is essential and what is inessential (§§562–4), and the upshot is that we make such a decision based on what the "point" of using the word is. So in §561, Wittgenstein judges that there are two different points in using the word in these two ways.

We come to learn the point of something (e.g. a game: see §§564–8) invariably by having experiences with it. Wittgenstein explicitly links this discussion of "the point of something" and games, in particular, back to meaning in §568. He comments, as an aside: "meaning as a physiognomy". This is an important remark.[26] Just as we come to see character as embodied in structural facial features by having experiences with that person (and not by something like a "science" of phrenology), we come to know something about the meanings of our words by having experiences with them.[27] But "having experiences with our words" just means "using them" (and seeing other use them etc.). So, again, this is what "meaning is use" comes to.

Meaning-blindness in *Philosophical Investigations* Part II

Part II of the *Investigations* is a potentially troubling portion of the book. G. H. Von Wright, for instance, does not consider it to be a genuine part of the *Investigations*, properly speaking. He is of the opinion that "Part I of the *Investigations* is a complete work and that Wittgenstein's writings from 1946 onward [when Part II was composed] represent in certain ways departures in *new* directions" (1982: 136). Nevertheless, I think that we can profit from some attention to this material. Whatever von Wright means by Wittgenstein's "new directions", there is a strong continuity between Parts I and II on the topic of meaning.

In section xi of Part II, Wittgenstein spends a good deal of time discussing "seeing aspects". Aspect-blindness involves "lacking in the capacity to see something *as something*" (p. 182). Human beings who are aspect-blind would apparently have a kind of defect "comparable to color-blindness". Speaking of the "double-cross image" (p. 176), Wittgenstein says that the aspect-blind man will not see the sudden change we ordinarily see. He will not suddenly say, "Now it's a black cross on a white ground!" (p. 182) when it "changes" from being a white cross on a black background for him, for this is the kind of experience he is lacking. It would never "change" for him.

Wittgenstein says that the aspect-blind person "will have an altogether different relationship to pictures from ours" (*ibid.*). This is significant for our purposes, because he then goes on to suggest that the importance of investigating aspect-blindness lies "in the connection between the concepts of 'seeing an aspect' and 'experiencing the meaning of a word'" (*ibid.*). The relationship to pictures (or to words) is vitally important to what we say about the meanings of those pictures (or words). This was part of the point of my discussion of meaning in the §§500s, above.

The meaning-blind person – Wittgenstein does not use this term in the *Investigations*, although he does in writings from the mid-1940s on[28] – is one who fails to have a certain "experience of meaning" when using a word. One of Wittgenstein's examples in other writings is of the word "bank".[29] There is an experience we have, when "going to the bank?" suddenly shifts its meaning from being a question about the ATM machine to one about the Monongahela River. The sentence has remained the same, and yet the meaning has changed: just as in the case of the double-cross (or the duck–rabbit). Wittgenstein seems to try to find expression for this experience and ones like it. Thus he discusses "accompanying phenomena of talking" (p. 186).[30]

In this midst of this discussion, he offers that, "[t]he familiar physiognomy of the word, the feeling that it has taken up its meaning into itself, that it is an actual likeness of its meaning – there could be human beings to whom all this was alien. (They would not have an attachment to their words)" (*ibid.*). The point of the discussion of (now thoroughgoing[31]) meaning-blindness here is to raise the possibility of those who use words in the way we do, while not having the kinds of experiences the rest of us typically have when saying the same things. Now, we might conclude that it is only the use of words that matters in the end, and so the meaning-blind person still means what we mean. Feelings are not essential to meaning.[32]

However, feelings and experiences we have while using words *are* typically important to us. This is one reason why Wittgenstein talks so frequently about the contexts in which our words come. We might have the notion that meaning-blind people are not quite human; they are like robots. This shows us something about what we call "using language" – just as the discussion of "private language" does. The discussion culminating in "meaning is a physiognomy" in the §§500s is not making a claim about how these kinds of relationships to our words are *essential*, but rather that they typically affect how we use language. So they are important *to us*.

Now in the end, though, to "how are these feelings manifested among us?" Wittgenstein replies: "By the way we choose and value words" (p. 186).[33] So, that we use this word in this context and are reluctant to do so in most others reflects some experiences we have had while using the word.

Maybe we do not want to call the meaning-blind person's language a legitimate "use of language". Wittgenstein is perhaps sympathetic to this response:[34] while no particular experience of meaning is essential, we might think that *some (indefinite) experience* is. People are not automatons, remember. But of course, the only reason we might feel this way is because – ultimately – it leads to using words in certain contexts, and the use of words is not in question here. We are assuming that their uses coincide with ours. So: why is this not a legitimate use of language? After all, "the practical consequences"[35] of the meaning-blind person's use of language are the same as ours, and if they are the same, then most often no questions (about meaning, for example) will arise. One might be left wanting more from the considerations of meaning-blindness. Is the meaning-blind person using language – using words with meaning – or not? I am suggesting that in the abstract there is no assumption of a fact of the matter here. Given a particular circumstance, we could look at its facts and come to some conclusion. What we have seen in this discussion are some of the considerations that will come to bear on such a decision. This is the sort of thing that Wittgenstein does time and again in the *Investigations*.

Conclusion

In *Investigations* §128, Wittgenstein notoriously says: "If one tried [or: wanted] to advance *theses* in philosophy, it would never be possible to debate them, because everyone would agree to them." At the very least, this suggests that he does not see his work as advancing theses. One such thesis would be some kind of theory of meaning, which would tell us what words mean as well as justify these claims. I believe it is safe to say at this point that we ought not think that Wittgenstein was advancing a theory of meaning. His comments about meaning in general (and about particular words' meanings) – in so far as he makes them – are on a par with our ordinary claims about meanings of words.[36]

But then, one is apt to wonder, what is Wittgenstein doing? In his review of the *The Blue and Brown Books*, O. K. Bouwsma seems *compelled* to ask (on the reader's behalf), "And it is a book in philosophy surely? Well, it is and it isn't" (Bouwsma 1965: 181). Earlier in the review, Bouwsma makes the following point: "Was Descartes right in his statement of the *Cogito* or not? What we want is an answer: Yes, or: No. And what do we get? Not even a weak answer such as 'Probably' or 'Not at all likely'" (*ibid.*: 179). Wittgenstein's writing can engender frustration in the reader if the reader has come to the work with certain preconceptions.

Peter Hylton expresses a kind of frustration, although he casts it in a different light and with a different subject. He says, of his own experiences with philosophy in general, "on the one hand, it completely absorbed me. On the other, its inconclusiveness frustrated me: I was only too well aware of the vulnerability of any philosophical claim, and could not convince myself that my own views might somehow be exempt" (1990: vii). Here the frustration comes from philosophy as a whole, not from Wittgenstein's instantiation of it.

What I would suggest is that Wittgenstein's writing is an attempt to lay bare the frustration Hylton cites. It is also an attempt still to say something about philosophy nonetheless. But if it is not to succumb to the same problems, it will have to be rather different. When we come to it, however, still somewhat ensconced in the assumptions of the philosophical outlook, then it is Wittgenstein's writing that can come to seem more frustrating (in the way Bouwsma indicates).

In his discussions of meaning, Wittgenstein has essentially called to our attention the ways in which we talk about the meanings of our words. In so doing, he undermines assumptions one might make about the nature of meaning. He does not leave us with a replacement account, but this in no way hinders our capacity to make meaning-claims.[37]

Notes

1. A nice example is Hallett (1967).
2. The edition referred to in this chapter is *Philosophical Investigations* (2001a).
3. Material in this section and the next is based on Chapters 2 and 3 of my "Wittgenstein and Myths of Meaning" (PhD dissertation, University of Illinois at Chicago: 2006).
4. Cavell finds this statement "remarkable". In "Notes and Afterthoughts" (1996) he continues, saying that Wittgenstein's claim here "doesn't seem obviously true". Goldfarb, in "I Want You to Bring Me a Slab: Remarks on the Opening Sections of the *Philosophical Investigations*", suggests that "Wittgenstein means to call up amazement" by saying that "this is the essence of human language" (1983: 268). It seems to me, however, that the ordinary, even uncontroversial, sound of such a statement serves to begin to push us into a philosophical discussion. It is in retrospect that his statement seems to have more weight – it is in *retrospect* that amazement seems more appropriate to me. (My reaction then might be: "*this* is what started us down that road?") Compare Floyd in her "Homage to Vienna: Feyerabend on Wittgenstein (and Austin and Quine)": "one of Wittgenstein's most important starting and ending points, namely, that what is least obvious, and sometimes most philosophically important, is that which we take to be obvious or trivial or *a priori*, the assumptions we take for granted at the outset, before a position is articulated" (2006: 130).
5. What I am saying here is similar to what Cavell says in his "The Availability of Wittgenstein's Later Philosophy" (1976b: 71). Here, he speaks of "the voice of temptation" that recurs in "Wittgenstein's dialogues". I am highlighting an instance of that temptation (for temptations are natural, I assume): the temptation to say something about the meaning of our words, to ask questions about meaning.
6. Just as above, I take what I am saying here to be similar to what Cavell says in "The Availability of Wittgenstein's Later Philosophy" (*ibid.*), specifically his talk of "the voice of correctness". Again, I see the responses highlighted here each as instances of the "voice of correctness".
7. Indeed, the first is more *philosophically* traditional, while the second is perhaps contrary to philosophical tradition.

8. In a sense, we are not the ones best situated to answer a question about the meaning of "five", anyway: the shopkeeper is, for example. But again, I do not think that the shopkeeper *could* answer such a question. Yet he can act; he can use these words.

9. The superfluity of talk about meaning can be seen as an instance of Wittgenstein's resistance to reliance on explanation, which he has already introduced with the assertion that, "Explanations come to an end somewhere." That is, at some point explanations must stop (or else we would never do anything but explain). Resorting to talk about meaning can be seen as an attempt to prolong explanation when we could get by without it; we know this because we often *do* get by without it.

10. For another useful discussion of the translation of *erklären*, see Lugg (2004: 83). Lugg's assessment agrees with mine here. A similar point is made for a broader context in Stern's discussion of the translation of *Erklärung* (2004: 110).

11. Such a case is: "The meaning of this sentence escapes me." Here, we are not talking about a *word's* meaning, so looking at the use of a word presumably would not help us. Also, the following is important: not all explanations work in all contexts, for all people. What the reader brings to the *Investigations* is always relevant. Since in general words do not come to us in isolation, *a fortiori* nor do Wittgenstein's. I believe that I am in agreement with Lugg's understanding of this "restriction" (see Lugg 2004: 83).

12. Savigny (1990) is right to note that this works as it does because of the stage-setting that has already occurred (or, as Wittgenstein puts it in §31, because its "place has been prepared").

13. Baker and Hacker disagree: they seem to regard what I am suggesting here as "absurd" (1980: 250). But it seems to me that they ignore the fact that Wittgenstein calls the act of pointing an explanation, not a definition. (I treat the distinction between explanation and definition in chapter 5 of my *Wittgenstein and Myths of Meaning*.)

14. Lugg (2004: 83) explicitly notes that Wittgenstein goes on to give a counter-example to the advice given in the first part of the section. See also Charles Travis's discussion of naming (1989: 89). For a contrasting view, see Savigny (1990: 242). Savigny sees the last sentence of §43 as an instance of the advice of this section. Even understanding §43 as he does (endorsing substitution of "use" for "meaning", effectively equating them), this is not an instance where "use" would be *said*. Pointing alone is sufficient to explain the meaning here.

15. Hunter (1971: 390ff.) remarks upon what he calls the "humdrum character" of what Wittgenstein is telling us in §43. I think that he is right in highlighting this character, although his reading of §43 differs from mine. He does not see Wittgenstein as giving a definition of "meaning", nor does he see him as giving us a theory of what meaning consists in. However, he does see Wittgenstein as endorsing the claim that we may substitute "use" (in a language) for "meaning" (*ibid.*: 382), as Savigny does (see above). Thus Hunter does see Wittgenstein as making some sort of claim about how we use the word "meaning": it can always be substituted for by the word "use". I see this claim as too "substantial". What is important (and right) about this reading is this: Hunter urges one not to talk about meaning.

16. This is similar to what Wilson offers: "What Wittgenstein says about meaning as use is not intended as a theory in any constructive sense but as a *corrective* ... We need to be reminded that it is *use* we look to in order to decide whether someone knows the meaning of a word or sentence" (1998: 46).

17. Recall the discussion in §38 of naming appearing queer and as an occult process. This appearance is something Wittgenstein is trying to avoid, obviously – he thinks it is misleading. I take it that "the mysterious" invites philosophical speculation, too.

18. Richter offers a gloss of §43 to the effect that "[knowing] to what objects the word refers (if any), whether it is slang or not, what part of speech it is, whether it carries overtones, if so what kind they are, and so on[– t]o know all this, or to know enough to get by, is to know the use of the word. And generally knowing the use is knowing the meaning" (2004: 117). Now, I would not necessarily disagree with what he says here, but as an interpretation of §43 it can be potentially misleading. My basis for saying that I would not disagree with this is how we use the word "meaning", not because of an account of meaning that Wittgenstein has offered. Wittgenstein does not say that "knowing the use is knowing the meaning".

19. And note that Wittgenstein does not go on, in these sections, to tell us what the meaning of any of these words actually *is*. Rather, he is telling us something *about* their meanings.

20. If what I am saying is correct, this is an obvious way in which §43 is not offering us anything like a theory of meaning. (Presumably a theory of meaning *is* meant to stand on its own.)

21. So again, we see the conversational nature of the *Investigations* crucially at play here. To try to remove §43 from that context (for it to stand "on its own") is to fail to appreciate this important aspect of Wittgenstein's work.

22. Compare §560, which I shall address below.

23. Lugg talks about §43 in a similar way, as does Wilson. Glock attributes to the *Investigations* the view that "the meaning of names is determined by their use" (1989: 238), and this amounts to the beginnings of an account of what meaning is. Baker and Hacker's (or, now: Hacker's) discussion in *Wittgenstein: Understanding and Meaning* is more ambiguous. Ultimately I think that their interpretation does amount to ascribing an account of meaning to Wittgenstein.

24. As I see it, this "tone and spirit" is expressed well in a discussion on Quine by Floyd in her "Homage to Vienna": "It is important to understand (just as it is with Wittgenstein) that these characterizations are not what they can appear to be. They are not definitions, restrictions, or *a priori* specifications representing a philosophical opinion. Instead, they present open-ended, flexible, metaphors, i.e., opportunities for reflection" (2006: 40). Also see, although in a slightly different, more focused context, the discussion concluding Conant's essay "Stanley Cavell's Wittgenstein" (2005).

25. It is quite possible that one is left unsatisfied by what (I am saying that) Wittgenstein has said about meaning here. If we *are* unsatisfied, if we still want to ask, e.g., "but what *is* the meaning of a word?" then it seems clear that Wittgenstein wants us to reflect upon this (to see what our motivation is, and what kind of "analysis" we're looking for). This seems to be a major aim of his, through these first forty-three sections of the *Investigations*.

26. Wittgenstein first starts talking about meaning and physiognomy in late 1946.

27. See §§535–9 for a related discussion. There is a great deal of importance throughout these sections.

28. Rhees mentions the term in his "Preface" to the *The Blue and Brown Books* (1965: xv–xvi). He seems to place a good deal of significance on it, as he relates it to our understanding of "the use of language". In Wittgenstein's writings, it

first appears in MS 130 (1946, around when "Part II" was being written), where he asks: "does the meaning-blind person understand human language?"

29. See, for instance, MSS 135 (pp. 36–7, 51–2, 70–71, 77–8, 158–9), 137 (pp. 20b, 26a, 44a–b, 82b–83a).

30. One of these, discussed here and elsewhere of course, is the experience typified by the expression "Now I know how to go on!"

31. That is, it is not just meaning-blindness for *one word* that is under consideration.

32. See also the discussion about pain and the beetle, §293.

33. Compare §29: "and how he 'takes' the definition is seen in the use that he makes of the word defined".

34. Rhees is of the opinion that Wittgenstein was unsure. See Rhees (1965: xv).

35. I take this phrase from §268, which is a nice encapsulation of Wittgenstein's discussion of "private language".

36. Minar says, in his "Feeling at Home in Language (What Makes Reading *Philosophical Investigations* Possible?)", that the obviousness of grammatical remarks is "the sole source of their philosophical weight" (1995: 415). It does seem to me that one concern of Wittgenstein's is the justification of a philosophical account. How would we justify a theory of meaning? Wittgenstein's remarks *are* capable of justification: this justification is reflected by us, by our shared language and behaviour. (We can disagree with his remarks, as well, without undermining a theory.) The facts, as we might put it, upon which we rely are descriptions of what we say and do. What we say and do is just what we fall back on, when we have left the context of our philosophical discussions. (What is to be noted, and is important, is that Wittgenstein is not against philosophical theories *a priori*, as it were. If some theory or account of meaning did have significance for us and changed our lives accordingly, then *for that reason* it would be fine. The same would apply to scientific results or theories: this is an important sense in which Wittgenstein is not "anti-scientific". *A priori*, as it were, *anything* might become significant for us.)

37. Thanks to Peter Hylton, Bill Hart, Andrew Lugg and Mauro Engelmann for helpful comments and discussions at earlier stages of my thinking on these topics.

Further reading

Tractatus, all the 3s, but especially 3.3, 3.326–7, 4.002, 6.211.

THREE

Language-games and private language

Lars Hertzberg

The Augustinian picture

Wittgenstein's *Philosophical Investigations* opens with a quotation from Augustine's *Confessions*. Augustine is giving an account of learning to speak:

> When they (my elders) named some object, and accordingly moved towards something, I saw this and I grasped that the thing was called by the sound they uttered when they meant to point it out. Their intention was shown by their bodily movements, as it were the natural language of all peoples; the expression of the face, the play of the eyes, the movement of other parts of the body, and the tone of the voice which expresses our state of mind in seeking, having, rejecting, or avoiding something. Thus, as I heard words repeatedly used in their proper places in various sentences, I gradually learnt to understand what objects they signified; and after I had trained my mouth to form these signs, I used them to express my own desires. (§1)[1]

Of course, Augustine is not recounting from memory, but rather expressing a commonly held view of the way we learn to speak. "This is what must have happened", he is saying. The central idea here is that the child learns to recognize an object and to associate a word with it.

Now Wittgenstein's intention is to lead us away from this view of learning to speak. The reason he quotes Augustine, who was one of the few philosophers he really admired, was evidently that in his opinion

Augustine had given an uncommonly lucid account of this view. Wittgenstein wants us to see that the proposed account does not work. For one thing, a large part of speaking is not a matter of *referring to objects* in the first place; for another, this story could not even explain how we learn that. We shall get back to this.

Focusing on language learning provides an occasion for looking closely at what is involved in mastering a use of words, at the place of words in our lives. Wittgenstein thought it important to recognize the limitations of Augustine's account, because whether or not we are aware of this, the fact that we tacitly assume its correctness tends to govern our thinking about words and meaning, and thus it has bearings on the way we think about many of the problems of philosophy.

The core of the Augustinian picture, as Wittgenstein describes it, is this:

> the individual words in language name objects – sentences are combinations of such names. – In this picture of language we find the roots of the following idea: every word has a meaning. This meaning is correlated with the word. It is the object for which the word stands. *(Ibid.)*

The quotation from Augustine and Wittgenstein's comment on it are followed by what seems like a bizarre little story about a shopkeeper who is given a slip of paper marked "five red apples":

> the shopkeeper … opens the drawer marked "apples", then he looks up the word "red" in a table and finds a colour sample opposite it; then he says the series of cardinal numbers … and for each number he takes an apple of the same colour as the sample out of the drawer. *(Ibid.)*

Thereupon Wittgenstein comments: "It is in this and similar ways that one operates with words". This remark may strike us as outrageous. "Of course we do nothing of the sort!" we want to say. What Wittgenstein is trying to create here, however, is what might be called a distancing effect: we are so accustomed to operating with words that we are not aware of the complexity of what is involved in doing this. But try to imagine someone who is just coming to master these words, or who suffers from serious memory problems, and you may become aware of the skills that underlie the successful application of even the most everyday words of our language. The important thing to note here is that each of these words requires a different kind of skill: the use of the word "apple" is linked to a certain class of object, here illustrated by its being placed in a specific drawer with a name on it; the use of colour words is linked to a sample (of course we do not all refer to one and the same colour chart, but in learning colour words we learn to match the colours of new objects with those of objects we have been shown before); the use of number words is linked to the counting of objects. Here we see that each of the words on the slip of paper is linked to the end result, the bunch of apples he hands over to his customer, by a different type of relation, mediated through a different way of proceeding.

This little thought-experiment instantiates an important feature of Wittgenstein's way of doing philosophy: he is not so much giving arguments as working on our habits of thought. That is, he is trying to make us aware of our tacit assumptions in order to liberate us from them.

The builders' game

All of this takes place in §1 of *Philosophical Investigations*. In §2 the perspective is widened to include a larger activity: *A* is building something, and calling out "Block!", "Pillar!", "Slab!" to his helper, *B*, who brings him the building-stones. Wittgenstein asks us to imagine this as a complete primitive language, and he says that this is a language for which "the description given by Augustine is right". By this he evidently means that each word in this "language" is linked to a particular type of physical object, as in Augustine's story. Actually, even this rudimentary language goes beyond Augustine's account, since *A* and *B* do not simply associate words with objects, but make use of the words in their activity: *A* uses the words to get what he needs, and *B* responds accordingly. This activity is what their "associating" words and objects consists in. The connection between, say, the word "block" and this particular shape of building-stone is constituted by the activity of the builders. *B* will not learn what it is he is supposed to do simply by having the building-stones pointed out to him and hearing their names, since that would require that he gets more out of the teaching than is contained in the act of pointing.

Wittgenstein calls the act of explaining a word by pointing to an instance of its application "ostensive teaching" (*PI* §6). He is concerned to show the limitations of what can be achieved by this method. The pointing by itself does not convey the activity that constitutes the use of the word (cf. *PI* §§28–36). There are different aspects to this: on the one hand, there is the question of what we do in order to pick out the object in question, as illustrated by the case of the shopkeeper. What features are relevant for the application of this particular word? On the other hand, there is the question of how one is supposed to respond when the word is used.

The point of the language-game metaphor is to bring these activities surrounding the uttering of a word into focus. We might compare a word to the ball in a game or the pieces in chess: we have not learned to understand the game by simply observing the ball or the chess king or being told what they are called (*PI* §31). We must get clear about the *role* of the object in the game. Balls, for instance, are used in a variety of games: in one game you try to get the ball across the goal line or into a basket, in another you hit it across a net, in a third you try to hit it as far as you can while the other side tries to catch it, in yet another you try to hit your opponent with it, and so on. If you simply concentrate on the fact that in each of these activities a similar-shaped object is in use, you will miss out on all these essential differences.

Most parents presumably play various word-games with their infants in which they point to objects and utter their names. Even if this is not a way of conveying the use of words, it does not mean that these games are useless. Maybe in this way the child becomes attentive to the ritualistic aspect of language, to the fact that similar vocal sounds are produced in similar situations. In *Philosophical Investigations* §7 Wittgenstein speaks about "those games by means of which children learn their native language".

It does not matter that most parents probably have no clear idea of what actual bearing their efforts at teaching have on what their children end up learning: children do learn to speak!

Other than objects

After this, Wittgenstein proceeds with a further widening of the perspective on language. He imagines the builders' game coming to comprise numerals, as well as the demonstrative pronouns "this" and "there" (*PI* §8). The type of activity surrounding the use of *these* words is wholly different from that surrounding the names of building-stones. In §15 the idea of proper names is added. Furthermore, while the original builders' game consists only of orders, he now imagines a game of reporting: the helper is to tell the builder how many stones there are in a pile (§21). An order and a report might sound exactly the same: they are distinguished only by their role in the game: an order means that the helper should, as we say, *make* it true; a report should *be* true. This brings us to the different roles of utterances. In §23 Wittgenstein points out that there are – not three (assertions, questions, commands) but – countless kinds of sentence, and he gives a list (seemingly random) of 24 different uses of sentences, among them: describing the appearance of an object or giving its measurements, singing catches, telling a joke, translating, thanking and praying.

After this, there follows a long sequence of remarks in which the points made in these initial passages are further refined and related to various debates in philosophy concerning the concept of meaning, existence, particulars. Wittgenstein is here more or less explicit in his criticism of his own thinking in the *Tractatus*, as well as that of Gottlob Frege. Thus Frege's requirement that a concept must have sharp limits if it is to be a real concept is replaced with the notion that what is important is that we can use a concept in practice. The word "game" itself is here used as a central example (*PI* §§65–71). There is no single characteristic or set of characteristics that all games have in common, at most different games are connected through a family resemblance, yet we mostly have no difficulty using the word "game" for various practical purposes. Thus the existence of common features is not required for a word to have a place in our life. The idea that the objects to which a word applies must have some features in common is due to a mistaken picture of what is involved in a word having meaning. According to Wittgenstein, this also throws light on language itself: a large variety of human activities are united by the fact that words (even many of the same words) are used in them, yet there are no specific common features making all cases of using words instances of speaking language.

If we think of speaking as playing language-games, the implication seems to be that in speaking we follow a distinct set of rules that could be formulated in words. But Wittgenstein points out that this may be too simple an idea of language. The sense in which a game has rules may vary from one type of game to another. In §83 Wittgenstein writes:

Doesn't the analogy between language and games throw light here? We can easily imagine people amusing themselves in a field by playing with a ball so as to start various existing games, but playing many without finishing them and in between throwing the ball aimlessly into the air, chasing one another with the ball and bombarding one another for a joke and so on. And now someone says: The whole time they are playing a ball-game and following definite rules at every throw.

And is there not also the case where we play and – make up the rules as we go along? And there is even one where we alter them – as we go along.

The sense in which our speaking is regulated, then, varies from one situation to another. In some contexts (say, in a court of law) the way to proceed is clearly laid down and we can give an account of it, in other contexts we may all proceed in more or less the same way without being able to spell out the principles involved (say, among a team of carpenters), yet again there are contexts in which we improvise, and where we reckon with others being able to go along with what we are doing (say, in spirited conversation).

This observation should serve as a warning against a certain way of going on with the concept of a language-game. It might be tempting to think that Wittgenstein is outlining a programme for philosophy, that of cataloguing the language-games that there are (at least the main ones) and listing their rules. This, roughly, was the direction taken by Wittgenstein's contemporary J. L. Austin (see Austin 1962). It is not just that such a task would be philosophically banal, since it would serve no purpose unless it were done in the service of addressing particular philosophical difficulties. In fact, it could not be done since the task would be indeterminate and open-ended. For one thing, language-games keep on changing, and for another, the question of what should be seen as constituting a different language game may itself be a matter requiring philosophical reflection.

In fact, the idea that our speaking is ultimately guided by formulated rules leads to an infinite regress. For the rules, being formulated in a language, would have to be applied, and this would then presuppose a different set of formulated rules for their application, and so on. What is basic to our speaking is not the knowledge of certain rules, but rather the fact that we have learnt to act in certain ways. This is a recurrent theme in Wittgenstein's later work. (There is an extended discussion of rule-following in the *Philosophical Investigations*, which is beyond the scope of this chapter.)

The so-called private-language argument

Wittgenstein's rejection of the Augustinian picture of language learning has an important implication, one that has been an object of intense discussion: the critique of the idea of a private language. This critique occurs, roughly, in *Philosophical Investigations* §§243–315. A core remark in this critique is §258:

Let us imagine the following case. I want to keep a diary about the recurrence of a certain sensation. To this end I associate it with the sign "S" and write this sign in a calendar for every day on which I have the sensation. – I will remark first of all that a definition of the sign cannot be formulated. – But still I can give myself a kind of ostensive definition. – How? Can I point to the sensation? Not in the ordinary sense. But I speak, write the sign down, and at the same time I concentrate my attention on the sensation – and so, as it were, point to it inwardly. – But what is this ceremony for? for that is all it seems to be! A definition surely serves to establish the meaning of a sign. – Well, that is done precisely by the concentrating of my attention; for in this way I impress on myself the connexion between the sign and the sensation. – But "I impress it on myself" can only mean: this process brings it about that I remember the connexion *right* in the future. But in the present case I have no criterion of correctness. One would like to say: whatever is going to seem right to me is right. And that only means that here we can't talk about "right".

This remark is a prime example of Wittgenstein's style of reasoning. It has the form of a compact dialogue between a protagonist (Wittgenstein himself, as it were) and an interlocutor, but without indication of which remark goes with which participant. Sometimes there are more than two voices, and it is only by sensing what Wittgenstein is driving at that one is able to keep the participants apart. In some remarks, the distribution of roles is controversial, but in the present case there is a large consensus on how the remark is to be read: the interlocutor – let us call her the diarist (D) – introduces the idea of a diary about a sensation, and she does not see any problem with this idea. The protagonist (W), on the other hand, is arguing that we do not really have any clear understanding of what D is describing here. What D is proposing has analogies with what an Augustinian account of learning the names of sensations would have to look like. That would have to mean that to learn the meanings of words like "pain", "hunger", "itch", and so on, is to associate them with particular sensations. However, unlike the case of physical objects, a sensation (consistently with this account) is present only to the person who has it, so a teacher cannot point to my sensations and tell me "That's a pain", nor can she inspect my sensations to check whether or not I have caught on to the correct use of sensation words. So if the Augustinian account is to apply, I must do the pointing and checking myself. But this is where W sees a problem. What is it to define a word to oneself? Of course, if one already has the use of a language for the purpose, there is no problem: I may undertake to use the sign "S" to refer, say, to "a tingling sensation in my lower lip". But the point about *D* is that she has no suitable vocabulary at her disposal. All she can do, it appears, is to undertake, inwardly, to use the sign "S" for this and only this sensation.

But what would it mean for *D* to "undertake" that? When I undertake to act in a certain way, what I proceed to do either is or is not in accordance with my undertaking. If "anything goes", I have not really made an undertaking. In the present case, however, there seems to be no basis for deciding what is or is not in accordance with the undertaking. Suppose the next day *D* has an inclination to write an "S": would she be right in doing so? Is it really the same sensation? The problem is not that her memory may deceive her, but that no standard has been established for deciding whether she remembers correctly or not. Calling two items instances of "the same kind" presupposes some standard of comparison, but in this case no such standard has been provided. The illusion that there is a standard comes from our imagining that in concentrating my mind on a sensation I am at the same time laying down a standard of application. If there is to be room for talk about a standard, there must be *room for judging* whether I am acting correctly or not, independently of my inclination to act in this way or that.

Wittgenstein's private-language discussion has a number of dimensions, and it has been read in a variety of ways. Here I wish to focus on one aspect of it. In the second remark following the one just quoted (*PI* §260), Wittgenstein writes:

> – Then did the man who made the entry in the calendar make a note of *nothing whatever*? – Don't consider it a matter of course that a person is making a note of something when he makes a mark – say in a calendar. For a note has a function, and this "S" so far has none.
> (One can talk to oneself. – Does everyone who speaks when no one else is present speak to himself?)[2]

Compare the case of the builder and his helper. If the helper brings a slab when the builder calls for a beam, the builder may correct him. If there were no correcting going on, there would be no room for speaking about moves as correct or incorrect. On the other hand, suppose the builder uses a slab when he really needs a beam. If he tries to fit it into the construction, he may notice that it does not work: the construction may become unstable or he is unable to go on. An onlooker can criticize his choice on purely technical grounds, since he can see the point of what the builder is doing. But when it comes to using the names of the building-stones, there is no such external standpoint from which to judge the use of the names independently of their role in the interaction between the builder and his helper. Thus, if the builder went on building by himself we could still make sense of what he was doing. However, if he were to call out the names of building-stones by himself, it would be hard to make sense of what he was doing as a case of saying something. His calls would only have *the appearance* of moves in a language-game. And something similar goes for the sensation diarist.

But do we never speak to ourselves? Of course we do, as Wittgenstein acknowledges. We will sometimes utter words out loud, say, in doing a calculation, or when trying to think of a person's name. However, this is done against the background of a shared language in which a distinction is made between getting it right and getting it wrong. Here we may wonder what the speaker means. (We may even correct someone who is doing maths out loud for himself.) Merely uttering words by ourselves, however, does not necessarily mean that we are speaking to ourselves in this sense; thus someone may be in the habit of repeating the last words he has heard under his breath without thinking of what he is doing. Here there is no question of what he means, and no distinguishing between right and wrong. What Wittgenstein is suggesting is that a sensation diary, without the background of a shared language, would be just as pointless as this type of speaking by oneself.

But if we cannot decide whether *one* person is right or wrong, some commentators have asked, what difference does it make if there are two people, or even a whole community? Cannot they all be wrong together? This question misses the point, however. After all, what would the community be wrong about? It is *its* language. It is not that a community is required to guarantee that something is correct, but rather: only between the members of a community trying to speak to one another is there any serious place for a distinction between right and wrong. Only there is there a space for disagreement and criticism concerning the use of words. This does not mean that there is always a way of resolving these disagreements, but that does not render it pointless to *seek* agreement.

But why, some have asked, cannot the sharing come later? Suppose a solitary individual starts up a diary, and then later she comes into contact with language-speakers and learns to explain her notes in their language. Would not that be sufficient to show that her notes had meaning to begin with; that there was a way of distinguishing right from wrong even before? But then the question is: what is she supposed to explain to them? She could not convey the point of the "diary" since the diary did not have a point. There would be nothing to appeal to in order to provide a space for the question whether her explanations were correct or not. So the idea that the language might already be there before it comes to be shared is unintelligible.

What are the lessons to be learnt?

Many readers of Wittgenstein who have taken his comments on private language to heart have assumed that its import lies in the light it throws on first-person psychological utterances – expressions of pain, feelings, intentions, beliefs and so on. However, it can also be argued – and there is some merit to the suggestion – that it really has a wider bearing on our thinking about what it means to be a speaker of language. On this view, the critique of the private diarist, together with the language-game metaphor, are meant to focus our attention on the actual situations in which people use words because they have something to say to one another, rather than, as has been the tradition in philosophy, limit our attention to the objects *about* which we are speaking. This means that speakers and listeners are placed in the centre of our enquiry. On this reading, the problems of philosophy are to be resolved, not by conceptual analysis in the abstract, but by listening in on the conversations carried out by particular people in particular situations, in order to take note of the role of the words of our language in those contexts.[3]

Notes

1. The edition referred to in this chapter is *Philosophical Investigations* (2001a).
2. I have deviated from Anscombe's translation in the last sentence.
3. I wish to thank David Cockburn for a number of helpful comments.

Further reading

Tractatus, 3.318–3.33.

FOUR

Wittgenstein on family resemblance

Craig Fox

Introduction

Family resemblance is one of Wittgenstein's best-known topics, although in all his philosophical work he spent relatively little time explicitly devoted to it alone. In this chapter, I shall give an overview of the treatment of family resemblance in the *Philosophical Investigations*.[1] It will become clear almost immediately that Wittgenstein's concern is not, as it is often portrayed, with the classic metaphysical debate between realists and nominalists.[2] Rather, he is discussing an aspect of our use of language. He is concerned to combat the accepted or perceived significance of the notion of "what makes language *language*" – or of the essence of language, one might say.[3] The assumptions that there must be an essence of language, that the philosopher should endeavour to give an account of it, and that such an account is a necessary philosophical step are intimately related to targets of Wittgenstein's throughout the *Investigations* as a whole.

Philosophical Investigations §65

We should observe right from the beginning that Wittgenstein's discussion of family resemblance begins in §65, as opposed to §66. This is sometimes overlooked, and to do so is to pluck Wittgenstein's treatment out of the context in which he placed it. In a work as conversational in style as the *Investigations*, this can be a most dangerous interpretive strategy. What comes in §66 comes as an explanation of an idea broached in §65:

[S]omeone might object against me: "You take the easy way out! You talk about all sorts of language-games, but have nowhere said what the essence of a language-game, and hence of language, is: what is common to all these activities, and what makes them into language or parts of language. So you let yourself off the very part of the investigation that once gave you yourself most headache, the part about the *general form of propositions* and of language."

And this is true. – Instead of producing something common to all that we call language, I am saying that these phenomena have no one thing in common which makes us use the same word for all, – but that they are *related* to one another in many different ways. And it is because of this relationship, or these relationships, that we call them all "language". I will try to explain this.

The discussion that begins with §66 is an explanation of the idea that it is because of the various kinds of relationships between our uses of words that we call all of the words together *language*. So we do not call language "language", for instance, in virtue of the fact that every word plays some particular role that it must play in order to be a part of language. Wittgenstein situates himself as not attempting to provide an account of the essence of language.[4] His suggestion, which is to be developed both in these sections and in the book as a whole, is that we have reason to think that a search for the essence of language is bound to run into (insurmountable?) difficulties and that it would be, besides, unnecessary.

This idea that the essence of language would be something useful is one that Wittgenstein has been working in opposition to from the very first section of the book. In §1, he offers a quotation from Augustine, in which we read of the young Augustine's entry into language. Wittgenstein uses this account to extract "a particular picture of the essence of human language. It is this: the individual words in language name objects – sentences are combinations of such names." A good deal of what he goes on to do serves to undermine this picture, which he seems to treat with the respect due to a serious threat.[5] He shows that while it works well for some examples, in many cases it comes to seem rather strained, not as applicable, useless, or downright wrong. One could choose to hold on to the picture in spite of these worries, but one does so at the risk of contradicting things we meaningfully say all the time. (In "working against the idea of the essence of language", I mean to say that he is giving us reasons to avoid such a notion. He has *not* shown, nor is he concerned to show here, that *there is no essence*.[6] Doing so would run into similar kinds of problems to the ones he is highlighting.)

A natural response to the beginning of the book, which Wittgenstein offers in §65, is then something along these lines: "All right, you've given us reason to believe this picture is not a good one. So what is the proper picture? Give us an account, yourself, that's not going to fall prey to the observations you've been making." Wittgenstein resists doing so – or at least, that is how I would like to read his remarks. Some commentators have thought that Wittgenstein did give us an account, albeit of a new kind.[7] I prefer not to read the sections on family resemblance in this way, because it does not square with what I take to be the aims of the book as a whole. I shall say more about this below. It should be noted that reading the *Investigations* in the way I am suggesting can be hard: this is precisely where many philosophers find Wittgenstein to be simply evasive and frustrating. Part of Wittgenstein's purpose here is to show why he is not avoiding doing something that could be worthwhile. Perhaps ironically, the frustration is actually continuous with what Russell highlights at the beginning of *The Problems of Philosophy*, that it is *difficult* to give answers to philosophical questions, because of all the "obstacles" that stand in the way (Russell 1912: 7–8) – that is, the frustration is part of the price we pay for engaging in philosophy.[8]

Philosophical Investigations §§66–7

Philosophical Investigations §66 begins the famous discussion of games:

> Consider for example the proceedings that we call "games". I mean board-games, card-games, ball-games, Olympic games, and so on. What is common to them all? – Don't say: "There *must* be something common, or they would not be called 'games'" – but *look and see* whether there is anything common to all. – For if you look at them you will not see something that is common to *all*, but similarities, relationships, and a whole series of them at that. To repeat: don't think, but look! …

Wittgenstein then goes on to portray some of this "looking" by surveying different features of different games. He concludes in this way: "And the result of this examination is: we see a complicated network of similarities overlapping and criss-crossing: sometimes overall similarities, sometimes similarities of detail." In §67 he writes, "I can think of no better expression to characterize these similarities than 'family resemblances'".[9]

Wittgenstein uses the term "family resemblance" as short-hand for a particular feature of the way we use (at least some) words: there are words such as "game" that we use to name a variety of kinds of things people do, even though there is no one feature common to all of these activities.[10] It would be natural to assume that since we call them all games, they must have something in common, in virtue of which we name them "games" – and while we appreciate the force of this assumption, Wittgenstein wants us to question it. The evidence that it need not be true is found in our everyday uses of words.

Do we in fact use the word "game" in the way Wittgenstein describes? Again, the evidence for the correctness of what he has asserted simply is our own uses of words.[11] It seems plausible to me to say that we do use "game" in this way. Baseball, hearts, tic-tac-toe, solitaire, "I spy", duck–duck–goose, chase, tag and so on are all games. I would be hard pressed to find a common element that isolates the essence of "game-hood". But further, it also seems plausible to me that using "game" in the way Wittgenstein describes is consistent with how I understand the word. Suppose I were to see three people simply standing on the side of Kedzie Boulevard, and as far as I can tell they are doing nothing else. I see someone I know watching these three people, and I approach her, asking what the people are doing. She tells me that they are playing a game. I would be at a loss: how is this a game? It does not seem as if they are doing anything. But if she were to tell me that it was like a staring contest, but instead it was a "stationary contest", then it would make more sense. I could then understand how this activity was in fact a game. Now what happened here was that one of those overlapping similarities was made clear to me. This explained why calling it a game was appropriate. It certainly does not matter that there is no ball, nor movement, nor a professional league that encourages its play. That is, some features of some games are lacking in this activity, while some features of some games are present; it is in virtue of these common features that it makes sense to me (and to my friend) to call what these people are doing "playing a game".

I have thus downplayed the significance of the question of whether Wittgenstein's description of our use of "game" is right. Although I think he probably is right in his description, what is significant is that it seems at least *potentially* right. But if it is potentially right (at least), then we can see that the assumption that there must be something in common to different games can be eliminated.

Many commentators have spent time addressing what we might call "the scope question". The scope question is this: to what extent are our uses of all our various words akin to family resemblances in the way described? Let us assume that we do in fact use "game" in the way Wittgenstein describes. This establishes one use of a word that need not have a common (and peculiar) element present in each of its correct applications. But is it the only one? Presumably not, since Wittgenstein's concern seems to be wider in scope than simply the use of "game" – after all, this is the beginning of an explanation of why he does not give us an account of the essence of language. Well then, is it the case that we use *all* words in this way? This is a sizeable claim, and one for which Wittgenstein would have to supply much more evidence if this were what he was trying to establish. He does not do so, though; he does not provide us with many more words of different types, for instance, and he does not make general arguments about how we use all words in this way.[12] (This is good, too: consider "biological mother". At first blush at least, it seems that there is a set of features that applies to all and only biological mothers.) How many words do we use like "game" and how many do we not?

My suggestion is that Wittgenstein does not intend to give an answer to the scope question. Rather, he uses the discussion of "game" simply to call to our attention the possibility of our using words in this way. Whether we use some particular word as we do "game" is a matter of linguistic practice. (Linguistic practices also change a good deal: it is important that I can imagine circumstances in which certain activities could come to be correctly described as games while presently they are not, and this need not mean that "our concept of 'game'" has changed – whatever this might mean.) What is important is that we have a reason to reject the assumption that we *only* use the same word in different contexts only because those contexts have something in common.

Wittgenstein introduces an important image in §67, that of spinning a thread, in order to illustrate the feature of family resemblance that he is emphasizing. The thread as a whole is meant to stand for our concept of a game. "We extend our concept ... as in spinning a thread we twist fiber on fiber. And the strength of the thread does not reside in the fact that some one fiber runs through its whole length, but in the overlapping of many fibers." That is, our concept is usable in all the various ways it is because of overlapping similarities between different contexts in which it is applicable. A better way to put this is to say that our concept of a game is gleaned from all the settings in which we correctly use the word "game" – and some of these settings are similar to others, while remaining perhaps dissimilar from yet others.

An objection is raised at the end of this section, one that a particular kind of well-trained philosopher might make. "There is something common to all these constructions – namely the disjunction of all their common properties." This is to say that what is common to games is that they are played with balls, or, they are contests of skill, or, they are played with cards, or, they employ a board, or, ... What is common would be this long "or" sentence. Wittgenstein discards this as "playing with words", for how would this property serve to highlight the essence of gamehood – or what all games have in common? The very formulation of it suggests that in fact there is nothing that all games have in common.

Philosophical Investigations §68

In §68 Wittgenstein speaks of concepts having or lacking frontiers [*Grenzen*]. He suggests that one *may* use a concept (perhaps my example of "biological mother") in such a way that it has very clear, rigid limits. Thus we know, for any given thing, whether it is correct to call it a "biological mother". We also know, of any biological mother, certain traits it will have. But "game", according to Wittgenstein, is not like this: its applications are not closed by a frontier. What does this mean? Suppose we were to come across people, much like the ones I spotted in Chicago, behaving in a strange way. But now, suppose that nobody was there to help me understand what was happening. A couple of days later, I see some more people, behaving in a similarly strange way – and I still cannot make sense of it. Familiar faces keep showing up on the street, and there always seems to be a lot of back-slapping and congratulations as they leave an hour or so later. Are these people playing a game? Perhaps they are, perhaps they are not. One would not be inclined to call it a game without more information about what was going on. But suppose it was something like a "stationary contest". Is this a game? With a rigidly delimited concept like "biological mother"[13] we can tell of any x whether "x is a biological mother" is true or false. But one might get into an argument over the "stationary contest". Maybe it is more "something one does when one is bored", or "something people are suddenly doing because they've heard of others doing it", or ... How would this argument go, between "pro-gamers" and "anti-gamers"? It would revolve around "similarity conditions", as they have been called (see e.g. Weitz 1956). Perhaps no consensus would be reached – it is certainly possible, at least. "What still counts as a game and what no longer does? Can you give the boundary? No ... none has so far been drawn."

The worry at this point, perhaps offered by one still attached to the "essence" (one common element) notion, is that if what Wittgenstein is saying is true, then this destroys our concept of game. It would seem then that we use words arbitrarily, and surely *that* cannot be good. Wittgenstein is unsympathetic to these kinds of fears: the lack of a boundary "never troubled you before when you used the word 'game'", he says.[14] In other words, the fact that we cannot decide about this "stationary contest" never affected your uses of "game" in most other contexts. It did not jeopardize your description of Monopoly when you told someone about it.

This worry runs deep, however. It comes right back to the original purpose of this discussion: the idea of an essence of language. For surely, one might think, our words must be "intimately linked" to the things they are about. That is part of how we talk about those things with those words. Linguistic freedom, one might say, is equivalent to linguistic anarchy: everyone using words in whichever ways they choose. (§68: "'But then the use of the word is unregulated, the "game" we play with it is unregulated.'" §70: "But if the concept 'game' is uncircumscribed like that, you don't really know what you mean by a game.") I decide this is a game, you decide it is not, and we are each neither right nor wrong. Linguistic anarchy is bad, because we ultimately would not be able to communicate with each other, as we shall not even know what we are talking about.

The "freedom" that Wittgenstein highlights does not lead to anarchy, he believes. This is an important point. He compares the situation to tennis. There is freedom in tennis: one may throw the ball any height when serving, one may hit the ball as hard as one chooses, and so forth. So there can be non-vicious freedom. It remains for Wittgenstein to establish how this might be possible for language. It also remains for him to assuage the fears about our "not knowing what we are talking about".

Philosophers have assumed that we need to have precise boundaries to our concepts in order to be able to use them properly and in order to satisfy philosophical goals. Kant, for instance, relied upon conceptual precision in his formulation of what makes for analytic and synthetic claims (see e.g. Kant 1997: A6–7/B10–11). If one concept is correctly said to be "contained" within the other, then the truth about this relationship is described as analytic. This distinction was all-important for his task of establishing the existence of synthetic *a priori* knowledge, of which $7 + 5 = 12$ is a prime example. A century later Frege, no philosophical friend of Kant's, also relied upon conceptual precision (see e.g. Frege 1972: §3). For him, the consequence of precision is a clear-cut demarcation between truth and falsity and a clear demarcation of conceptual content, essential for building his symbolic language that would make the language of science rigorous. But Wittgenstein wants to highlight these kinds of assumptions as unfounded. While for Kant or Frege they seemed like uncontroversial assumptions, Wittgenstein highlights that they are assumptions of rigour being imposed upon our uses of words.[15] He discusses Frege explicitly (see Frege 1997: §56), in particular his notion that a concept with vague boundaries is not really a concept at all. Wittgenstein asks: "But is it senseless to say: 'Stand roughly there'?" He goes on to illustrate that it is not simply senseless to say something vague, that vague boundaries[16] can be perfectly acceptable in some circumstances. From my saying "stand roughly there", I shall be able to pick you up after I go and get my car – in spite of any vagueness inherent in what I said. So it is not senseless for one to say "stand roughly there". We can understand how we might use these words.[17] This serves to link the words to our lives, as opposed to an abstract rigorous standard – for this is how *we* use *our* words.

People do various things with words, and part of what we do with the word "game" is to teach others how to use it. We might do this by relying upon certain established games as exemplars, and then by permitting the learner to extrapolate on the basis of these. (See §69.) When one "goes on" with the word, one might make a mistake. A child refers to the mother's doing her taxes as a game: he is told that no, doing taxes is not a game – as much as it might resemble doing a crossword puzzle or playing hangman when viewed from afar. Another child gets seriously upset when she has to pay rent in Monopoly: she is told that it is only a game, after all – she does not actually owe her brother any money. In these ways and others, children learn the word "game".

Philosophical Investigations §§72–3

In §§72–3, Wittgenstein describes some of this "going on".[18] He introduces it with the words "seeing what is common". For when we go on with a word, if we do it correctly, then presumably we have seen what is in common for the various (correct) applications of the word. He examines colour words here. First, he says, "[s]uppose I show someone various multicolored pictures and say: 'The color you see in all these is called "yellow ochre"'". Then he contrasts this with a case in which "I show him samples of different shades of blue and say: 'The color that is common to all these is what I call "blue"'". One can see the relevance of what we might call "colour teaching" to the discussion up to this point: while certain samples are going to obviously be classified as "yellow ochre" or "blue", it is easy to imagine cases where even the experienced colour-word user will be unsure. When we imagine the colour-word learner, though, we envision her trying to "see what is in common" to the beginning examples.

In this way, we might arrive at the idea that "to have understood the definition means to have in one's mind an idea of the thing defined, and that is a sample or a picture".[19] And thus one might come to the view that in fact the "family-resemblance" situation should not be applicable. One just needs to have the appropriate idea in one's mind, and then the applications of the word will be straightforward (almost simply "read off the idea", as it were). But to see the idea in one's mind as the general kind of idea that it is, is to see it as "blue in general", for instance.[20] In this way we know that the particular *shape* we might imagine or the particular *shade* we might imagine is not significant (as it is when I am trying to find my other shoe, for instance). We are supposed to use the conception of "blue in general" to enable us to describe countless kinds of things as "light blue", "dark blue", "royal blue" and so on. But now we see how this notion – "having in one's mind an idea of the thing defined" – does not do the work one might have assumed it would. We are still confronted with the very greenish-blue sample and the decision of whether to call it "green" or "blue".

Again, Wittgenstein resists the "anarchic conclusion" that we do not know what blue is. We are tempted to say this at all only because of some assumption about the necessary precision of our concepts. In §75 he says, "What does it mean to know what a game is? What does it mean to know it and not be able to say it? Is this knowledge somehow equivalent to an unformulated definition?" To think that it is, that we have just not been able to formulate the definition yet, for whatever reason, is still to be committed to the "precision of concepts" view. It is to refuse to see that everything we say about games (or about blue) does tell us perfectly adequately what games are (or what blue is). "Isn't my knowledge, my concept of a game, completely expressed in the explanations that I could give?" To think that something more, something better is in the offing is to succumb to a tempting illusion. This is the illusion Wittgenstein is trying to break in these sections on family resemblance.

Conclusion

I have already indicated a number of ways in which an assumption about the precision of concepts can enter into traditional philosophical concerns. In §77, Wittgenstein briefly mentions some others. Speaking of attempts to make that which has some inherent vagueness more precise,[21] he says, "this is the position you are in if you look for definitions corresponding to our concepts in aesthetics or ethics". The suggestion, which is not developed here at all, is that "good", for instance, might have a "family of meanings" similar to the way "game" does.

I mentioned above that Wittgenstein's "family-resemblance" discussion was intimately related to goals with the *Investigations* as a whole. I highlighted Wittgenstein's description of the result of our reflecting upon our use of game in §66: "we see a complicated network of similarities overlapping and criss-crossing". This description could indeed be applied to Wittgenstein's discussions overall. In the "Preface" (*PI* ix–x), he describes how he could never "weld his results together" into a traditionally arranged book, with everything proceeding "from one subject to another in a natural order and without breaks". It was due to "the very nature of the investigation" that this would not be the case. "For this compels us to travel over a wide field of thought criss-cross in every direction."

The "family-resemblance" discussion can thus be seen as a model for many of Wittgenstein's other discussions in the *Investigations*. In it, he (i) challenges the assumption that language has an essence, (ii) challenges the assumption about the precision of concepts, (iii) warns against role that "mental objects" can play for philosophical explanations, and (iv) provides an illustration of his philosophical methodology, in which he considers not only paradigmatic cases of language uses but anomalous ones as well. [22]

Notes

1. The edition referred to in this chapter is *Philosophical Investigations* (2001a).
2. For a mere sampling from the literature, compare some of the discussions in: Bambrough (1961), Wennerberg (1967), Simon (1969), Khatchadourian (1958), McCloskey (1964), and Griffin (1974). It should be noted that Bambrough's paper really set the pace for discussions of family resemblance in the secondary literature.
3. One might try to use such a notion as the basis of an account of how our words mean what they do, for instance. Wittgenstein is trying to combat such a project as well.
4. This is contrary to appearances, at least, in Wittgenstein's earlier work, the *Tractatus*. See especially 4.5–6. The phrase used in §65 (*die allgemeine Form des Satzes*) is exactly that used, for instance, in proposition 6 of the *Tractatus*.
5. Compare Russell (1956) in his "Philosophy of Logical Atomism". He talks of "Socrates" standing for the man, "mortal" standing for a quality, and "Socrates is mortal" standing for a fact. Words or sentences stand for different types of things, then. Although there are multiple types of relationships between the symbol and what is symbolized, at bottom he retains this picture of symbol and object (*ibid.*: 186–7ff.).

6. For instance, compare what I am saying with Hallett (1977: 140–41). Sluga seems to make a similar error in his, "Family Resemblance" (2006).

7. See accounts, for example, by Bambrough, Wennerberg, Teichman (1969), Khatchadourian, Ewing (1971), Baker & Hacker (2005: 145–6). However, compare accounts by Dilman (1978–9) and Lugg (2004).

8. Of course, Russell and Wittgenstein have quite different notions of what counts as a legitimate philosophical question and of what would ultimately count as an answer.

9. It is perhaps best not to take the term "family resemblance" too literally. One might think: here is a group of people, and they all have that Smith nose – that is family resemblance. This is *not* what Wittgenstein is getting at. Rather, his picture is that some Smiths have the Smith nose, some have the Smith smile, some have the Smith hairline, some have the Smith build, and so on. But it is very likely that no one Smith has all features. Nonetheless, when taken as a whole, the members of this group of people are said to share a family resemblance. (Gert [1995] points out that the term "family resemblance" is helpful at least in this way: one is surely not a Smith *in virtue of* certain family resemblances.)

10. Being a bit more precise, we might rephrase this as follows: there need be no one common feature to all and only these activities.

11. For a similar point, see Minar (1995: 415).

12. Further on in §67, he does give us "number" as another example. This might seem to conflict with mathematical constructions of the numbers from a common basis (say from the natural numbers), although I do not think that it does. For we do not use the construction of the integers from the naturals to justify our speaking of both kinds of number *as numbers*. In other words, we use the word "number" for real numbers, rational numbers and integers because of certain overlapping similarities – not because of some mathematical construction or analysis.

13. I am assuming that "biological mother" will count as a rigidly delimited concept. I am not actually sure that it would. I can imagine circumstances in which its boundaries are expanded as well. Charles Travis seems to be of the view that any concept is boundary-less in the relevant way (Travis 1989: chs 1–2).

14. There is a fruitful comparison to be made here between what Wittgenstein is saying about language use and what he says elsewhere about Frege and contradictions in mathematics. I cannot pursue this connection further here; for some particular examples, however, see Wittgenstein's *Remarks on the Foundations of Mathematics* (1978b: II, 58; III, 12; III, 80; IV, 60).

15. "We are not *striving after* an ideal, as if our vague sentences had not yet got a quite unexceptionable sense, and a perfect language awaited construction by us" (§98).

16. If I stand 1 foot from where he pointed, is that in accord with the order? If I stand 10 feet away? What about 20? What if he pointed to a location on a map? We would generally know in particular circumstances.

17. Note that *this* is the basis for the claim about the words making sense. He is simply relying upon our ordinary notion of sense.

18. Knowing "how to go on" is of course an integral part of the Wittgenstein's discussion of rule-following.

19. One potential target here is a view (such as C. I. Lewis's) that identifies a meaning with a criterion in mind.

20. It might be worth putting some of this discussion alongside that of "seeing as" in *Investigations*, Part II, xi ff.

21. I use the expression "inherent vagueness" – but this should not be misunderstood. The application of "game" is vague to whatever degree it is because that is how we use our words. That is, it is not vague because the idea of a game somehow is "necessarily" vague. I still say "inherently vague" reflecting the fact that for *me*, it is: our uses of "game" have been around much longer than I.

22. I am very appreciative of helpful comments by Bill Hart on a draft of this chapter.

Further reading

Tractatus, 4.5–6, 5.21–5.41.

FIVE

Ordinary/everyday language

Rupert Read

Wittgenstein is in practice generally thought to be some variety of "Ordinary-Language" Philosopher, that is, a philosopher who takes ordinary language (as opposed to scientific language, to "technical" language, or to its bastard child, "super-scientific" ("metaphysical") language) to be our keystone in philosophy; and who thinks that philosophy can proceed therefore by means of paying careful attention to the way we normally actually speak, and prohibiting uses that conflict with the way we normally actually speak.

And indeed, what "ordinary/everyday language" is taken to be opposed to is critical. The key point of this chapter is however to suggest, *contra* what still tends to be the prevailing wisdom, that the crucial mistake in "Wittgenstein studies" has generally been to misidentify the contrast class that Wittgenstein intended. I call it "the crucial" mistake, for the mistake has (had) enormous consequences, as I shall seek briefly to demonstrate.

We should begin with the single most important passage in *Philosophical Investigations* for understanding Wittgenstein's employment of the term "everyday":

When philosophers use a word – for instance "knowledge", "being", "object", "I", "proposition", or "name" – and try to grasp the essence of the thing, one must always ask oneself: is the word ever actually used in this way in the *language*, which is after all its home? // What *we* do is to bring words back from their metaphysical to their everyday use.[1]

The first thing to say about this famous passage is that it opens with a *question*; and that the sentence that follows does not answer the question (or at least, does not "reveal" it to have been a merely rhetorical question). The question ought to be regarded (at the very least provisionally) as a genuine question, motivating one in one's subsequent philosophical activities. Thus it is always (for those of us who wish to follow Wittgenstein's method) initially an open question whether or not the philosophical remarks that we are interrogating can be seen as involving "home-spun" or "home-baked" language uses, or not. I shall return to this critically crucial presumption of interpretive charity below.

Furthermore, Gordon Baker makes a vital move in helping us to understand what is going on in this potentially deceptive passage, when he suggests that we ought to regard the concept that one as it were starts from or with, here, as the metaphysical.[2] Rather than presupposing (what there is precious little textual warrant for in Wittgenstein) that the everyday is some secure area of language that we can look to for forceful guidance as to how logic will "permit" us to speak, we might rather be guided by the fact that predecessor versions of this remark in earlier texts of Wittgenstein's *Nachlass* all feature the word "metaphysical", but oscillate between *various* other words as its possible contrast-class (Baker 2004: ch. 4, 100ff.).

Thus we *start* with the question as to what one is trying to do when one uses a word (such as "being" or "object" or "this", etc.) in a sense that does or is something entirely extraordinary, or that strives to establish an essence where it is non-obvious that an essence can be established. What is happening when words are used in a way that we struggle to grapple with, in an effort "to grasp the essence of the thing"? For example, when "this" is said to be a name, in fact the truest or reallest name of all, and when (what we call) names are said to be only degenerate cases of names (cf. *PI* §§38ff.).

Philosophy is about trying to make sense of things. (Trying to weave uses that we do not (as yet) find our feet with in with our existing grasp/ use of our concepts.) Things that, it is said, *must* be the case, although there does not seem to be a secure warrant for the "*must*". Such "things", such essentializings, we provisionally call "metaphysical".

If the philosopher with whom we are in dialogue[3] can convince us that he has developed a novel use (that *has* a use), then we should allow that this is part of the language. If, on the contrary, we can convince him that he has not specified a use for his words, then he allows that what he has come up with is nothing that has a sense. Non-sense.[4] An idle wheel. Language, as Wittgenstein memorably puts it, "on holiday" (see again *PI* §38).[5]

Here, then, it is crucial to point up an ambiguity in the word "use" in *Philosophical Investigations* §116 (an ambiguity with a family relation to that in the word "*satz*" in the *Tractatus*), again to avoid being deceived by it. We can speak of metaphysical uses of language, in the sense of uses of words where the speaker intends to do metaphysics with his words (intends to provide an essentialist definition, to say what *must* be the case), or in the sense of uses of words where we suggest to the speaker that he is willy-nilly employing his words metaphysically (such that they are "flickering"[6]). But none of this turns metaphysical uses into a *kind* of use of words, in the sense that there are uses of words to (e.g.) ask things as opposed to state things, or (e.g.) to do history as opposed to to do science. Metaphysical use is, roughly, only a variety of use in the same kind of way as a decoy duck is a variety of duck.

"Metaphysical use" is not intended by Wittgenstein in *Investigations* §116 to be (as it were) a genuine category of language-use.[7] In the phrase "everyday use", the term "everyday" is, for Wittgenstein, pleonastic. (It is worth noting that the terms "everyday" and "ordinary" are in fact rarely used by Wittgenstein. In that regard, they are akin to his term "form of life", and rather unlike his term "language-game".) The term "everyday" or "ordinary" is employed by Wittgenstein chiefly as a *reminder*: to use these words is to remind one(-self) of something that one so utterly swims in that one can forget it completely.[8] Less one's spectacles, more one's cornea.

One is not reminded as if of a fact; it is more like the kind of "reminder" one experiences when (for instance) one has a near-death experience.[9] Not the reminder that one is mortal – for that, although easily forgotten, is nevertheless not so hard to remember. Rather: the reminder *that one is alive*. The kind of reminder wherein ground suddenly becomes figure. The kind of "reminder" delivered, for example, by a suddenly *vivid* experience of something perfectly … ordinary.

A little more work remains to be done in order correctly to home in on the requisite contrast-class for everyday/ordinary, in order to clarify their meaning for Wittgenstein. And that is: to be quite clear on the character of what is counterposed to the everyday, here, in order to enable it to be spoken of at all.

Let me quote Ed Witherspoon on this:

> [W]hen Wittgenstein is confronted with an utterance that has no clearly discernible place in a language-game, he does not assume that he can parse the utterance; rather, he invites the speaker to explain how she is using her words, to connect them with other elements of the language-game in a way that displays their

meaningfulness. Only if the speaker is unable to do this in a coherent way does Wittgenstein conclude that the utterance is nonsense; ideally, the speaker will reach the same conclusion in the same way and will retract or modify her words accordingly. Applying Wittgenstein's conception of nonsense therefore requires an intense engagement with the target of criticism; an examination of the words alone is not enough. When Wittgenstein criticizes an utterance as nonsensical, he aims to expose, not a defect in the words themselves, but a confusion in the speaker's relation to her words – a confusion that is manifested in the speaker's failure to specify a meaning for them.   (2000: 345)[10]

This is an excellent exposition of what it amounts to, to "return" words to the language.[11] One must use words in ways that one is oneself more or less comfortable with, and can take *responsibility* for. One must *acknowledge* one's own words, fully. Fairly accusing another of speaking nonsense is never a matter of merely noting their departure from accepted modes of speech. It is a last resort, and always provisional, when charity gives out: it is accusing them of speaking in such a way that they themselves will come to admit amounts to not successfully saying any one thing, and hovering between possible senses.

But Witherspoon does not go quite far enough in acknowledging the implications of this radical method of "returning" one to oneself, this method of resolution. Where he writes "Ideally", he should, I believe, have written "Essentially". Compare on this Wittgenstein: "We can only convict another person of a mistake … if he (really) acknowledges this expression as the correct expression of his feeling. // For only if he acknowledges it as such, *is* it the correct expression. (Psychoanalysis.)" (*BT* 410). In other words: the ultimate *criterion* of a successful effort to criticize something as a departure from "everyday" language must be: the subject's own consent.[12] So: *if* the subject is (for example) coining a new metaphor, expressing herself poetically, founding a new branch of science with a real empirical tether or expression, exploring/developing a new type of numbers, seeking to remind one that certain "things" are things/ideas/claims that we do not (at least, not yet) regard as so much as making sense, or in any other way knowingly breaking with conventional modes of expression, or indeed knowingly speaking nonsense with some distinct end in view, then our effort at (a purely) *philosophical* criticism must cease.

We can exemplify the discussion now by casting a look at something that Wittgenstein asks himself, about philosophy, and about psychoanalysis as it has actually developed (in *Culture and Value*): "Why shouldn't

I apply words in ways that conflict with their original usage? Doesn't Freud, for example, do this when he calls even an anxiety dream a wish-fulfillment dream? Where is the difference?" (*CV* 44).[13] Now, we should immediately be on our guard here: Wittgenstein does *not* in fact consider the Freudian move here-abouts an unproblematic one, as we know for instance from his explicit treatment of the extension of the term "wish-fulfillment" in the *Lectures and Conversations on Aesthetics, Psychology and Religious Belief*. Freud uses words in ways that conflict with their original usage *without fully admitting (or realizing) that he is doing so*, and this for Wittgenstein is a sign that what we have in Freud is a mythology, a persuasive and potentially dangerous effort to get one to think in a different way about something, about important aspects of our lives and minds and words, without (as it were) full disclosure.

To expand on this a little: the point must be that Freud *takes himself* to be a scientist, and thus thinks he is licensed in using technical terms, in using terms in (in this case) a "bloated" manner. Thus the problem with Freud is *not* – and this is crucial – the extended use *itself*; it is that the extended use is *not* in fact scientifically justified,[14] but (moreover) that there is then a systematic unclarity, in that Freud continues to act as if it is a scientific claim that is in question, in his work.

If there is to be extended use of terms beyond what we are used to, then it had better either be (e.g. scientifically) justified, or at least clear about its own groundlessness. If a philosopher uses a word in an "extended" sense, as Wittgenstein himself of course not infrequently does, then he has to take full *responsibility* for such a use. That extended use cannot be *grounded*, as an extended use in science can be (think for instance of the kind of grounding that became available, over time, for even the remarkable linguistic innovations of Copernicus or Einstein).

Wittgenstein is asking, in effect, why a human scientist or a philosopher should not simply do what natural scientists do: where is the difference between himself or Freud on the one hand and a (natural) scientist, with whom there can be no quarrel in principle concerning her use of technical terms, on the other? In other words: it is fine for people to bifurcate from ordinary usage, generally, so long as they have a good reason for doing so; but there is something *prima facie* problematic or difficult or at least voluntaristic about himself or Freud doing so.

What, exactly? This is his answer:

In a scientific perspective a new use is justified by a theory. And if the theory is false, the new extended use has to be given up. *But in philosophy the extended use does not rest on true or false*

> *beliefs about natural processes. No fact justifies it. None can give*
> *it any support.* (CV 44)

This quotation makes quite clear the vital difference that Wittgenstein sees between the use of technical language in the natural sciences and in philosophy. Science is everyday language that uses technical terms, that for instance "bloats" terms relative to their standard usage, on the grounds of the theoretic efficacy of so doing, whereas a philosopher or a "human scientist" cannot similarly undergird such a "bloated" use without setting up a theory or some such that stands in tension with the way we already competently express ourselves. (If a "human scientist" gets us to speak in a new way, this is a creative or a political achievement, not a scientific one.)

In short: this quotation demonstrates very efficaciously the point that I have been arguing throughout. Wittgenstein generally counterposes ordinary or everyday language *not* to scientific language – scientific language is simply one "branch" of ordinary language – but to language "outside language-games" (cf. *PI* §47). To metaphysical language. To what is latently nonsense. To *nothing*. To nothings that powerfully and persistently[15] masquerade as somethings about which nothing further can intelligibly be said.

Is there not perhaps a danger in saying that all sensible language use is ordinary-language use, as I now appear to be doing: for, if everything sensible/sensical is ordinary, is this term not in danger of becoming rather empty? Perhaps it is turning into a metaphysical term itself.

This risk is inevitable. Wittgenstein's own manner of speaking is not immune to the very vicissitudes that he detects in the philosophical language that he is interrogating. That is why Wittgenstein's own language is transitional,[16] and his "method" through-and-through therapeutic. But, crucially: there is no dogmatic insistence, upon my part or Wittgenstein's, that the terms "ordinary" or "everyday" be used thus; there is merely a motivated suggestion that so to use them, while providing absolutely no guarantee (there can be none) of avoiding metaphysical pitfalls, will conduce to one's chances of finding one's way about – of finding some peace.

Moreover, as already indicated, there are plenty of non-ordinary uses – of uses that run the risk of being metaphysical – that are desirable/necessary, or at least potentially so. Poetic employments of words, novel scientific vocabulary-shifts and so on– and, indeed, *many (most?) of the discursive practices of Wittgenstein (etc.) himself.* Wittgenstein's own "extended" uses of words can be justified, if at all, only by their successfully expressing his struggle with language, and/

ORDINARY/EVERYDAY LANGUAGE

or actually effecting the ("therapeutic") work on others (or on himself) that they intend.

All words are the same – there are no magic words, no words that mean something irrespective of our decisions-in-action as to what words (will) mean.[17]

> We are under the illusion that what is peculiar, profound, essential, in our investigation, resides in its trying to grasp the incomparable essence of language. That is, the order existing between the concepts of proposition, word, proof, truth, experience, and so on. This order is a super-order between – so to speak – super-concepts. Whereas, of course, if the words "language", "experience", "world" have a use, it must be as humble a one as that of the words "table", "lamp", "door".   (*PI* §97)

They – words – all just mean what we have them mean (although that is not the same as saying, "They all just mean *whatever* one desires or 'wills' them to mean at any given moment"!). The words that philosophers tend to fixate upon are, for Wittgenstein, *perfectly ordinary*. Or, better still: their use is perfectly *humble*. It is only in so far as we want them to be used metaphysically that illusions otherwise get generated. And there remains the interesting question of what the status is of the task of coming to see and feel and "present" these words *as* ordinary.

Thus, once we get clear on the contrast-class that Wittgenstein intends, our task in philosophy instantly becomes a lot clearer – and a lot harder. What *we* do, then, is to try to "bring words back" to their "everyday uses" by means of trying to get others (and ourselves) to think – to see – that they (we) do not need anything other than those "everyday uses" in order to do all that one really can do with language. (And: to think that the idea of it being possible or necessary to do anything other than what these words are after is in fact only the fantasy of an idea. Once again: "the everyday" is *not* counterposed to science. It is "counterposed" only to metaphysics, to myth – to decorated and attractive forms of nothing. Its antithesis is: nothings that charm and delude us into thinking that they are somethings.) It is no longer possible to proscribe forms of words and to think that one is making philosophical progress by means of doing so. For the contrast-class to the everyday is *only*: a lived delusion.[18]

Neither is it best put as a set of failed attempts at science that nevertheless succeed in being or doing or saying something greater than or different from science. For there is no such thing as succeeding in expressing or stating nonsense. There are only – particular – failures to mean clearly.

If one thinks that *"the"* everyday is something that can be mined, explored, made explicit, then one becomes a word-policeman, like logical positivism,[19] like the "Oxford" Wittgensteinians such as, arguably, Peter Strawson[20] and certainly Peter Hacker, and in one way or another like most "Wittgensteinians", at least until recently.[21] But this is a complete misunderstanding of Wittgenstein's "method", which, to repeat, is above all to seek to show to readers that they themselves need to settle on how they are going to use a word. (See Chapter 12, "Therapy".[22])

If one thinks that usage can be one's definitive guide to what is legitimately philosophically sayable, then one in effect turns philosophy into a branch of sociolinguistics: this is no part of Wittgenstein's brief.[23] One then finds oneself saying things like "The meaning of a word really is its use in the language", and thus falling into essentialism – into metaphysics![24] If one thinks that bifurcations from ordinary language in this sense are illegitimate, then one moreover puts forth a conservative doctrine, and disallows linguistic innovation.[25] This kind of interference with (for instance) scientific innovation is again quite alien to Wittgenstein's thought.[26]

The underlying absurdity of the traditional idea of "ordinary-language philosophy", an absurdity mirrored in only superficially different forms in the doctrine of "category mistakes", in logical positivism, in "descriptive metaphysics", in "conceptual geography/topography", and so on, is the absurdity of thinking that there could be any such thing as stating the content of the ordinary/everyday. For: the ordinary/everyday is everything. It is all there is … It is, as it were, all that is the case.[27] What kind of standpoint must one be fantasizing, in order to make clear its contents? Ironically, of course, one must be fantasizing a *metaphysical* standpoint, an Archimedean point, as it were, outside all language and thoughts. In order supposedly to overview the contents of the ordinary, one has to imagine an entirely mythical perspective "from sideways on".

Thus the great temptation to contrast the ordinary with something tangible, such as the scientific. And thus the yo-yo back to the point at which we began: the deeply tendentious identification of Wittgenstein as someone opposed to linguistic innovation, and ruling out "cognitive science" or whatever *a priori* on the alleged ground that it "violates the logic of our language". About as convincing as saying to someone that they cannot start calling whales mammals, because they were once upon a time a paradigm case of "fish".[28] This kind of silliness is given a superficial patina of interpretive support by Wittgenstein's (deep, and genuine) antipathy to scientism. But note: it is an antipathy to scien*tism*. Not to science! Not, in other words, to whatever is actually scientific (usually, at least something!) in the actions of scientists.

I called the misidentification of the contrast-class to "ordinary" intended by Wittgenstein "the crucial mistake" in the inheritance of Wittgenstein's philosophy. The appellation is justified, because this mistake of mythological dimensions has in effect meant that an apparently extremely diverse range of philosophers who have taken themselves to inherit from Wittgenstein have, in the most crucial respect, failed to do so. These philosophers certainly include Gilbert Ryle, the logical positivists (including even the most subtle of them such as Schlick and the later Carnap), the "ordinary-language philosophers", Tony Kenny, Peter Hacker and his followers such as Hanjo Glock; and many more. These philosophers have thought that Wittgenstein was *ruling out* various ways of expressing ourselves as untrue to our language/our conceptual scheme, or as incompatible with sense.

Furthermore, the range of philosophers negatively affected by this failure to inherit from Wittgenstein is much wider: it includes very many philosophers who take themselves to be in some crucial respect opposed to Wittgenstein because they do not accept the philosophical validity and force of categories such as (respectively) "category mistake", "violation of logical syntax", "wrong use of our language" (or "not a way we (can) use words"), "transgression of the bounds of sense", "violation of the rules of grammar", and so on. They – rightly – refuse the right of the would-be language-police – for example Ryle, Ayer, Carnap, Flew, Strawson, Hacker (or even Searle, with his efforts to "clarify" the functional categories of speech) – to stop them from using words in novel ways, introducing technical distinctions that go beyond the language of the layman, and so on. And they see and hear these would-be language-police as the spokespeople or followers of Wittgenstein. And so, understandably, they (believe that they) reject Wittgenstein.

There is a smaller group of philosophers who understand the employment that Wittgenstein practises to powerful myth-breaking and liberating effect of the terms "ordinary" and "everyday" – as opposed to metaphysical. This group includes Gordon Baker, Stanley Cavell, Cora Diamond, Katherine Morris – and J. L. Austin. Austin is standardly thought to be the greatest exponent of "ordinary-language philosophy". Perhaps so: but, if so, "ordinary-language philosophy" need not fall into "the crucial mistake" that has been my topic in this chapter. Alice Crary (2002), Eugen Fischer (2005) and Tommi Uschanov (2001) have in recent years argued convincingly[29] that Austin has been horribly misinterpreted as relying on ordinary usage to win philosophical arguments, when in fact his appeal to the ordinary is fundamentally drawn from/the same as Wittgenstein's: the ordinary is simply whatever is available to us that we ourselves can satisfactorily adduce without falling into what we ourselves regard as dogmatic essentialism/equivocation/lack of sense/metaphysics. Austin's greatest works are entirely compatible with Wittgenstein's use of the term "ordinary". Austin would for instance applaud Wittgenstein's remark that "[O]ne can only determine the grammar of a language with the consent of a speaker, but not the orbit of the stars with the consent of the stars. The rule for a sign, then, is the rule which the speaker *commits himself* to" (Baker 2003: 105).

And this should hardly surprise us. For the kind of insight that Austin provokes in us, when he suggests famously for instance that it is what *we want to contrast with* reality that determines what force the word "real" has, rather than the other way around, is of the same genre as Wittgenstein's suggestion that we understand what is ordinary or everyday not by virtue of a substantive ascertainment of their content but by virtue of what we want to contrast with them. Namely, the utterly extraordinary, the "beyond" to the "limits" of sense: metaphysics/nonsense. All actual language that is language that we ourselves are not brought to recognize as only a failing attempt to mean is someone's everyday language. Scientific language, just as much as the language of the grocers or of the test match or of the text message. The (probably endless) task of philosophy is to prick the balloon of uses of language that are entirely unsupported, and thus to deprive them of further attractiveness. To give us peace, by "returning" us to ourselves.

But why make these "counter-intuitive" claims? Why say that (e.g.) using Einstein's relativity theory can count as ordinary language in operation?

The (Wittgensteinian) distinction between ordinary or everyday on the one hand and metaphysical on the other is a distinction *that subserves a "therapeutic" purpose*. In itself, it is of no moment. It is *not* an attempt to categorize or theorize language – although it will doubtless often be *heard* as such (as it nearly always was for instance even from the mouth of one as subtle and as innovatively inheritative of Wittgenstein as Austin); and working through the inclination so to hear it will itself be of signal therapeutic worth ... And the purpose is: to focus one's attention on one's target in philosophy. Namely: "uses" of language that are *systematically* unclear, and that are not satisfying even to their purveyors. (Einsteinian talk in itself does not in general suffer from that defect. It is, to one initiated in it, perfectly clear and ordinary, and moreover it is an appropriate case for my present purposes, in that it is arguably itself a tool for clarifying what is unclear in non-Einsteinian talk when it takes in conditions such as those that apply when velocities that are an appreciable fraction of that of light are in play.)

Why, though, am I so down on metaphysics? Is this not tantamount to condemning many of the marvellous products of the human mind to the scrap heap?

Not at all. Note once again that calling something "nonsense" is for Wittgenstein as I am interpreting him a provisional judgement, and a last resort, rather than being something that one is entitled to do with certitude, and even does with abandon, as is the case for Ryle, Ayer, Hacker and others. Note therefore that (as discussed below) a proper understanding of the metaphysical versus ordinary contrast is compatible with finding many of the great works of Western philosophy *not* to consist of metaphysics, at their greatest (one could for instance say this of Berkeley [see Diamond 1991], Kant, Nietzsche and Heidegger, among others). And note finally that one can have the very deepest of *respect* for what one believes to be in the end a heroic and natural[30] but nevertheless mythically flawed human endeavour; I hope I follow Wittgenstein, in having such respect for the metaphysical systems and so on of a good number of the great philosophers of the Western canon.

What about *literature*? Is my line of thought not tantamount to thinking that much great literature is nonsense?

Possibly. But nonsense is not, as I noted earlier, always a term of *criticism*. Most of what Wittgenstein himself wrote, it follows from the argument being pursued here, may be best construed as through and through transitional. As not ordinary working language, but (one might venture to say) metaphysics that knows it is metaphysics and can end all metaphysics. Do I *criticize* Wittgenstein's work, then, as (an imaginative engagement with and in) nonsense? Far from it.

Similarly with literature.[31] Literature is often language *on display*. The *form* of such language is paramount. It both is and is not language, we might say. We might call literature the imagination of language, or perhaps the dream of language. Inasmuch as we are inclined to identify the work that language does, or the communications that it accomplishes, as essential to (its being) language, we may conclude that much poetry, and also some of the greatest "prose" of the likes of Shakespeare, Faulkner, Woolf, Joyce and Beckett, among others, partakes of the character of non-language, or of non-sense at least. As being at *least* as akin to beautiful or brilliant decoration or to eternally possible and never-actual meaning as to expression or communication of a content. Is that cause for *criticism*? Again, hardly. *It is the very* achievement *of these authors*; and of a good number more besides.

And what about my own discourse here? Is it everyday/ordinary (or not)?

Well, yes and no. Or (once again): it depends upon your purpose. As Wittgenstein puts it: it is as you please.[32]

It has significant *affinities* with "metaphysical uses" of language: crucially, in that it is not used with a genuine contrast-class.[33] It is *knowingly* used in this way. It is in that regard comparable with Heidegger's famous self-conscious employment(s) of nonsense, pilloried by Carnap but explored and provisionally defended/charitably interpreted by Wittgenstein and his followers.[34]

On the other hand, Wittgenstein's own writing is in an important sense much more accessible than (say) Heidegger's. Wittgenstein does not try to create a new jargon – *on the contrary* (that was what he was most afraid of, and sought to avoid). He himself goes so far as to say this:

> When I talk about language (words, sentences, etc.) I must speak the language of everyday. Is this language somehow too coarse and material for what we want to say? *Then how is another one to be constructed?* And how strange that we should be able to do anything at all with the one we have! // In giving explanations I have already to use language full-blown (not some preparatory, provisional one) ...   (*PI* §120; trans. mod.)[35]

And this:

> The philosophy of logic speaks of sentences and words in exactly the sense in which we speak of them in ordinary life when we say e.g. "Here is a Chinese sentence", or "No, that only looks like writing; it is actually just an ornament"[36] and so on. // We are talking about the spatial and temporal phenomenon of language, not about some non-spatial non-temporal phantasm. But we talk about it as we do about the pieces in chess when we are stating the rules of the game, not describing their physical properties.
> (*PI* §108)

Wittgenstein urges us, at times such as these, to try to see his own employments of words as ordinary/everyday. But it remains the case that there is an urging or a trying required here.

So: it is as you please. You must take responsibility for the ways you use words.[37] As Wittgenstein takes responsibility for the provocative use he makes of the words "ordinary"/"everyday" in speaking of language/ life, juxtaposing them principally to "metaphysics"/"nonsense", rather than to (say) "scientific"/"technical", and relying on the unfolding of the strange concept of "metaphysical"/"nonsensical" to *teach* us what he means by "ordinary"/"everyday". We might say: he speaks the language of everyday, albeit in a somewhat non-everyday *way*, in order to draw attention to its *form*, that we live and breathe in, and so that normally escapes our attention. What he draws attention to is not one thing rather than another. It is rather the actuality of anything at all being thought or said, which is itself something that metaphysics tends to try to put into question.

Why have I given so few examples of ordinary or everyday language in this chapter? Has the chapter not been in significant part very ... abstract? Un-ordinary? Tendentious?

But the very term "example" here is a misnomer, in its implication that there is content prior to the examples, that "examples" only ever illustrate something greater than themselves. This is the very kind of assumption that a proper Wittgensteinian emphasis on ordinary language will overcome.

This chapter is designed to subserve a therapeutic purpose, and in trying to subserve that purpose, and to liberate us all from the compulsion to seek a solid guarantee of what words mean (in order, one in effect fantasizes, to save one from the hard work of actually doing the therapy), I have taken the risk of using numerous odd modes of expression, of engaging in metaphorical and perhaps metaphysical uses ("uses"?). What is the alternative? I could stick resolutely to using what is without doubt ordinary language (cf. *TLP* 6.53), but this would be unlikely to be satisfying/effective. Or I could stick to pointing out would-be instances of metaphysics (cf. again *TLP* 6.53), but this would hardly amount to a chapter with the title "Ordinary/everyday language".

Why have I given so few "examples" of ordinary/everyday language in this chapter? One might risk the following reply: because, in context,[38] *everything* is ordinary. This is the way we look at things. (And in the spirit of *PI* §122, we should now perhaps ask: is this a worldview?) Everything that *is* anything. There is no such thing as proprietorily pointing to *the* everyday. To do so would be as absurd as trying to point to one's visual field, or to point out the universe. As I have suggested we say: "the everyday" is itself, ironically, if it is to be useful, perhaps best heard as a "non-everyday" "category". A transitional category. It is *not* some things rather than others.

So would the better way to proceed after all not simply be by giving "examples" of metaphysical uses of language? But the scare quotes cannot be dropped: *there are none*. Metaphysics is an aspiration or a falling only. It is *not* an achievement-term.

Let me end[39] by giving Wittgenstein the last word, and by giving a kind of example – an example drawn from the anti-private-language considerations, an example of "language on holiday", an example that Wittgenstein explores with particular verve and draws a key lesson from, for our purposes here:

> It's true that I say "Now I am having such-and-such an image", but the words "I am having" are merely a sign to someone else; the description of the image is a *complete* account of the imagined world. – You mean: the words "I am having" are like "I say!: ...". You are inclined to say it should really have been expressed differently. Perhaps simply by making a sign with one's hand and then giving a description. – When, as in this case, we disapprove of the expressions of ordinary language (which are after all performing their office), we have got a picture in our head which conflicts with the picture of our ordinary way of speaking. Whereas we are tempted to say that our way of speaking does not describe the facts as they really are. As if (e.g.) the proposition "He has pains" could be false in some other way than by that man's not having pains. As if the form of expression were saying something false even when the proposition *faute de mieux* asserted something true.
>
> For *this* is what disputes between idealists, solipsists and realists look like. The one party attacks the normal form of expression as if they were attacking a statement; the others defend it, as if they were stating facts recognized by every reasonable human being.
>
> (*PI* §402, trans. mod.)

Notes

1. *Philosophical Investigations* §116. Editions referred to in this chapter are *Philosophical Investigations* (2001a) and *Zettel* (1988). The ("non-literal") translation here is mine, based on the Anscombe translation. I believe that the Anscombe translation has unwarrantedly overly encouraged many readers to search for a "language-game theory" in Wittgenstein, in which one would

     segment ordinary language from scientific language from metaphysical language and so on, and thus immediately commit oneself to a kind of relativism and the prospect of language-policing in order to secure the "boundaries" of these "language-games".

2. See his powerful essay, "Wittgenstein on Metaphysical/Everyday Use" (Baker 2004: ch. 4), strongly recommended for anyone serious about getting straight on Wittgenstein's use of the concepts of everyday/ordinary.

3. Frequently, of course, this one: oneself.

4. Often, another good word for this can be precisely: metaphysics. When metaphysics is empty, a hovering only.

5. Cf. also Wittgenstein's various remarks on language "idling", memorably explored by James Guetti in his "Idling Rules" (1993).

6. What flickers borrows from the context that it seems to promise to drop into while never truly doing so.

7. One might truly call an *isolated* language-game one involving metaphysical *use* of words. But philosophers are rarely content to allow metaphysics to remain isolated. They wish it in some way to *revise* the rest of language – or, at least (as in the case of the metaphysics of ordinary-language philosophy) to "undergird" its not being in need of revision, and to conserve it.

8. Katherine Morris's essay, "Wittgenstein's Method: Ridding People of Philosophical Prejudices" (2007) is of considerable use in this connection. She points out subtly and in detail (*ibid.*: esp. 78) how Wittgenstein has no objection whatever to someone violating ordinary usage, but, as Baker puts it, "What is pathological in [the metaphysician's] thinking is not the deviance of his philosophical utterances from everyday speech-patterns, but the unconscious *motives* which give rise to [this] behaviour" (Baker 2004: ch. 10, 208). This was, I believe, just what the generation of John Wisdom had in mind with the analogy to psychoanalysis.

9. The kind of reminder that is the staple of the philosophy of Walker Percy, and it resonates in a number of major philosophical works of art, such as Terence Malick's film, *The Thin Red Line*.

10. Compare also Baker (2003: 235). (Of course, it is often oneself as often as others who falls into "metaphysical use": "returning" words to the ordinary is a personal, and not just a critical, struggle. As it were: being resolute ain't no walk in the park ...) And compare too the following: "[Sensation] is a ghost word. But that does not mean that it may not be used. I don't want to prohibit the use of any words unless they are misleading. *They are misleading when they in fact mislead us.* You may use all sorts of misleading expressions without harm if only you remember what they mean and when they become dangerous" (Klagge & Nordmann 2003: 394, emphasis added).

11. Although it is vital to note a key codicil: everyday language is itself moulded by philosophical–metaphysical ideas and hence there is no straightforward return to it. Such "return" is always a *project*. This is one reason for my repeatedly scare-quoting the word "return".

12. Thus – and this is critically important, in every sense of the word "critically" – criticism in philosophy must begin by seeking to recover the place from which the other's words are coming. (Compare for instance OC §37, and Wittgenstein's response to Moore more generally.) Trying to figure out what the other was trying to say is of course an everyday practice that need not attach one to any confusion or delusion.

13. This segment of this chapter is loosely based on material published previously in my "Throwing Away 'The Bedrock'" (2004).

14. Compare here *Zettel* (§§447–9). Roughly: there is no language-game of philosophy, whereas there is of normal science. Agreement in philosophy is thus a radically different kind of animal from agreement in science. The former, we might venture, is *never* agreement in opinions. Because opinions, assertions, are not, in philosophy's case, of the essence.

15. The distinction between metaphysics and the ordinary is *not* easy to make, and cannot be made once and for all. Compare this remark of Wittgenstein's (and cf. also *PI* §109): "Why are the grammatical problems so tough and seemingly ineradicable? – Because they are connected with the oldest thought-habits, i.e. with the oldest pictures that are engraved into our language itself … // People are deeply embedded in philosophical … confusions. And to free them from these presupposes pulling them out of the immensely manifold connections they are caught up in … – But this language came about … as it did because people had – and have – the inclination to think *in this way*" (Typescript 213 §§422–3). As Kuusela comments: "[I]f everyday language is itself molded by philosophically problematic thought habits … , then one evidently cannot appeal to it in any straightforward way to settle philosophical disputes. Rather, when describing ordinary uses one is in constant danger of producing descriptions that are themselves informed by philosophical prejudices and pictures. Accordingly, Wittgenstein's conception of everyday language seems radically different from that of the ordinary language philosophers" (2008: 278).

16. For more on this term in such contexts as this, see Cora Diamond's work on and around the *Tractatus*, in particular.

17. Compare here my remarks on the "flatness" of language in my article in *Essays in Philosophy*, at www.humboldt.edu/~essays/read.html (accessed April 2010).

18. For explication, see Part II of my *Applying Wittgenstein* (2007a). This connects of course to why philosophical work of this kind is unavoidably personal in character – a work on oneself, and on others each with their quiddities.

19. I am thinking of course here of verificationism's banishment to meaninglessness of a great deal, including for starters ethics and aesthetics.

20. Obviously, I cannot adequately defend here Strawson's inclusion in this list, at which some might baulk, and I concede that there are some of Strawson's essays that do not fit this characterization of him. One case against Strawson's inclusion might be most naturally summed up as follows: Was Strawson not a descriptive *metaphysician*? How could a *metaphysician* be a mere word-policeman? But policing the use of words, dogmatically or conservatively insisting upon their being used in certain ways, is merely one more variant of metaphysics. It is the simple negation of the *fetishization* of linguistic innovation (as if to capture nature's ontology) inherent in scientism. Strawson generally seems to believe that the bounds of sense mark off from us a tangible substantial realm – in this way, he falls foul of the therapeutic exploration of the nonsensicality of "substantial nonsense" and of "limits" to thought already inherent in Wittgenstein's *Tractatus*.

For a strong and beautifully argued defence of ordinary-language philosophy (in the very person of Strawson) amounting to a more satisfactory case against its inclusion in the list here, see Avner Baz's (forthcoming a) "In Defence of Ordinary Language Philosophy". It is certainly possible that ordinary-language philosophy is by and large innocent of the charge, or at least that plenty of ordinary-language philosophers (including at times Strawson) do not fit the paradigm of what has come down to us as ordinary-language philosophy (I allow already that of Austin, for sure, and would say the same of Ebersole).

Establishing whether it is or not inevitably lies beyond the scope of this chapter.

21. What these philosophers/philosophies have in common is: no time for the suggestion that philosophical work has an ineradicably personal character. Thus the "Oxford Wittgensteinians" in effect allow for an allegedly Wittgensteinian "research programme" of setting down the grammar of our language, ruling out the transgressions of its rules allegedly present in various benighted scientistic thinkers, and so on.

22. See also Baker's remarkable paper, "A Vision of Philosophy" (2004: ch. 9).

23. Compare here: "Should we record the actual use of a word, variable and irregular though it be? This would at best produce a history of the use of words. Or should we set up a particular use as a paradigm? Should we say: Only this use is legitimate, and everything else is deviant? This would be a tyrannical ruling" (Baker 2003: 277–8). This passage is devastating for any "ordinary-language philosophy" interpretation of Wittgenstein.

24. I steal this example from Baker (2004: ch. 4, 103).

25. It is worth pointing out parenthetically that there need be nothing problematically conservative about the idiom of "return" that this chapter is promoting. The "return" to ordinary language is just an effort to come back from a state of indecision to something more like mastery of one's own language. The "return" is made for *forward-looking* reasons, one might usefully say.

26. For a clear picture of why, one need look no further than Kuhn's philosophy of science (and/or OC).

27. Needless to say, I do not mean by these remarks to buy into any kind of idealism. The topic under discussion/the field of view here is *language*.

28. For development of this thought, see particularly Phil Hutchinson's philosophy of the emotions (Hutchinson 2008).

29. See also Baz (forthcoming a).

30. As Wittgenstein and Cavell repeatedly stress, metaphysics involves deep *human* urges. For discussion, see the latter stages of Cook & Read (2010).

31. I discuss an important example in *ibid*.

32. And, to deflate the issue quite a bit, in any case: what is everyday to some people is often not everyday to others. Think of (say) the thought-community that is "at home" in relativity theory; and of the (much-larger) thought-community that is not.

33. On this, see again my "Throwing Away 'The Bedrock'" (2004), and Baker (2004: ch. 10, 98). (One might usefully say: there is no fact of the matter as to whether my discourse here is ordinary or not. One might characterize this metaphilosophy as "non-cognitive".)

34. See for instance Baker's "Wittgenstein's Method and Psychoanalysis", (2004: ch. 10, 208ff.) and James Conant's and Ed Witherspoon's writings on Wittgenstein and Heidegger.

35. See my "Wittgenstein and Marx on 'Philosophical Language'" (2000), *passim*, for detailed reading of this remark with regard to the everyday versus philosophical/metaphysical contrast. Cf. also *Philosophical Investigations* §134; and §412 on the unparadoxicality of things we say, of "the everyday", even when it includes seeming attempts at metaphysics.

36. Cf. *Philosophical Investigations* §16. We should also ask ourselves whether, for example, language employed as a wall-decoration is really language, at all. Questions such as this will with efficacy "return" us to our everyday language, as if we then know it for that first time.

37. As Cavell and Kuusela have it: philosophy is a quest for justice, and is saturated by ethics. We might even venture that, for Wittgenstein, ethics is first philosophy. See for example Kuusela (2008).
38. And, roughly: what a new metaphor and so on so far "lacks", we might say, is a context that exhausts and ordinary-izes it.
39. Many thanks to my colleagues Oskari Kuusela (especially), Angus Ross, Phil Hutchinson, Garry Hagberg, Alun Davies, Simon Summers and Gavin Kitching for very helpful readings of drafts of this chapter, and to Avner Baz for inspiring comments.

Further reading

Tractatus, 3.326–7, 4.002, 4.11–4.1273.

SIX

Wittgenstein on rule-following
Roderick T. Long

The rule-following paradox

I shall begin by misdescribing the moral of Wittgenstein's rule-following paradox, because I take the misdescription to be a helpful one, more of a ladder than a stumbling-block (although it should be borne in mind that it is always possible to trip on a ladder).

The moral of the rule-following paradox, then, is that what rule one is following when one acts is (radically) underdetermined by anything in either one's actions or one's thoughts. Underdetermined by anything in one's actions, since every actual sequence of behaviour is finite, and so is capable of being extended in an infinite variety of ways, each one corresponding to a different rule, all such rules being equally consistent with the behaviour thus far exhibited. (Worse yet, even an *infinite* sequence of behaviour, were one possible, would not settle the matter, since such a sequence would be consistent with both a flawless execution of rule *A* and a bungled attempt to apply rule *B*.) And underdetermined by anything in one's thoughts, because no matter what the agent may have before her mind's eye, as it were, it does not count as such-and-such a rule unless the agent reliably applies it in such-and-such a way:

> I cannot know what he's planning in his heart. But suppose he always wrote out his plans; of what importance would they be? If, for example, he never acted on them. ... Perhaps someone will say: Well, then they really aren't plans. But then neither would they be plans if they were *inside* him, and looking into him would do us no good. (*LWPP I* 234–5)

Nothing in the mind seems to settle what I mean; everything depends on how a given mental item gets expressed in practice. But no amount of external conduct settles what I mean either. A move in chess, for example, is not simply a matter of "moving a piece in such-and-such a way" (the machine-like option), but neither does it consist in "one's thoughts and feelings as one makes the move" (*PI* §33).

Nor will it help to identify grasping a rule with the *combination* of some interior mental item and some sequence of bodily behaviour; we cannot impose specificity on one cloud of ambiguity by tying it to another such cloud. And obviously nothing the agent *says* will help either, since whatever the agent says will just be one more bit of variously interpretable behaviour.

Yet surely we do succeed in meaning and intending things and in following rules – despite its apparently being impossible for us to do so. Hence the paradox.

The form of scepticism with which the rule-following paradox threatens us seems still more vertiginous than the familiar Cartesian variety. The latter merely cuts us adrift from the objective world while leaving our subjectivity intact, whereas Wittgenstein's paradox invades our subjectivity, casting into obscurity not merely other people's mindedness but our own. How can there be so much as a fact of the matter concerning what I mean or intend if nothing in either my mind or my conduct settles what it is I am doing? In facing the rule-following paradox, we seem to lose our grip on our own self-understanding.

Yet it is, of course, no part of Wittgenstein's aim to cut the ground away from under us; he is, on the contrary, always out to remind us of the ground on which we stand and have always stood. And in the present case, the point of the rule-following paradox is not to undermine our confidence in our ability to understand ourselves and one another, but rather to liberate us from a muddled picture of what such understanding is like.

Against self-applying rules

Wittgenstein invites us (*PI* §185)[1] to imagine a case where we have asked someone to continue a sequence of numbers in accordance with the rule "add 2 each time" and she seems to be doing so. The problem with the *spoken phrase* "add 2 each time" is that it can be interpreted in a variety of ways, can express a variety of rules, all equally compatible with the person's behaviour thus far. When we initially suppose that reading her mind would clear up our worries, what we are supposing is that there is some item in her mind that *cannot* be interpreted or applied in different ways, something that carries its own interpretation or application with it. But that supposition is dissolved by imagining ourselves peering telepathically into the subject's mind and seeing, say, the thought "add 2 each time" inscribed there in big shining ectoplasmic letters – whereupon the subject cheerfully proceeds to do something else (i.e. something *we* would not describe as adding 2 each time). We then see that what one means by the *thought* "add 2 each time" depends on how one actually applies it in practice, no less than what one means by the spoken words does.

The upshot is not that there is something mysterious or impossible about following a rule, but rather that there *would* have to be something mysterious or impossible about it if following a rule involved what we are tempted to think it involves: a *self-interpreting* or *self-applying* rule. This is in effect what we are hoping to find when, in imagination, we peer telepathically into the subject's mind – only to find, to our dismay, merely more stuff that requires interpreting and applying. As Wittgenstein puts it, we are tempted to suppose that "the act of meaning the order had in its own way already traversed all those steps: that when you meant it your mind as it were flew ahead and took all those steps before you physically arrived at this or that one" (*PI* §188).

If we think that what makes rule-following possible *must* be the rule's somehow having its application already built into it, then careful reflection on rule-following is bound to turn vertiginous, because – with Wittgenstein's guidance – we soon recognize that there is no such self-applying rule to be found: "any interpretation still hangs in the air along with what it interprets, and cannot give it any support" (*PI* §198). But what Wittgenstein infers from this is not that grasping a rule is impossible or mysterious, but rather that "there is a way of grasping a rule which is *not* an *interpretation*, but which is exhibited in what we call 'obeying the rule'" (*PI* §201).

It is thus a mistake to suppose that, having failed to find the magical meaning-determining item either in the agent's thought or in her conduct, we should start to look for it *somewhere else* – say, in the agent's *behavioural dispositions*, or in the practices of the agent's *linguistic community* (to pick two examples not exactly at random). It is true enough, of course, that for Wittgenstein the agent's ability to mean and intend as she does, and to engage in rule-guided activity, depends crucially on various facts about what he would call her "natural history", including her behavioural dispositions and linguistic community. But these can no more function as *independently specifiable* determinants of the agent's meaning than her thought or conduct can.

If a behavioural disposition is thought of as a disposition to exhibit various *bodily movements* in various situations, then it too will underdetermine which rule the agent is following, since a description in terms of mere bodily movements is going to have a hard time distinguishing between, say, (i) an intention to add 2 most of the time but 3 occasionally, and (ii) an intention to add 2 in all cases, coupled with a tendency to make mistakes in calculation.

As for the practices of the agent's linguistic community, any ambiguity in specifying which rule an individual is following is simply going to be reproduced at the collective level as an ambiguity in specifying *which practice the linguistic community is following* – since, for the same reasons, the community's noises and movements are going to be consistent with an infinity of possible practices. To follow a rule is to engage in a certain kind of social practice, to be sure; but what practice that is cannot be identified independently of a reference to following *that rule*.

Wittgenstein warns us against supposing that "because only the actors appear in the play, no other people could usefully be employed upon the stage of the theatre" (*RFM* VII.18). The error against which he warns us is that of confusing a process's *presuppositions* with its *content*. It is true that our grasp of mathematical propositions, for example, depends upon facts about our natural history, but that does not mean that mathematical propositions themselves are "anthropological propositions saying how we men infer and calculate" (*RFM* III.65). In the present context: dispositions, community practices and the like are stagehands in the theatre of meaning – indispensable stagehands, to be sure (and indispensable not just practically but conceptually) – but they are not the actors.

Of course if we describe the agent's disposition, or the community's practice, as a *disposition to add 2 each time*, or a *practice of applying the phrase "adding 2 each time" to adding 2 each time*, then the underdetermination problem vanishes; but it is equally true that if we describe the agent's thought as an *intention to add 2 each time*, or simply describe her conduct as *intentionally adding 2 each time*, then the underdetermination problem vanishes once again. *And that in a way is the answer.* But in such cases we have not identified any factor *distinct* from her rule-following that determines which rule-following it is.

The fundamental mistake that Wittgenstein is trying to disentangle us from is precisely the assumption that in order to make sense of such rule-governed activities as understanding, meaning, intention, action and the like, we must be able to analyse them in terms of something more basic – an assumption that leads us to make a mystery out of the ordinary and then to generate further mysteries in a vain attempt to dispel the first one. The rule-following paradox exposes as a confusion the familiar philosophic distemper of seeking the coherence of human life and practice in something external to such life and practice – from the epistemologist's search for the indubitable, self-certifying foundations of knowledge to the Hobbesian's search for a force or institution that will impose cooperative order upon society without presupposing such cooperative order for its own establishment and maintenance.

In the regular course of life, Wittgenstein reminds us, we do not generally find ourselves mystified at what we (or even others) mean or intend; we entangle ourselves in mystery only when we try to dig *beneath* our ordinary experience in order to uncover foundations for what needs no such foundations.

Is meaning arbitrary?

Yet if what we mean is not grounded in anything beyond itself, how does it escape being arbitrary? Wittgenstein might well say it does not escape, since he often uses the term "arbitrary" precisely to mean "not grounded in anything beyond itself". But there is nothing pejorative about this sort of arbitrariness; indeed, it is the kind of arbitrariness that *logic* is seen to have once we assimilate Frege's lesson that logic is not to be grounded in psychology – while avoiding Frege's mistake, or at least the mistake Frege's language might encourage, of attempting to ground logic in a metaphysical "third realm". (Talk of a third realm is innocent enough so long as it is understood as a description of various logical features rather than as a reference to a realm of entities purportedly underlying and explaining those features.)

Psychologism and Platonism both attempt to ground logic in something distinct and more basic; but for Wittgenstein it is incoherent to seek anything deeper than logic, since this could only be something to which logic does not apply, and so something we cannot so much as speak of or do anything with. "I must *begin* with the distinction between sense and nonsense. Nothing is possible prior to that. I can't give it a foundation" (*PG* I.6.81)

Of course rule-following *can* be arbitrary in the more ordinary, voluntaristic sense too; it depends on the details of the case. Some practices are localized and dispensable; we can take or leave their rules as we will, for any reason or for none (although we ordinarily cannot keep the practices while dropping the rules). Other practices are woven more deeply into the fabric of our lives; abandoning their rules, while possible, would mean a major disruption. Still other practices may be so bound up with rational agency itself that no avenue of abandonment (short of a bullet to the head) is intelligible to us.

The thought that the rule-following paradox *must* make all meaning arbitrary (in the voluntaristic sense) can draw support from Wittgenstein's insistence that it is "no act of insight, intuition, which makes us use the rule as we do", and that it "would be less confusing to call it an act of decision" (*BB* II, 5). But Wittgenstein attempts to forestall such a misunderstanding by immediately adding: "though this too is misleading, for nothing like an act of decision must take place, but possibly just an act of writing or speaking".

How is rule-following like and how is it unlike an "act of decision"? We can see how it is like a decision by reflecting on the following remark: "In all language there is a bridge between the sign and its application. No one can make this for us; we have to bridge the gap ourselves. No explanation ever saves the jump, because any further explanation will itself need a jump" (*L: C 1930–32*, 67). Wittgenstein's thought here is closely akin to Lewis Carroll's parable in "What the Tortoise Said to Achilles" (1895). The Tortoise grants Achilles some premises from which a certain conclusion follows, but refuses to grant the conclusion. When Achilles points out that if the premises are true, the conclusion must be so as well, the Tortoise seemingly accepts Achilles' claim, *adding it to his premise set*, but still resisting the conclusion. And each time that Achilles insists that if the most recently expanded premise set is true, so must be the conclusion, the Tortoise responds by expanding his premise set once again to incorporate Achilles' latest insistence (without drawing the conclusion).

The Tortoise is in effect demanding to be provided with a self-applying rule, one that will all by itself bridge the gap from premises to conclusion without *his* having to do anything. And of course each new insistence from Achilles, *when interpreted as one more premise*, simply "hangs in the air along with what it interprets" and brings the conclusion no nearer.

Achilles would do better to answer the Tortoise with a remark of Wittgenstein's as recorded by Rush Rhees: "I don't try to make you *believe* something you *don't* believe, but to make you *do* something you won't do" (Rhees 1970a: 43). No pile of premises, no matter how towering, can substitute for the *action* of actually drawing the conclusion. Rule-following is like an act of decision because our action when we follow a rule is free from logical determination by anything external to it; we "obey the rule *blindly*" (*PI* §219).

Yet the decision comparison is also, as Wittgenstein notes, misleading. Talk of "decision" makes it sound as though we are conferring meaning on something, just as talk of "insight" and "intuition" makes it sound as though something is conferring meaning on us. *Both* metaphors bifurcate meaning into a receiving and a bestowing element – dough on the one hand, cookie-cutter on the other. But what is this meaning-bestowing decision but another attempt at a self-applying rule? If a "decision" is needed to specify which rule I am following in my action, what specifies which decision I am making? Or if the decision does not need its meaningfulness bestowed from without, why does the action need to receive its meaningfulness from the decision?

It is also misleading, then, to describe Wittgenstein as teaching that there is "no fact of the matter" as to what we mean or what rule we are following; the slide from "no *independent* fact" to "no fact" is unwarranted. Ontologically, what "makes it true" that I am following rule A rather than rule B is simply *my following rule A*. Epistemically, the feature of my conduct that others pick up on in order to detect that I am following rule A rather than rule B is, once again, simply my following rule A.

Of course their ability to see the rule in my actions – what Wittgenstein would call their "sane human understanding" (*PR* 18) – depends on their sharing the right sort of natural history with me. But there is no neutral, regress-proof vocabulary in which to specify uniquely what that shared natural history is without invoking the very sorts of meaning-facts that the natural history was supposed to explain.

In the beginning was the deed

I began by describing the moral of the rule-following paradox as follows: what rule one is following when one acts is (radically) underdetermined by anything in either one's actions or one's thoughts. But I also began with a warning that this description was not quite accurate.

We can now see where the inaccuracy lies. *Of course* there is something in one's thoughts that settles which rule one is following: namely, the intention to follow that rule. And likewise, *of course* there is something in one's actions that settles which rule one is following: namely, one's intentionally following that rule. But one can earn the right to these commonsensical banalities only by ceasing to think of thought and action as independently specifiable; and to win our way to that insight we need to work our way through the rule-following paradox.

A living, conscious being is neither a ghostless machine nor a machineless ghost; but nor can it be understood as a mere *gluing together* of these two non-living items, ghost and machine. Aristotle defines soul as the form of the organic body and organic body as body informed by the soul – neither specifiable independently of the other (*De Anima* II.i.412a19–b26). In similar spirit, Wittgenstein affirms that "the human body is the best picture of the human soul" (*PI II* 178), while nevertheless denying that "the soul itself is merely something about the body" (*RPP II* 690; quoting Nietzsche, *Thus Spoke Zarathustra* I.4). A living being is an integrated, organic whole – in Aristotelean terms, a *hylomorphic unity* – of which soul and body are distinguishable but inseparable aspects (not ingredients).

By extension, we cannot arrive at the notion of action by gluing together one ghostly item – a mental image with no behavioural import – and one machine-like item – mere bodily movement with no psychological import. Action too is an indivisible whole, of which thoughts and movements are aspects but not separable ingredients. "Thinking is not an incorporeal process which lends life and sense to speaking, and which it would be possible to detach from speaking rather as the Devil took the shadow of Schlemiehl from the ground" (*PI* §339). Action, in short, is more than the sum of its parts; the very identity of my thoughts depends on how I express them in action – but which action I am performing depends on what thought I am expressing in it. The difference between thoughtful action and mere bodily movement is thus not a *distinct ingredient*; the mistaken search for such an ingredient is in fact yet another quest for a self-applying rule.

The rule by which we play a musical score, Wittgenstein tells us, "is not contained in the result of playing, nor in the result plus the score (for the score might fit *any* playing by *some* rule)", but "only in the *intention* to play the score" (*L: C 1930–32* 40). Yet this claim that the rule is "contained … in the intention" might seem to be contradicted by Wittgenstein's later remark that "The rules are not something contained in the idea and got by analyzing it. They constitute it" (*L: C 1932–35* 86). But we should not assume that the same fixed sense of "contained" is in play in both passages; after all, an expression has meaning only in a proposition (*TLP* 3.314), that is, only in the context of significant use (3.326).

In the later passage, the sense in which the rule might be thought of as "contained" in the intention is being contrasted with Wittgenstein's preferred formulation that the intention be "constituted" by the rules. The contrast between "contained" and "constituted" suggests that "contained" as used here bears the implication that the intention is *distinct from* and *more than* the rules it carries within it – an implication that Wittgenstein is concerned to reject. In short, "contained" marks the ghostly while "constituted" marks the organic interpretation.

In the earlier passage, however, the rule's being contained in the intention is being contrasted with its being contained in something narrower – "the result of playing", or "the result plus the score"; here it is "contained" that marks the organic, this time in contrast with the machine-like. And so the inconsistency vanishes; both passages endorse the organic unity of action against mentalistic or behaviouristic alternatives.

The redemption of metaphysics

The claim that human agents, and human actions, are indissoluble, irreducible hylomorphic unities sounds suspiciously like a metaphysical thesis. Has Wittgenstein not set his face against such theses? If so, how can such a thesis be one of the upshots of his rule-following paradox?

As with "contained", so with "metaphysics": the meaning of the term depends on the context of significant use. Stanley Cavell has characterized Wittgenstein as seeking to de-psychologize psychology (1976a: 91). In like spirit we may say that Wittgenstein's project also seeks to de-metaphysicize metaphysics.

Part of what Wittgenstein customarily calls metaphysics, but which we may perhaps call *metaphysicism*, is the error of treating essentially logical or grammatical principles as though they were descriptions – contingent in form though not in intent – of some extramental reality (for example the tendency, frequently discussed by Wittgenstein, to treat logical constraints as though they were like physical constraints, only super-rigid). As such, metaphysicism is the twin of psychologism, the error of treating logical or grammatical principles as descriptions of some psychological reality (e.g. explaining the laws of inference in terms of psychological association). Indeed, metaphysicism and psychologism are perilously entangled, for each tempts us to accept it as the remedy for the other.

Plato's Forms might be seen as an example of metaphysicism. On such a reading, Plato saw, rightly, that logical concepts are not reducible to anything physical or psychological or empirical, and his exaltation of the Forms is thus his attempt to convey the irreducibility of logic; but in describing the irreducibility of logic in terms of a realm of irreducible entities, he slid into treating logic as grounded in, and reducible to, the natures of these entities, and so lost his hold on the very position he was trying to defend. Another example might be Duns Scotus's theory of individuation. Scotus may be interpreted as wishing to claim that all objects are irreducibly particular and so do not need to derive their particularity from some added ingredient such as prime matter; but rather than expressing this idea by saying (as later Scholastics would) that objects do not have or need a principle of individuation, or even that each object is its own principle of individuation, he arguably slid into reifying the object's irreducible particularity, treating it as a special metaphysical ingredient – "thisness", *haecceitas* – and in effect treated the object's particularity as reducible after all, that is, to the particularity of its *haecceitas*, thus depriving the object of its genuine *haecceitas* precisely by giving it a pseudo-*haecceitas* conceived in the manner of metaphysicism.

Just as much that passes under the name of psychology is in Wittgenstein's eyes mere psychologism, so much that passes under the name of metaphysics is doubtless mere metaphysicism. Still, Wittgenstein is trying to rescue and clarify our psychological concepts, not eliminate them; and the same is arguably true for metaphysics as well. When Wittgenstein remarks that "grammar tells us what kind of object anything is" (*PI* §373), and characterizes his grammatical investigations as exploring "the 'possibilities' of phenomena" (*PI* §90), he is essentially *assigning to grammar the traditional task of metaphysics*. In doing this he is not so much *rejecting* metaphysics (as he would be if he were to insist that *nothing* can perform the traditional task of metaphysics) as he is *logicizing* metaphysics. (Of course this involves reconceiving – logicizing – the task as well.)

The irreducibility of logic may be called a metaphysical thesis, so long as such terminology is not misunderstood; metaphysical it may be, but it is precisely the antidote to most of the errors that have been termed metaphysical. Indeed, one function of the rule-following paradox is arguably to help us distinguish between nonsensical metaphysicism and sensible (because logicized) metaphysics. Wittgenstein writes:

> But I don't mean that what I do now (in grasping a sense) determines the future use *causally* and as a matter of experience, but that in a *queer* way, the use itself is in some sense present. – But of course it is, 'in *some* sense'! Really the only thing wrong with what you say is the expression "in a queer way". ... In our failure to understand the use of a word we take it as the expression of a queer *process*. (*PI* §§195–6)

To Wittgenstein's mind there's nothing *inherently* wrong with a metaphysical-sounding statement like "When we grasp a sense, the future use is already present." It depends how we take it. When we take it "in a queer way", we are thinking of the presence of the future use as a fact that is *independent* of the ordinary business of rule-following, a transcendental process in which that business is grounded. This is to fall into metaphysicism. But if we take the presence of the future use as an illuminating description of rule-following itself, rather than of something else that serves as rule-following's ground, we are innocent of metaphysicism; we have recovered the proper grammar for such locutions. "The rules are not something contained in the idea and got by analyzing it. They constitute it." That means: the presence of the future use is not something in which grasping a rule is grounded; it is simply the grasping redescribed.

The idea of action as irreducible and basic, not decomposable into ghostly thought and machine-like movement, may be further explicated by means of the distinction Wittgenstein draws in the *Tractatus* between signs and symbols, where a sign is a mere mark or sound while a symbol is that same mark or sound employed with a particular meaning – so that "bank", meaning the edge of a river, and "bank", meaning a financial institution, would be the same sign but different symbols. For Wittgenstein, a symbol is *neither* a mere sign, *nor* a sign plus some ghostly accompaniment (like Schlemiehl's shadow); it is the sign *in significant use* (*TLP* 3.326). Nor, on pain of a rule-following regress, can significant use itself be analysed either in sign-talk or in ghost-talk. What the symbol adds to the sign cannot be specified independently; hence the symbol is not built up from the sign *plus* something further. Rather, the symbol is basic, and the sign is a sort of abstraction from it, the "perceptible aspect of the symbol" (*TLP* 3.32). There is no getting *behind* or *beneath* the symbolic level. Because logic is basic, symbolizing is basic; because symbolizing is basic, the organic unity of action is likewise basic.

Note

1. Editions referred to in this chapter are *Philosophical Investigations* (2001a) and *The Blue and Brown Books* (1960).

Further reading

Tractatus, 5.21–5.41.

SEVEN

Thinking and understanding
Phil Hutchinson

Introduction

Consider some questions: What is thinking? What is understanding? What affords us the right to say of someone that they are thinking? What are the criteria of correctness for employment of the word "understanding" (i.e. what grounds do we have for predicating of someone understanding)? Is there something common to all instances of "thinking" and of "understanding" that helps us here? Indeed, could there be some *thing* or *process* underlying instances of thinking and understanding (respectively) that could satisfy us?

Two more questions. What view(s) did Wittgenstein hold on "thinking" and on "understanding"? Did Wittgenstein offer us an answer to the questions "What is thinking?" and "What is understanding?"?

One of the areas of philosophy to which Wittgenstein is taken to have contributed most is philosophical psychology, and he certainly had things to *say* about thinking (and thought) and understanding (see e.g. *PI* §§138–55 for a discussion of "thinking" and §§327–76 for a discussion of "understanding").[1] But does that mean he held or propounded, *qua* philosopher, (philosophical) views on these issues? Wittgenstein is taken by many to have held that much of mental life, what we call thinking, is linguistic in some deep way, and thus being committed to the notion that that which cannot speak cannot think. Consider the following passage from Matt Cartmill (a sadly indicative example, selected for its availability – i.e. its Google-ability – online):

Many Western thinkers have ... insisted that because animals can't talk, their mental lives are defective in big ways, or even nonexistent. "Thinking", wrote Wittgenstein, "is essentially the activity of operating with signs". That view of thinking naturally appeals to college professors, who sometimes get so consumed by operating with signs that they wander around their campuses talking to themselves and tripping over shrubs. And since non-human animals aren't very good at operating with signs, many professional types have been reluctant to grant that beasts can have mental lives at all. (Cartmill 2000: 8)[2]

According to Cartmill, Wittgenstein's view is emblematic of a particular (linguistic) brand of prejudicial view about thinking. *Is Cartmill correct?* Now, one might expect the answer to this question to hinge on whether or not Wittgenstein holds the view that thinking is essentially linguistic; I wish to suggest that it does not. Rather, I shall argue that the answer hinges on whether Wittgenstein holds or propounds any views at all, *qua* philosopher, on thinking.

In what follows I shall briefly examine some of Wittgenstein's remarks, putting them into their proper context. For much of this chapter, I shall proceed in a manner that might seem to suggest that one can treat "thinking" and "understanding" interchangeably. I do so advisedly; the grammar of – that is, the sensical uses to which we put – these terms is different.[3] However, the sorts of confusions we are led to in our philosophical considerations of these (grammatically distinct) terms stem from our being unconsciously in thrall to a particular picture; they are confusions that often have the same source and character.

There is, then, a pattern discernible in Wittgenstein's treatment of mental terms, terms that have traditionally been treated as if they were names of mental processes. Wittgenstein is concerned to relieve us of our temptation to theorize inner mental processes, a temptation that seems grounded in the hope that such processes will serve as the "thing corresponding to [the] substantive" (cf. *BB* 1, 5). He pursues his therapeutic goal by reminding us that such mental terms might not refer to any *thing*. He reminds us that it is not the case that all substantives correspond to things; and nor must they do so in order for them to be meaningful. Indeed, he draws our attention to our language use, so that we are reminded that some terms are employed without there being or having to be anything common to each and every employment of such terms; for, some terms might be best characterized as "family resemblance" terms (see *PI* §67). Further, Wittgenstein exposes the "craving for generality" (*BB* 16–20), which serves to drive our desire for finding or positing inner processes, processes that we hope might serve a general explanatory role for all the many and variegated instances of "thinking" or "understanding". He shows how this craving for general explanations goes hand in hand with a contemptuous attitude toward the particular case (*ibid.*). Wittgenstein believes that the treatment of these prejudices will be effected by facilitating his interlocutor's realization that she is in the grip of a particular picture that has lain in her unconscious, led to her cravings and constrained her thought in such a way that she has been blind to other possible pictures and counter-examples. Once she acknowledges the picture, once it is brought to consciousness, it loses its thought-constraining grip; for the picture's capacity to fetter thought rested in the interlocutor's failure to be aware of its role in her considerations.[4]

So, the craving for generality, which arises from being in thrall to a particular picture of the way things must be – say, a latent picture of the necessary form of explanation – might lead us to overlook those substantives that do not correspond to things. In overlooking such substantives, we assume that there *must always* be some *thing* to which each substantive corresponds and which bestows meaning on the term in question. This picture of substantives-as-necessarily-corresponding-to-things has exerted such a grip that when philosophers have failed to find a material or tangible *thing* to which the substantive in question might correspond, they have often succumbed to the temptation to posit "processes", "states", ethereal "*things*", or theoretically postulated quasi-hypothetical "*things*" (cf. *PI* §36).[5] Such prejudice regarding substantives amounts to a general prejudice about meaning, a prejudice that has led us to overlook or discount the particular case – for example, the case of a meaningful substantive that does not correspond to a thing.

If we shift our focus away from substantives in general and onto the particular concepts of "thinking" and "understanding", we can see how the same prejudice might be what leads many philosophers to assume that these terms correspond to processes. The temptation is to assume that it is a process that underpins all the many and variegated instances of "thinking". This temptation is manifested in the positing of a process that, it is proposed, serves as the grounds or the ultimate justification for all our predications of "thinking": such positing might be materialist – we claim that all instances of thinking correspond to brain processes that involve the intervention of the neocortex;[6] it might be ethereal – we claim that processes are non-material; or it might be theoretically postulated quasi-hypothetical – we theoretically postulate processes on the model of computational processes.[7] Whichever of these – if any – we find most tempting, the assumption has remained that the answer to the question "What is thinking?" will be answered by pointing at the process to which the word "thinking" corresponds: this assumption has led us to think that there is a genuine question to be answered here.

If we are freed from the grip of this picture, by the picture having been brought to consciousness – the picture that has led to the hankering for generality, the concomitant disdain for the particular case and the assumption that there must be something, a process, underpinning all instances – we see that an investigation of our use of the terms "thinking" or "understanding" (a grammatical investigation) will furnish us with all we need to know about the meaning of these terms; and furthermore, that questions such as "What is thinking?" have yet to be given adequate sense.[8]

Now, Wittgenstein's efforts to relieve us of the temptation to posit mental processes have been interpreted by some as implying an endorsement of behaviourism. This interpretation is incorrect. Wittgenstein considered behaviourism to not merely be as confused as cognitivism, but to have its roots in the very same prejudice. Consider *PI* §308:

> How does the philosophical problem about mental processes and states and about behaviourism arise? – – The first step is the one that altogether escapes notice. We talk of processes and states and leave their nature undecided. Sometime perhaps we shall know more about them – we think. But that is just what commits us to a particular way of looking at the matter. For we have a definite concept of what it means to learn to know a process better. (The decisive move in the conjuring trick has been made, and it was the very one we thought quite innocent.) – And now the analogy which was to make us understand our thoughts falls to pieces. So we have to deny the yet uncomprehended process in the yet unexplored medium. And now it looks as if we had denied mental processes. And naturally we don't want to deny them.

So, here Wittgenstein identifies that which constrains our thinking, that which "we thought quite innocent", as being the assumption that mental processes are taken to be processes on the model of those processes that we have encountered in other domains and with which we are familiar ("we have a definite concept of what it means to learn to know a process better"). The issue is not, as many have assumed, that Wittgenstein is some sort of behaviourist and rejects processes *tout court*. Rather, it is that he wants to bring to consciousness our hitherto unconscious assumption that when we talk of "mental processes", we do so on the assumption that these are akin to processes with which we are already familiar and which we already understand (through our having grasped the concept of "process" and previously employed it in other domains).

We might put the point Wittgenstein is making as follows: when communicating with our (cognitivist) interlocutor we might say to her: "talking of mental processes is fine, so long as you either (a) acknowledge that you are employing the concept of 'process' in a new way, a way that does not necessarily imply continuity with nor draw upon your employment of that concept in other domains; or (b) you furnish us with a justification for your claim that the notion of 'process' that you are invoking in the term 'mental process' *is* continuous with previous uses of that term in other domains". And the same might be put to a behaviourist; they, too, owe us an account of their use of the term "process" if we are to take seriously their rejection of it.

There is no revisionism here. What we, as Wittgensteinians, should want to do is bring to consciousness our interlocutor's hitherto unacknowledged *assumption* that mental processes are akin to, are shadows cast by, or are modelled on the sorts of processes we encounter in other domains and about which we have understanding.

Of course, the upshot of this strategy is that while we have not denied our interlocutor her recourse to the invocation of mental process – for we have not "policed" her language use – we have problematized the move she makes. For in making her aware that her use of the term "process" left many questions unanswered, in departing from previous uses of that term, we are inviting her to provide us with the rules according to which she now employs the term. In short, we are asking her to commit to a grammar for her use of the term "process" when she talks of mental processes. When we ask her for such she will probably realize (we have facilitated her realization as to) how little explanatory work her initial invocation of the term "process" had done; that it served, at best, only to defer her attempts at explanation.

Authors such as Cartmill (and, to reiterate, he is not in a minority on this matter) depict Wittgenstein as continuous with conventional philosophy and thus as offering a specific answer to the question: "What is thinking?"; answer: "Thinking is essentially the activity of operating with signs". How can such commentators be so mistaken in their reading of Wittgenstein? The short answer is that they read him selectively, and thus fail to get to grips with his distinctive approach to philosophy. Failure to read Wittgenstein through the hermeneutic of therapy – i.e. failure to be attuned to the therapeutic voice(s) in which Wittgenstein speaks – leads almost inevitably to a reading of him that takes him to be making positive proclamations, to be advancing philosophical doctrine. If one reads him in this way, one will probably find moments in his work where one discerns Wittgenstein-the-behaviourist, Wittgenstein-the-proto-computationalist, or Wittgenstein-the-language-policeman. In response to such readings, we might venture that commentators such as Cartmill are themselves in the grip of a picture, which leads them to read Wittgenstein as they do.[9]

Let us therefore take the expression of Wittgenstein's that Cartmill quotes and examine the ways in which we might read it. This will ultimately lead us to a discussion of how Wittgenstein practises therapy in *The Blue Book* (with regard to "thinking") and in *Philosophical Investigations* (with regard to "understanding").[10]

"Thinking is operating with signs"

"Thinking is operating with signs". So wrote Wittgenstein in the early 1930s.[11] Taken in isolation, one could be forgiven for seeing this as a paradigmatic instance of that which non-Wittgensteinians find most objectionable in Wittgenstein's post-*Tractatus* philosophy. As an identity claim, which (taken in isolation) it appears to be, it seems, at least, somewhat vague or obscure.[12] Surely, it can give rise to a number of divergent interpretations. In what follows we shall consider some of the most prevalent. Ultimately we shall see that this "slogan", which is from what is often referred to as Wittgenstein's "middle period", is consonant with his later discussions of "thinking" and of "understanding", only in these later discussions he foregoes the coining of slogans in favour of more indirect ways of facilitating reorientations in thought. (See Chapter 12 on "Therapy".)

(Proto-)Computationalism

Wittgenstein's slogan might be read as indicating that he held and/or propounded a proto-computational theory of mind. In this case, Wittgenstein anticipates those for whom he is usually taken to have provided the resources for criticizing: Jerry Fodor, Fred Dretske and their like. On this "reading" of the remark, Wittgenstein is taken to be saying that when a person thinks, what takes place is that mental representations with (psycho)semantic content have been triggered; the signs of which Wittgenstein is taken to be speaking are the concepts of psychosemantics and the activities of which he speaks are taken to be the mental processes. So, it is not the person who is putting the signs to work but their mind, their computational modules, as it were. This, then, is what thinking is. The adding up, the composing of the poem and so on, are being done "in our minds" prior to our putting the sum or the poem on paper and it is our "minds" that are directing our movements as we do this. "We" are mere agents of "our" computational processes.

Of course, this "reading" does not actually "get off the ground", for, to say the least, it does not sit well with Wittgenstein's other remarks; his remarks about philosophy, for example (see Chapter 12, "Therapy"). In short, this "reading" relies on treating Wittgenstein's slogan in abstraction from its immediate textual context (the context provided by the discussion in which the remark is embedded) and the wider context provided by having grasped his philosophical method(s): the therapeutic, non-theoretical, non-doctrinal and non-metaphysical nature of Wittgenstein's philosophy. Wittgenstein is not in the business of propounding theories of mind and mental content.

Behaviourism

A more common interpretation of the remark goes something like this: the remark is from Wittgenstein's "middle period", when as well as flirting with positivism Wittgenstein had some decidedly behaviourist leanings. So, Wittgenstein is offering us a behaviourist thesis, such that what it is for a person to think is for that person to, literally, put signs to work: a person thinking *just is* a person speaking, writing, typing, sliding across the beads of the abacus, and so on. If we took this to be Wittgenstein's claim, it would then be quite clear why Wittgenstein is a philosopher "we" – early twenty-first-century analytic philosophers – can largely pass by. For, is not the problem with behaviourism, such as this, that it cannot account for my calculating in my head, for my thinking to myself that Reuben is a complete ass, for my thinking to myself that Spot is a somewhat odd-looking dog, and so on?

Surely, much of what we call thinking simply takes place "in the head" without any outward behavioural manifestation (or even disposition to act), much less some sort of behaviour accurately described as "the (activity of) operating (or calculating) with signs". If Wittgenstein is a behaviourist, then he seems to be missing out that which is arguably most characteristic of thought: its representational quality. However, as we saw above, Wittgenstein explicitly rejects behaviourism as having its roots in the same confusions as cognitivism. This reading of the remark, therefore, ignores the therapeutic voice in which Wittgenstein speaks and ignores his explicit remarks about behaviourism.

The grammar of "thinking" and *logical* behaviourism

As noted in the opening section, above, Wittgenstein is not seeking to advance philosophical doctrines. If we take this much on board from what he writes about his conception of philosophy, we might respond to the above two readings by remarking that Wittgenstein is not seeking to furnish his readers with a theory of mind or a theoretical answer to the question as to what it is to think. Wittgenstein, we might say, is simply not in the business of providing an answer to the question "What is thinking?" but is rather pointing out to his readers the grammar (the uses) of certain psychological concepts. He is, on this "grammatical" reading, availing us of the rules of grammar with which, as language users, we must act in accordance so that we might avoid uttering nonsense when employing the word "thinking". The upshot of such a reading is that Wittgenstein transpires to be a *logical* behaviourist. He is not committed to the substantive behaviourism of psychological behaviourists such as B. F. Skinner, but he is, on this reading, claiming that the logic of psychological concepts – their grammar – is exhausted by the extent to which they denote (pick out or are expressive of) a certain family of behaviour (operations with signs) or dispositions, rather than serving as reports on, descriptions of or labels for inner states or process.

What motivates this reading is the thought that Wittgenstein has established that meaning is use, that to mean something by our employment of a word on an occasion is to have used that word in accordance with its grammatical rules (the rules that allow us to distinguish between sense and nonsense and which are read off the sensical uses of those terms).[13] The grammatical rules for the sensical use of the word "thinking" are made perspicuous for us by Wittgenstein's grammatical remark "thinking is operating with signs". For, to use the word "thinking" in a way that cannot be accommodated by the notion of "operating with signs" is to fail to make sense, through having violated the grammatical rules – the grammar – of the word "thinking". It is akin to using the word "bachelor" in a way that cannot be accommodated by the notion of "unmarried man".[14]

Wittgenstein's behaviourism is said to be logical (rather than Skinnerian substantive psychological) because he is not, on this reading, seeking to downplay or even deny mental life, as it were – that one can have thoughts without outward manifestations or dispositions. He is not collapsing together "thought" and "behaviour", but rather he is saying that psychological concepts should be analysed in terms of behavioural dispositions or tendencies. There is no metaphysical commitment. There is no commitment to what is (or is not) going on "in the mind". Rather, there is a commitment to the grammar or the logic of mental predicates, such that the conditions for the applicability of the word "thinking", on an occasion and in a context, are perspicuously represented by the grammatical remark: "thinking is operating with signs".

While one sees this version of Wittgenstein (and this brand of "Wittgensteinianism") presented in the literature often, it is, I suggest, problematic (and a "Wittgensteinianism" that finds at best only superficial support in Wittgenstein's work). Not only did Wittgenstein explicitly reject behaviourism, but also there are good reasons to resist depicting him as either engaged in or advocating a policing of the grammar of our language, in this way (see Baker 2004: *passim*; Hutchinson & Read 2008).

Propaganda for a certain way of thinking about "thinking": liberating slogans

We have now worked through three ways of "reading" Wittgenstein's remark "thinking is operating with signs". The first two ways of "reading" the remark were shown to stem from a desire to extract positive doctrines about thinking from Wittgenstein's texts. In this sense, we might say that commentators such as Cartmill are so in thrall to a particular picture (of the philosopher's task) that they fail to observe that which would show their interpretation to be a non-reading of Wittgenstein (Wittgenstein's remarks about his (therapeutic) vision of philosophy). Such authors fail to take seriously Wittgenstein's remarks about his conception of philosophy. We might say, they show contempt for the particulars of Wittgenstein's texts in their desire to read him as making general claims about the nature of thinking and providing us with a general answer to the general "question": "What is thinking?".

The third way in which one might interpret Wittgenstein's remark reads him as elucidating the grammar of "thinking". This initially appears more promising. However, it puts Wittgenstein in the role of legislator or policeman regarding the grammar of terms such as "thinking", a role that one finds no support for in Wittgenstein's text. (See, for example, his remarks about the importance of gaining the consent of the speaker regarding the grammar of the terms they employ; cf. *BT* §410; Baker 2003: 105;[15] also see Baker 2004: ch. 2, 55ff.)

So how might we better understand Wittgenstein's slogan: *thinking is operating with signs*? First off, we should take care to read it in the right voice, as it were. Wittgenstein's method is therapeutic, he seeks to absent prejudice, prejudice that constrains us in our thinking about "thinking" and in our attempts to understand "understanding". I submit, therefore, that coining the slogan, "thinking is operating with signs", is done in an attempt to expose and redress the prejudicial view of "thinking" as being a process of a familiar sort – i.e. a process on the model of processes with which we are already familiar – which accompanies what we thus take to be the outward manifestations of thinking, such as speaking, writing, furrowing one's brow and so on.[16] So, Wittgenstein is offering us neither a theory of the mind – proto-computational or behaviourist – nor is he stipulating or mapping for us the grammar of "thinking" or "thought", from which one might infer that he is committed to logical behaviourism. Rather, he is furnishing us with a slogan in an attempt to jolt us out of our settled, prejudicial way of thinking about "thinking". On the reading I here propose, the prejudice is not merely something along the lines of: "mental processes must accompany outward (visible and/or tangible) manifestations of mental life"; it is a more nuanced prejudice than this. The prejudice comprises the (unconscious) commitment to the thoughts that

  (a) mental processes are assumed to be processes on the model of processes with which we are familiar from other domains (cf. *PI* §308); and
  (b) these processes play an explanatory role, such that they provide the justificatory grounds for predicating mental life of a person behaving in a certain way and they thus explain what thinking is: they are the essence of thinking.

Wittgenstein is not *providing* us with a new *account* of (the grammar of) thinking but is *suggesting* to his interlocutors a *way of thinking* about "thinking" that might relieve us of our current prejudice and help guard against certain temptations to produce metaphysical theses.

Now, this might elicit a response from Wittgenstein's interlocutor that this – Wittgenstein's suggested way – is simply inadequate, for it tells us nothing about the *nature* of thinking over, above and beyond the instances of people doing things that we ordinarily take to be instances of them thinking: talking, writing, calculating, communicating and so on. What does the interlocutor's response amount to here? Well, the interlocutor's response seems motivated by her frustration at Wittgenstein foregoing attempts at explanation. And the response and its motivating frustration seem to rest on an *assumption* that there *must* be something common to all these activities we call "thinking"; the response rests on the *assumption* that there must be some *thing* or discrete process to which the word "thinking" corresponds.

How might we counter the interlocutor's response? Well, we might reply by saying that the interlocutor has merely *assumed* that thinking is *not* a family-resemblance term; we might suggest to them that they are simply proceeding on the *assumption* that thinking is a term for which there is something common to all its instances. We should ask them, therefore, to provide support for this assumption.

The interlocutor will surely respond to us here that neither we nor Wittgenstein have *reason* to *assume* that "thinking" *is* a family-resemblance term. Given this point, the interlocutor might suggest to us now (feeling somewhat happy with themselves at "turning the tables" and finding us guilty of assumptions) that we might do some theorizing as to what thinking *is* rather than glibly and blithely *assuming* that it is a family-resemblance term. In taking themselves to have exposed *our* assumption that "thinking" is a family-resemblance term as just that, an assumption, the interlocutor now suggests that our refusal to engage in hypothesizing as to what all the disparate and variegated instances of "thinking" have as their grounds is itself merely born of (Wittgensteinian) prejudice. Accusations such as this one are often buttressed by the thought, claim or hope that the correct theory will one day be supported by some neuroscience.

Again, we come up against another common accusation levelled at Wittgenstein. He is taken to be anti-science, when he is actually anti-*scientism* – the thought that science can answer all possible questions. This is an important misconception to rebut. Wittgenstein, we might say, wants to relieve us of the bias that leads us to assume that "thinking" denotes a process of a particular sort, which serves as an explanation. He does not want to do this because he has some "knee-jerk" objection to the idea of mental processes, nor because he does not like science (what would such a dislike amount to or look like?) and therefore wants to undermine cognitivism/cognitive neuroscience. Rather, Wittgenstein is concerned to facilitate our realization that the appeal to processes cannot achieve that which we hope for in making such an appeal.

Let us consider those occasions where we say of someone that they are thinking, or that we say of ourselves that we are/have been thinking. Such instances are many and variegated; they are specific to particular and varied practices, and intelligible in specific contexts and on occasions. This untidiness, this occasion- and context-specificity, this contingency, leads us to want something more general and necessary. Why do we want something more general? Why do we, as Wittgenstein puts it, crave generality? Well, as our interlocutor might (somewhat exasperatedly) respond, "how else do we know what *thinking* is?!"

To put this concern another way, our interlocutor's exasperation stems from a sense of incredulity at the thought that we would, as philosophers, want anything other than to discover some general necessary underpinning to all these many, variegated and seemingly contingent instances of "thinking". "Surely", our interlocutor would probably exclaim, "it is the discovery of something common to – underpinning – all instances of thinking that affords us the assurance that we use the word 'thinking' correctly! For, how otherwise might we know what counts as a correct and an incorrect application of the word (predication of) thinking?"

How might Wittgenstein or a Wittgensteinian respond to the interlocutor's incredulity and her concomitant craving for a general explanation? Well, the response ought to be to show her that the theorizing of inner processes cannot do the work she desires of them (they cannot satisfy her craving), for they necessarily abstract from that which gives instances of "thinking" (and "understanding") their sense: the practices in which those instances are embedded, in contexts and on occasions.[17] Correctness and incorrectness in our applications of the word – our predicating of a person (or beast) that they are – "thinking" do not demand of us that we theorize grounds for all applications of the word thinking.

Facilitating aspect shifts through immersion in imaginary scenarios: understanding Wittgenstein's grocer

When we reach the *Philosophical Investigations* Wittgenstein seems to have grown cautious regarding the employment of slogans.[18] Instead, he immerses us in imaginary scenarios. In the main, the extended discussions of certain concepts are similar: there are reminders regarding certain aspects of our language use and the role of context and practices. Wittgenstein again talks of the craving for generality and of the desire to theorize grounds that cannot fulfil the role that they putatively serve. And there are extended discussions of the concepts of "thinking" and of "understanding" (*PI* §§138–55 and §§327–76, respectively). However, slogans such as "thinking is operating with signs" slip out of the picture and imaginary scenarios, such as the "trip to the grocer", take their place. Wittgenstein is now less inclined to coin slogans in an attempt to jolt his reader out of her settled assumptions regarding "thinking" or "understanding"; instead, he tries to facilitate his interlocutor's (and reader's) realization that she is in the grip of a picture that leads her to crave more than observable instances of "thinking" or "understanding" offer her. In terms of "understanding", we find *Philosophical Investigations* opening with the following imaginary scenario.

> Now think of the following use of language: I send someone shopping. I give him a slip marked "five red apples". He takes the slip to the shopkeeper, who opens the drawer marked "apples"; then he looks up the word "red" in a table and finds a colour sample opposite it; then he says a series of cardinal numbers – I assume that he knows them by heart – up to the word "five" and for each number he takes an apple of the same colour as the sample out of the drawer. – It is in this and similar ways that one operates with words. – "But how does he know where and how he is to look up the word 'red' and what he is to do with the word 'five'?" – Well I assume that he *acts* as I have described. Explanations come to an end somewhere. – But what is the meaning of the word "five"? – No such thing was in question here, only how the word "five" is used.   (*PI* §1, para. iv)

It has been noted that the trip to the grocer that Wittgenstein presents us with in the opening remark of *Philosophical Investigations* is apt to strike readers as somewhat odd (see Mulhall 2001; Hutchinson 2007). The grocer seems dumb (or extremely miserable and rude); moreover, he seems in need of colour charts so that he might associate the word "red", as written on the note passed to him by the shopper, with the colour of the apples, which he keeps in drawers. Is there a reason for such an eccentric presentation of an otherwise familiar and mundane scenario? I submit that there is. Wittgenstein structures the story of the trip to the grocer as such to reflect the form of a dominant picture of "inner mental processes". Wittgenstein tries to tempt his reader/interlocutor into asking for more, into asking for something that will serve as grounds for predicating of the grocer understanding. His interlocutor in *Philosophical Investigations* obliges: "But how does he [the grocer] know where and how he is to look up the word 'red' and what he is to do with the word 'five'?" Wittgenstein thus succeeds in tempting the interlocutor into undermining her own prejudices. As Stephen Mulhall writes, commenting on this passage in his book

Inheritance and Originality: "If the public, externalised versions of such procedures were not in themselves enough to establish the presence of understanding to the interlocutor's satisfaction, why should their inner counterparts?" (2001: 45).

Let us consider this for a moment. Can it be that inner processes would be more satisfactory to Wittgenstein's interlocutor in virtue of their being simply inner? If we theorize modules and elicitation files matching mental images of colour with files having semantic content, then why should this satisfy the interlocutor when the grocer, having done the same externally in the scenario, failed to so satisfy her? Surely, "going inner" is not enough?

The subtlety of Wittgenstein's example does not stop there. Mulhall writes,

> If Wittgenstein's shopkeeper's way with words strikes us as surreal and oddly mechanical, to the point at which we want to question the nature and even the reality of his inner life, and yet his public behaviour amounts to an externalised replica of the way we imagine the inner life of all ordinary, comprehending language-users, then our picture of the inner must be as surreal, as oddly mechanical, as Wittgenstein's depiction of the outer. (*Ibid.*: 46)

Of course, one of the driving forces behind the interlocutor's question (her craving for more) is the thought that the outer behaviours described by Wittgenstein in this scenario are merely contingent, merely accoutrements: for, obviously we can imagine a grocer who simply picks up five red apples (without the use of colour charts etc.) and of whom we are happy to say that they have understood the request. This makes the interlocutor assume that something general must be going on "behind the scenes" – in the grocer's head – that affords us the right to attribute to him understanding. What this scenario does, therefore, is facilitate one's realization that what is at issue is not whether certain practices are internal or external, mental or physical, but rather what would *count* for us (for Wittgenstein's interlocutor) as a grounding for an attribution of "understanding". The craving for generality leads us to look for general grounds underlying all instances of understanding.

Now, could such a craving be itself grounded in the philosopher being in thrall to a particular picture lying in the unconscious and constraining their thoughts? That picture might be such that it leads such philosophers to assume that substantives gain their meaning by corresponding to things; all instances of the substantive are, therefore, meaningful inasmuch as they are instances of a correspondence between the substantive and the general thing. And where a philosopher with such a craving cannot see the general thing, she proceeds to theoretically postulate one (again, cf. *PI* §36).

So (to stay with the concept of understanding), when Wittgenstein returns to discuss "understanding" later (§§327–76), he again draws our attention to the prejudices that he considers apt to befall us when doing philosophy:

(a) our *assumption* that all instances of a word must have something in common;
(b) our *contempt* for the particular case and our concomitant *craving* for generality;
(c) our *bias* against the worth or significance of a family of contingent instances – i.e. the tendency to see contingencies as merely accoutrements – and our desire for essentialism and "metaphysical necessity"; and
(d) our seeing our theoretical postulations as providing the grounds or ultimate justification for that which initially warranted their theoretical postulation.

The fourth entry in the list is worth elaborating. It is a point Wittgenstein makes in numerous places in his later writings.[19] When we theorize something underlying all instances of "thinking" or "understanding", that which licenses the theorizing are the very observed instances for which we hope to provide (through our hypothesizing the underlying processes) ultimate justification.[20] How can the processes that have been theorized into existence *from* the observable instances of someone thinking serve as ultimate justification – as grounds – *for* those very same observable instances that have afforded their theoretical postulation?

We might, therefore, summarize Wittgenstein on "thinking" and "understanding" as follows: he is interested in neither providing inviolable metaphysical grounds for attributions of "thinking" or "understanding" (realism) nor in undermining our day-to-day practical ability of employing the words "thinking" and "understanding" (scepticism). Both scepticism and realism (and idealism) begin with the assumption that leads Wittgenstein's interlocutor to ask her question regarding the grocer in *PI* §1. That is, they begin by assuming that what is there, our practices, our form of life, is not enough. Wittgenstein seeks to practise therapy such that he relieves one of the desire to make realist claims or sceptical claims or produce cognitivist or behaviourist theories. He seeks to remind you of what you already know: that your practices of ascribing "thinking" and "understanding" are satisfactory (and where you might err, you do so not for want of a theory of mental processes) and that the yearning for something beyond practices can never be more satisfying than the observable practices in which they are embedded.[21]

Notes

1. Editions referred to in this chapter are *Philosophical Investigations* (2001a) and *The Blue and Brown Books* (1965).
2. The passage is taken from Cartmill's paper "Do Horses Gallop in Their Sleep?" (2000). The reader will gather from the tone of the passage and "side-swipes" at college professors and so on that the paper is not intended as a serious piece of research or critique but rather as a somewhat light-hearted report for non-specialists. However, Cartmill is a professor of Biomedical Anthropology and Anatomy, and has published widely, including papers in the philosophy of science; this paper was written for and published in the *Key Reporter*, the journal of the Phi Beta Kappa society. And, his attempts at humour aside, he intends the quote from Wittgenstein and the extrapolations he makes from that quote entirely seriously as being representative of Wittgenstein's views. In this respect, as I noted above, Cartmill is sadly indicative of widely spread and widely held views regarding Wittgenstein's views on thinking.
3. We might say that "understanding" is a species – along with "wishing", "believing", "desiring" and so on – of the genus "thinking". See Baker (2004: ch. 8).
4. My way of putting things here should not lead one to conclude that the therapeutic relationship must be between two people. The tussle can be with (tendencies within) oneself.
5. See Paul E. Griffiths (1997) for a recent prominent example of a philosopher succumbing to this temptation to theoretically postulate a quasi-hypothetical "*thing*" to which emotion terms correspond. See Hutchinson (2008: ch. 1) for a critique.
6. It is important to note that one does not have to deny this in order to see it as problematic as a candidate *account* or *explanation* of "thinking". This will become clearer below. For now it will suffice to say that there is a difference between correlating "thinking" with brain-processes-involving-the-intervention-of-the-neocortex or identifying a causal relation between brain-processes-involving-the-intervention-of-the-neocortex and what we call thinking and an answer to the question "what is thinking?"
7. See Coulter & Sharrock (2007) for a recent critique of such endeavours.
8. It is, therefore, important to note that the "grammatical investigation" comes late in the therapeutic process, after much of the work has been done. It is, however, part of that therapeutic process. It is not a positive, constructive add-on to Wittgenstein's negative therapeutic practice (*pace* Hacker 1986: 151, 177–8; 1996: 232–8; 2001a: 23, 31, 37; 2001b: 333–41) and Kenny (1984: 45). See Hutchinson & Read (2008). Neither is it a central or primary tool in the armoury of the "Wittgensteinian" philosopher (*pace* those who see strong continuity between Ryle's methods and Wittgenstein's, e.g. Jeff Coulter). We need to have been relieved of some of our confusions and yearnings so that we might be in a position to see the worth of an investigation of the grammar of a term.

9. This picture might be one that restricts their view of the philosopher's task (an underlying picture of philosophy-as-a-theoretical-discipline); or it might be one that constrains their "reading" of Wittgenstein (an underlying picture of Wittgenstein-as-ordinary-language-philosopher).

10. I do not suggest here that he deals exclusively with one of these in one book and one in the other. Both concepts come in for extended treatment in both *Philosophical Investigations* and *The Blue Book.*

11. This formulation and very similar can be found in the *The Blue and Brown Books* (see pp. 6 & 16) and in Wittgenstein's dictations to Friedrich Waismann, which can be found collected in Baker (2003).

12. If you are wont to cry foul here on the grounds that you think no one could seriously treat this as an identity claim, you might like to consider how some (even some who claim to be "Wittgensteinians") take the remark "meaning is use".

13. It is somewhat odd that so many exegetes gloss the wording of Wittgenstein's famous remark about meaning and use, at *Philosophical Investigations* §43. See Hutchinson (2007) for discussion of this.

14. For an in-depth discussion of "grammar" in Wittgenstein, see Baker (2004: chs 2 & 3). In the latter of these two chapters, Baker offers an alternative to the standard understanding of what constitutes a genuinely Wittgensteinian grammatical investigation.

15. Also see Baker (2003: "On the Character of Disquiet", 69–77; also 233–7, 277–9, 303–5).

16. To an extent I follow Baker (2004: ch. 8) in this respect. However, Baker takes the prejudice to amount merely to the assumption that mental processes must accompany outward manifestations of thinking.

17. Of course, this might take a lot of work!

18. This might be because he later considered them less effective as therapeutic devices than he had hoped in the early 1930s; it might be that he was worried that such slogans might be taken as substantive claims, thus replacing one myth with another. If the latter was what motivated the move away from slogans, we can say with the benefit of hindsight that he was right to be worried (cf. the quote from Cartmill with which we began).

19. See *The Blue Book* p. 47, para. 2; *Philosophical Investigations* §§293 & 304; and *On Certainty* §307 for some examples.

20. For an example of this move being employed in contemporary philosophical discussion see Pleasants (1999: ch. 6) and Hutchinson (2008: ch. 1).

21. Thanks are due to Jeff Coulter, Eugen Fischer, Hanjo Glock, Oskari Kuusela, Rupert Read and Wes Sharrock. The paper was presented at conferences held at the University of East Anglia, Norwich, UK and at the Indian Institute of Technology Bombay, India.

Further reading

Tractatus, 5.54–5.5422.

EIGHT

Psychologism and
Philosophical Investigations

Kelly Dean Jolley

Introduction

In her study of Husserl's logic, Suzanne Bachelard writes

> [F]or the logician, the problem of psychologism is not just one
> problem among other problems: it is a determining problem; for
> either the logician welcomes psychological justifications, or he
> considers such recourse to psychology a radical vice. The choice
> is decisive for the logician. (1968: iii)

The choice is decisive for Wittgenstein in *Philosophical Investigations*.[1]
It is a book of logic (a "conceptual investigation" or "grammatical
investigation") and from front to back in it, Wittgenstein considers
psychologism a radical vice. And "vice" is the exact word: psychologism
is not treated as a false theory but as a failure more radical – a failure
so much as to recognize logic at all. But the fact that psychologism is a
radical vice does not mean that combating it is easier than it would be
were it a false theory. It means that combating it is more complicated
and requires more patience than would combating a false theory. Wittgenstein not only has to struggle against certain beliefs in his reader but
also against his reader's philosophical character.

Some background: Gottlob Frege

Before looking at Wittgenstein's treatment of psychologism, it will help to consider Frege's description of psychologism and his response to it. The *locus classicus* is the beginning of Frege's paper, "Thoughts". Frege explains that

> People may very well interpret the expression "law of thought" by analogy with "law of nature" and then have in mind general features of thinking as a mental occurrence. A law of thought in this sense would be a psychological law. And so they might come to believe that logic deals with the mental process of thinking and the psychological laws in accordance with which this takes place. That would be a misunderstanding of the task of logic, for truth has not here been given its proper place. Error and superstition have causes just as much as correct cognition. Where what you take for true is false or true, your so taking it comes about in accordance with psychological laws. A derivation from these laws, an explanation of a mental process that ends in taking something to be true, can never take the place of proving what is taken to be true ... In order to avoid any misunderstanding and prevent the blurring of the boundary between psychology and logic, I assign to logic the task of discovering the laws of truth, not the laws of takings things to be true or of thinking. (1977: 1–2)

Frege distinguishes between logic and psychology. He notes that we may be tempted not to distinguish them or not to distinguish them properly if we do not take care with the phrase "law of thought". "Thought" can be taken as either a mental occurrence (the psychological sense) or as something that is true or false (the logical sense). Taken as a mental occurrence, a thought is neither true nor false; it just occurs, it just is. It is an event in the mind, a psychological event. As such, a thought is surely subject to psychological laws and comes about in accordance with them. But having come about in accordance with psychological laws does not confer a truth-value on the thought – in particular it does not confer truth on the thought. Now, Frege is implicitly deploying an act/content distinction: "thought" in the psychological sense is an act – a taking to be true. The act is neither true nor false. But the content of the act, "thought" in the logical sense, will be one or the other. It will be either true or false. Frege's point is clear: a law of thought, where "thought" is taken in its psychological sense, governs psychological acts; but a law of thought, where "thought" is taken in its logical sense, governs truth.

One important feature of Frege's discussion is that he does not attack psychology in attacking psychologism. Frege has no doubts about the reality of an "inner realm" (his term); in fact, he has a fairly clear view of the inner realm and a definite conception of its denizens. Frege dubs the denizens of the inner realm "ideas". Ideas are neither true nor false; they either occur (in the inner realm) or do not. Ideas are private, existing in only one inner realm. No one can have my ideas and I can have no one else's. Whatever else may be true of Frege's anti-psychologism, it is not behaviouristic: he is not denying the inner realm. He is instead denying that the inner realm has a certain kind of significance. It lacks that kind of significance because of what is true of the denizens of the inner realm. Ideas, ideas like takings to be true, are neither true nor false, and are private. They are not governed by the laws of thought in Frege's sense. So what Frege is denying is that the inner realm has any significance *qua* inner realm for logic. I shall return to this.

Frege contrasts the inner realm with the outer realm and the third realm. The outer realm is the realm of biscuits and hyacinths, of the beasts of the field. Its denizens are neither true nor false, but they are public. The third realm is the realm of thoughts, the place where those things that are true or false timelessly refuse to moulder. Unlike the denizens of the outer realm, thoughts are not netted in the causal nexus.

In *Foundations of Arithmetic*, Frege states three principles that he says he keeps throughout the book: "always to separate sharply the psychological from the logical, the subjective from the objective; never to ask for the meaning of a word in isolation, but only in the context of a proposition; never to lose sight of the distinction between concept and object" (1980: x). When explaining the second principle, known as the Context Principle, Frege notes that failing to keep it forces us to look for the meanings of words in the inner realm; we look for "pictures or acts of the individual mind" – ideas. In so doing, we fail to keep the first principle, since we fail to separate sharply the psychological from the logical. Failing to separate them sharply, we psychologize logic and meaning. In fact, one very useful way of thinking about Frege's three principles is to see them as his bulwark against psychologism – whether about logic, or meaning, or whatever. Certainly they function in this way for Wittgenstein – not only in the *Tractatus*, where the struggle against psychologism looks rather patently Fregean, but also in *Philosophical Investigations*, where the nature of the struggle is rather more latently Fregean. But we need only pay attention for it to become patent there, too.

A fundamental misunderstanding

Consider Frege's third principle and consider the following remark: "It shews a fundamental misunderstanding, if I am inclined to study the headache I have now in order to get clear about the philosophical problem of sensation" (*PI* §314). For Wittgenstein, philosophical problems are conceptual problems, and, as such, are to be distinguished from empirical problems. Wittgenstein's distinction is a Fregean inheritance: empirical problems are problems involving objects. So, Wittgenstein is in his own way asking his reader never to lose sight of the distinction between concepts and objects. Section 314 warns against losing sight of the distinction and of the grave consequences of doing so. ("It shews a fundamental misunderstanding ....") The philosophical problem of sensation is a conceptual problem, one rotating around the use of "sensation". To get clear about the problem requires conceptual investigation, an investigation of the use of "sensation". But the interlocutor Wittgenstein addresses is in danger of losing sight of that, and is inclined to introspect, to peek into the inner realm, and to examine an idea – the headache he has now. To so incline is to incline towards radical vice. For whatever might be revealed to introspective study, it will not be of the right sort to help with the philosophical problem. For what could be revealed to introspective study? That the interlocutor now has a headache; that it is intense; that the pain seems to shoot into his eyes and to make them sensitive to light; that noise worsens the pain; and so on. All things worth knowing, surely; but how could the puzzlement of a philosophical problem be vulnerable to such information? Wittgenstein thinks that it could not. No information about ideas helps in getting clear about concepts. But why would anyone think that it could help? One reason is a misconception of the significance of the inner realm; another is a misconception of conceptual investigation. Take the last first. It is easy to think that empirical investigation and conceptual investigation differ only in what they investigate – the first, empirical matters, the second, conceptual matters. On this way of thinking, the two investigations are congeners, and they differ in what they investigate – in much the same way as a homicide investigator and a narcotics investigator differ. Each is an investigator and each investigates in a similar way; the difference is in what they investigate: one investigates murders, the other illegal drug activity. So, on this way of thinking, conceptual investigation is treated as the investigation of the non-empirical, but investigation that is otherwise like empirical investigation. But where is the non-empirical to be found? Well, ideas, as denizens of the inner realm, a private realm, look as if they might be of the right sort to be non-empirical. And this is the second misconception. The inner realm comes to seem as if it houses the non-empirical objects that are the targets of conceptual investigation. Conceptual investigation thus is hard and mysterious because it seems to require introspection instead of extrospection, and because the inner realm is peculiar when compared to the outer realm. Wittgenstein perhaps canonically expresses this misconception in *The Blue Book* (in his discussion of what is required to fulfil an order to fetch a red flower): "These … activities [understanding, meaning, interpreting, thinking] seem to take place in a queer kind of medium, the mind; and the mechanism of the mind, the nature of which, it seems, we don't quite understand, can bring about effects which no material mechanism could" (*BB* 3). Another word Wittgenstein deploys nearby is "occult": the inner realm, the mind, seems an occult place peopled with occult items, ideas; and we do not quite understand either. But we press forward, believing that the difficulty of conceptual investigation is not the product of its difference from empirical investigation but rather the difference of its occult objects and their occult realm. Objects in the outer realm are not occult, the outer realm we quite understand. The inner realm, however, is spooky, and so, too, are the objects in it. Conceptual investigation is just empirical investigation of the spooky. (Think of Dorothy, first in Kansas, the outer realm, and then in Oz, the inner realm. Oz is strange and so are its objects – not just lions and tigers and bears, but witches and munchkins and ruby slippers. Empirically investigating Oz is hard: all is bewitched.)

Note that Wittgenstein in *Philosophical Investigations* §314 turns Frege's third principle – part of the bulwark against psychologism – to a purpose that Frege himself might well not have clearly expected. Frege cared principally to defend logic and mathematics from psychologism; Wittgenstein cares about that, too, but not principally – at least not in *Philosophical Investigations*. There Wittgenstein cares principally to defend psychology from psychologism. Wittgenstein in §314 uses Frege's third principle as a bulwark against psychologizing psychology. The philosophical problem of sensation is a problem about our psychology, but Wittgenstein warns us off trying to solve it by peeking into the psychological, the inner realm.

Anti-psychologism is *not* behaviourism

This leads into a crucial complication affecting Wittgenstein's anti-psychologism. By refusing to psychologize, by refusing to assign to the inner realm a particular philosophical significance, Wittgenstein seems suspiciously like a behaviourist – as if he denies the existence of the inner realm altogether or denies it any significance. Wittgenstein acknowledges the potential for confusion. In §307 he allows the interlocutor to voice a suspicion: "'Are you not really a behaviourist in disguise? Aren't you at bottom really saying that everything except human behaviour is a fiction?' – If I do speak of a fiction, then it is of a grammatical fiction." Wittgenstein's response to the suspicion is denial, but denial with an explanation. Wittgenstein does not treat the inner realm or ideas as fictions. But he does, again, treat assigning to the inner realm or to ideas a peculiar significance as itself an error, as fictitious. He treats the assignment as a grammatical fiction, meaning that he thinks that the surface grammar of the language tempts us to think that the inner realm or that ideas really can be assigned a peculiar significance. (Think again of the person who believes that introspecting her current headache will allow her to solve the philosophical problem of sensation. Wittgenstein has no quarrel with her headache or with her ability introspectively to determine various facts about it. But nothing she can determine about it determines the concept of "sensation". The headache is a sensation; the concept of "sensation" is not. That the headache is a sensation makes it seem as though it should be a revelator of the concept. But it is not.) Seeing what Wittgenstein is doing against a Fregean background should make what Wittgenstein is doing intelligible while also crucially distancing it from behaviourism. Frege's three principles and Wittgenstein's keeping to them explain his apparent behaviourism. Just as Wittgenstein refuses to rummage among ideas for the meanings of words, so, too, he refuses to rummage among ideas for the meanings of human actions. Throughout *Philosophical Investigations*, Wittgenstein treats the inner, treats ideas, with what might be called integral neglect. Meanings are not to be found in the inner realm, among ideas. But there is an inner realm. And is it populated with ideas. Neither the inner realm nor its denizens are fictions. All is not darkness within. Wittgenstein is no kind of behaviourist, simple or complicated, Skinnerian or Rylean. (Unfortunately, the publication of Ryle's *Concept of Mind* before *Philosophical Investigations*, and the general association of Ryle's work with Wittgenstein's, still strongly colours the understanding of Wittgenstein's actual position. Ryle may have been in his book some kind of complicated behaviourist; Wittgenstein in his was not.) Wittgenstein's concerns with human behaviour, with outer criteria, and so on, are the products of his resolution not to confuse the logical with the psychological, of his effort to investigate psychology non-psychologistically. Wittgenstein's investigations are conceptual – logical, not psychological.

Conclusion

I should add a word of caution. I have been using Frege's distinction among realms as if Wittgenstein believes the distinction to be unproblematic. That is not true. But the various criticisms (explicit and implicit) that Wittgenstein makes of the distinction in *Philosophical Investigations* are not really my concern at the moment. What I have been concerned to do is to frame Wittgenstein's anti-psychologism helpfully, as well as to differentiate it from behaviourism. Frege's distinctions aid in that task.

Frege warns himself to sharply separate concepts from objects. For him, to fail to sharply separate them is a radical vice, a fundamental confusion about what logic is and what psychology is. Sharply separating concepts from objects is decisive for the investigator. And if the investigator investigates concepts, he investigates something absolutely different from objects and investigates what he investigates in an absolutely different way. A person can choose to do logic or to do psychology, but he cannot choose to do both at once, to leaven his logic with a little psychology or regiment his psychology with a little logic. The choice is decisive.

Note

1. Editions referred to in this chapter are *Philosophical Investigations* (2001a) and *The Blue and Brown Books* (1958a).

Further reading

Tractatus, 4.1121, 5.541–5.5421, 5.5571–5.641.

NINE

Moore's paradox revisited

Avrum Stroll

Introduction

In October, 1944 G. E. Moore gave a talk to the Moral Science Club in Cambridge that contained a sentence that has become known as "Moore's paradox". In the ensuing sixty plus years, Moore's paradox has generated an extensive literature. Wittgenstein, who at times made caustic remarks about Moore's intelligence, immediately wrote to Moore, urging him to publish his "discovery". In his letter, Wittgenstein explained why he thought that Moore's finding was so important.

> You have said something about the *logic* of assertion. Vis: It makes sense to say "Let's suppose: p is the case and I don't believe that p is the case", whereas it makes *no* sense to assert "I-p is the case and I don't believe that p is the case." This *assertion* has to be ruled out and is ruled out by "common sense", just as a contradiction is. And this just shows that logic isn't as simple as logicians think it is. In particular: that contradiction isn't the *unique* thing people think it is. It isn't the only logically inadmissible form and it is, under certain circumstances, admissible. And to show that seems to me the chief merit of your paper.
>
> (Cited in Monk 1990: 545)

As Ray Monk has pointed out, this was not how Moore himself saw it. He thought that, as the paradox did not issue in a formal contradiction, it was an absurdity for psychological, rather than logical, reasons – an interpretation that Wittgenstein vigorously rejected.

Following these divergent interpretations, subsequent writers on the paradox have fallen into two categories: those who claim that Moore's sentence (which I shall present below) is a paradox but are not sure why it is; and those who think, as I do, that its appearance as paradoxical is apparent only, and that when the assumptions underlying the remark are clarified it can be seen not to have a significant use, let alone to be paradoxical.

The paradox

In the 1944 essay, Moore formulated the paradox in this way:

Smith left the room but I don't believe he has.
    It is generally agreed that the two sentences:

(i)   Smith left the room
(ii)   I don't believe he has (left the room)

are not logically incompatible in the way that the following locutions are:

(iii)   Smith is Mary's husband
(iv)   Smith is not married to Mary

That it is, there is concurrence by nearly all commentators that if (i) and (ii) were uttered singly, each would be perfectly meaningful and, of course, depending on the context, each could be true. Accordingly, it is agreed that (i) and (ii), when taken individually, are not logically incompatible.

Moore also pointed out that the past-tense counterparts of the paradoxical sentence are not incompatible. For example,

(v)   It was snowing and I did not believe that it was snowing

does not give rise to an absurdity. Some critics have thus argued that it is the word "I" used in the present tense that is the cause of the perplexity. Wittgenstein's view (in so far as that can be elucidated from his arcane remarks) suggests that the assertive nature of the paradoxical sentence arises from "I" used in the present tense. This is a position that many exegetes have accepted. It is also generally agreed that even if Moore's paradoxical sentence does not involve a *formal* contradiction, many commentators, following Wittgenstein, have agreed that there is a kind of logical tension between

(vi)   Smith left the room

and

(vii)   I don't believe he has

when these are combined into a single unit. There is a further consensus in the scholarly community that a distinction should be made between words taken independently of their use and words in use. The paradox on this view does not arise from a consideration of the sentences themselves; but rather from the use of those sentences made on a particular occasion by someone. It is also agreed by those who accept Moore's complex sentence as being paradoxical that, when combined into a single unit, (v) and (vi) are *logically* incompatible, but not in any formal sense of the term. As we have seen, Moore did not accept the point that the absurdity was logical.

Assertion and belief

But once such accords have been accepted, disagreement sets in. The dissenting parties fall into two categories: those who find – as apparently Wittgenstein did – that the paradox turns on the concept of *assertion*, and those who think it turns on the concept of *belief*. As his letter to Moore states: "You have said something about the *logic* of assertion."

Wittgenstein's view seems to have been that the paradox arises because the two parts of the paradoxical sentence entail assertions, that is, a speaker is both asserting that Smith left the room and also asserting that he does not believe he has. It is admittedly difficult to construct an argument from his letter to Moore. But in so far as one can, it would seem that his claim is that the two assertions cancel each other and hence nothing significant has been said. Many persons agree with him. His view anticipates a slightly different idea due to Donald Davidson, called "The Principle of Charity". According to Davidson, the default position of assertive talk is that it is making a truth-claim (or truth-claims). So if one is asserting that Smith left the room and is also asserting that he does not believe that he did, the combination of the two cannot count as an affirmation of truth. It will be noted that Wittgenstein contends that the paradox shows that the notion of contradiction (or of logic in general) has to be broadened to extend to cases where a perceived tension is more than formal. Davidson can be interpreted (although this is not the main thrust of the Principle of Charity) as saying something similar. In effect, both are claiming that in asserting p one is making a truth-claim; Wittgenstein's view in addition seems to stress that one who is asserting p and then saying he does not believe that p is both asserting and not asserting p, and that the complex sentence that results from such a pairing has no everyday use and thus is nonsense.

The second position concentrates on belief, rather than on assertion. The contention here is that any affirmation or claim entails that the speaker believes it. When a speaker says that Smith has left the room, he is implying (in a formal sense of "imply") that he believes that what he is saying is true. Thus, when a speaker also states that he does not believe that Smith has left the room, the absurdity one feels can be traced to an incompatibility between two affirmations of belief.

My sense is that commentators on the paradox have split more or less evenly on this issue, some holding that it is the concept of assertion and some holding that it is the concept of belief that lies at the heart of the paradox.

Annulling the paradox

I think both views are incorrect, and here are some arguments to that effect. Let us begin with the view that in certain specific circumstances one is making an assertion. Several dictionaries overlap in their definitions of "assertion" and its verbal form "assert". *Webster's Third New International Dictionary*, for example, gives several entries for both terms. One of its entries for "assertion" says: "insistent and positive affirming or maintaining or defending (as of a right or attribute)". With respect to "assert", it says "to state or affirm positively, assuredly, plainly, or strongly". It adds that "assert" puts "stress on the fact of positive statement; it may imply noteworthy assuredness or force on the speaker's part".

In *Philosophical Investigations* §116,[1] Wittgenstein remarks that "one must always ask oneself: 'Is the word ever actually used this way in the language-game which is its original home?'" – and then mentions: "What *we* do is to bring words back from their metaphysical to their everyday use". In using the term "we" he is obviously referring to himself and a new conception of philosophy. But in the case of Moore's paradox, has Wittgenstein appealed to how "assertion" is used in the language-game of everyday speech? Unfortunately, I do not think he has. In his letter to Moore, he says "this *assertion* has to be ruled out and is ruled out by 'common sense', just as a contradiction is". Wittgenstein seems to have interpreted Moore as saying two things: that Moore is speaking about logic and also about assertion. As he writes: "You have said something about the *logic* of assertion." As I mentioned, my interpretation of his letter to Moore presupposes that Moore's paradoxical sentence contains two assertions that run counter to each other and that is why common sense rules it out. Wittgenstein, of course, recognized that the paradoxical sentence has no significant use, but instead of pursuing the point further, he insisted that Moore was demonstrating that there are multifarious forms of contradiction of which formal contradiction – $(p.-p)$ is only one example. Instead of asking why the paradoxical sentence lacks a significant use, I think he was misled by a philosophical conceit about logic and contradiction to speak in ways that he himself, in other contexts, would have disavowed.

Some exegetes have argued that the paradoxical sentence has a use. They claim, for example, that a schizophrenic may say: "I hear voices telling me what to do, but I do not believe that such voices exist." According to such persons, such a locution parallels Moore's paradoxical sentence. I do not find such examples convincing. If a schizophrenic is hallucinating, that person is convinced that voices are present; so he or she would not say "I don't believe that such voices exist." The example assumes that the person is hallucinating and is at the same time aware that he or she is not hallucinating, and this seems to be inconsistent with the ordinary meaning of "hallucination", which implies that the person suffering from such a malady is not aware that the events being experienced do not really exist.

Some examples

In disagreement with both Moore and Wittgenstein, I shall offer four illustrations, arranged in an ascending order of disinclination, to describe a situation as one in which a person is entertaining something that counts as a truth-bearer, such as an assertion, judgement, assumption or belief. To simplify matters, let us restrict the discussion to putative cases of belief. Here is the first example. I rise in the morning and look out of a window in the parlour as I am normally accustomed to do. The light is good, there is no haze or fog or any other impediment to seeing the nearby environment; but I notice it is raining. I turn to my wife and say: "It is raining." According to Wittgenstein, I have made an assertion, but does it *follow* from my saying that it is raining that I believe it is? In my opinion the answer is no. One can grasp the intuition the negative answer taps by contrasting this case with a second example. I rise in the morning and look out of the window. The light is poor. It is hazy and I can barely see the outside terrain. I look harder; it seems to me that it is raining but I am not sure. I say to my wife "I believe it is raining."

The second scenario describes a case where I can truly be said to be believing something. But the former in contrast does not. The contrast brings out that the true ascription of belief requires that the scenario be a special one, as in the case described where the visual situation is not optimal. But in the first scenario no special impediments obtain. There is thus no evidential or circumstantial ground in support of the claim that I believe it is raining. Many philosophers would insist that my saying it is raining logically entails that I believe it is raining.[2] But in my view this entailment relationship is not *in general* found in ordinary speech, although there may be special circumstances, such as I have just described, where the ascription of belief is in order. It is true in the first case that my saying it is raining is based on what I notice; yet my saying in that case that it is raining is not an expression of belief. Instead, my noticing that it is raining is one of those features that make ordinary communication between various persons possible. When the circumstances are special, such as in the second case, then true ascriptions of belief may be apposite.

Consider now a third example that we can contrast with the first. In the first scenario, I was certainly *aware* that it was raining. The point of the example was to bring out that such awareness is not tantamount to belief. But now let us look at a variation of that case. In saying to my wife that it is raining, I am speaking to a perfectly normal person – someone who has two eyes, two feet, a nose, and two hands. Now, in speaking to my wife, am I aware that she has two eyes and two hands in the way that I was aware that it was raining when I looked out of the window? I say no. In the former situation I notice that it is raining and my noticing that this is so is the basis for my saying that it is raining. But I do not notice, nor indeed do I say or imply in any way, that my wife has two hands, when I inform her that it is raining. In looking at my wife while saying it is raining, do I believe she has two hands? I think not. If I had some reason to suspect that some dramatic circumstance had occurred affecting her hands, I might say in that kind of circumstance "I believe my wife has two hands."

Here is a fourth case. I am aware, as I look out of the window, that water is running down the glass. I am thus aware that the water is moving. Do I therefore believe that motion exists? Suppose I turn to my wife and say "Motion exists." Or, even more oddly, that I say, as Parmenides did, "Motion does not exist." What would her response as a person of common sense be? No doubt perplexity. But am I even aware that motion exists? The answer again is no. It is no because we would need a *very* special situation for saying otherwise. And what apart from a philosophical context would that be? When I notice water running down the glass, do I therefore believe that the glass is a physical object? To believe that the glass is a physical object would be to entertain a metaphysical thesis in which the notion of a physical object plays a central role. Such a view would contravene Berkeley's immaterialism. But do I, a person of common sense, hold any such view? Once again, the answer is no. From the fact that I notice that water is running down the glass it does not follow that I hold any philosophical thesis at all.

The difference between noticing that water is running down a pane and holding a philosophical theory about motion is brought out brilliantly in a series of passages by Wittgenstein. He writes:

> Children do not learn that books exist, that armchairs exist, etc. etc. – they learn to fetch books, sit in armchairs, etc. etc.
>
> (OC §476)

> Are we to say that the knowledge that there are physical objects comes very early or very late? (§479)

Many philosophers have contended that the ingredients of common sense are implicit beliefs that their activities as philosophers are designed to make explicit. On their view, I have a latent awareness that my wife has two eyes and two hands, and that this submerged awareness is a form of implicit, perhaps dispositional, belief to that effect.

The function of a philosopher, as they see it, is to make articulate the submerged beliefs that ordinary persons hold. For Moore, common sense consists of such propositions as "The earth exists", "Time is real", "I was once smaller than I am now", and so forth. He describes such beliefs as "obvious truisms", and adds that they are so obvious as hardly to be worth stating. Yet he does state them, and in so doing seems to be suggesting that although they are not in the forefront of anyone's attention, they are nonetheless "there", somewhere in the human psyche. There is thus the strong implication from his practice that he is trying to make those unexpressed beliefs explicit. And in adopting such a position, he is presupposing that when anything at all is said, and independently of the context in which it is said, one must be believing what is said. It is views such as this that I am rejecting. My thesis is that such words as "belief" and "assertion" play limited roles in the description of human action, and are essentially context dependent.

Moore's famous sentence is seen to be paradoxical only because the context dependence of its key terms is ignored or misrepresented. This is a lesson, though not the only lesson, that the later Wittgenstein has tried to teach us. His own discussion of Moore's paradox shows that this is a lesson it is easy to forget.

Notes

1. The edition referred to in this chapter is *Philosophical Investigations* (2001a).
2. P. H. Nowell-Smith, for example, says: "In saying 'no foxes eat hens' (a speaker) gives me to understand both that no foxes eat hens and also that he believes this" (1962: 9). R. Crawshay-Williams puts the point this way: "It is axiomatically understood ... that if anyone asserts a proposition, he wishes it to be interpreted as believing it to be true (or probable or acceptable in some sense)". He supports this view with the following remarks: "In other words, we almost invariably base our discussions upon an unstated agreement to adopt as one of our premises the double implication 'A says that p' implies 'A asserts that p,' and this in turn implies 'A believes or holds that p'" (1957: 183). In opposition to these authors, I think that most of the time when persons say something it would be incorrect to claim they are either making an assertion or implying that they believe what they are saying.

Further reading

Tractatus, 5.541–5.5421.

TEN

Aspect perception

Avner Baz

The seeing of what he calls "aspects", or the "seeing of something *as* something", preoccupied Wittgenstein during the last two decades of his life, and arguably earlier than that. His later manuscripts and type-scripts are filled with hundreds of remarks on this subject.

With a few exceptions (cf. *PI* §§534–9),[1] Wittgenstein never came to incorporate his remarks on aspects, or some selection of them, into what we now have as the first part of the *Philosophical Investigations*. Nor did he ever come to organize these remarks, or some selection of them, in some other way into a philosophical whole. This is important to keep in mind. While the remarks that make up what we now know as the first part of the *Investigations* were carefully and deliberately designed, over many years, to make their reader work, the numerous remarks on aspect perception show us Wittgenstein himself at work – making his way in a conceptual landscape that he himself found hard to find his way in. Witness here his saying to Maurice Drury, not long before his death, and after many years of thinking about aspect perception: "Now try and say what is involved in seeing something as something; it is not easy. These thoughts I am now having are as hard as granite" (quoted in Monk 1990: 537). Part of what concerns me in this chapter is the nature of the difficulty Wittgenstein found himself facing in thinking about aspects.

Wittgensteinian "aspects" – initial characterization

What are Wittgensteinian "aspects"? And what is it to see, or perceive, such an aspect? The first few remarks of section xi of part II of the

Investigations are probably as good a place to seek initial orientation as any other:

> Two uses of the word "see".
>
> The one: "What do you see there?" – "I see *this*" (and then a description, a drawing, a copy). The other: "I see a likeness between these two faces" – let the man I say this to be seeing the faces as clearly as I do myself.
>
> The importance of this is the difference in category between the two 'objects' of sight.
>
> The one man might make an accurate drawing of the two faces, and the other notice in the drawing the likeness which the former did not see.
>
> I contemplate a face, and then suddenly notice its likeness to another. I *see* that it has not changed; and yet I see it differently. I call this experience "noticing an aspect".

Let us see what may initially be gathered about what Wittgenstein calls "aspects", taking our cues from the above remarks:

1. Aspects are contrasted with "objects of sight" of a different "category". What are these other objects of sight? A red circle over there would be one example (*PI* §195a), a knife and a fork would be another example (§195b), a conventional picture of a lion yet another (§206b). Another type of object of sight that Wittgenstein contrasts with aspects is "a property of the object" (§212a). In short, aspects contrast with what is "objectively" there to see, in the sense that any competent speaker with eyes in his head would see it under suitable conditions, whereas one could fail to see this or that aspect without thereby showing oneself incompetent. In this sense, aspects "teach us nothing about the external world" (*RPP I* 899). But this last remark, while illuminating, has to be taken with caution, for it is going to matter here what one understands by "teaching something" and by "the external world".

2. The objects of sight with which aspects contrast may be described, and often will be described (or otherwise represented), in order to *inform* someone else who for some reason is not in a position to see them – in order to teach her, precisely, something about the external world. The other person asks "What do you see *there*?" She asks, because she cannot, for a more or less contingent reason, see for herself. By contrast, the person with whom we seek to share what we see when we see an aspect is standing there with us and

is seeing *as clearly as we do* the object (the two faces) in which we see the aspect (the likeness between the two faces). Indeed, as Wittgenstein says, the other person could even make an accurate representation of the object while failing to see the aspect. In giving voice to the seeing of an aspect, we accordingly normally seek, not to "inform the other person" but rather, as Wittgenstein puts it, to come in touch with, or "find", the other (*RPP I* 874). The seeing of aspects makes for a particular type of opportunity to seek intimacy with the other. Like beauty, Wittgensteinian aspects are importantly characterized by it being possible for a fully competent speaker (and perceiver) to fail to see them even though he sees as well as anyone else the objects in which they are seen, and by its making sense to *call upon* such a person to see them. This, for Wittgenstein, is connected with another feature of aspects: their being "subject to the will" (see *RPP I* 899, 976; *RPP II* 545). Wittgensteinian aspects are subject to the will not so much, or primarily, in the sense that we can see them at will, but precisely in the sense that it makes sense to call upon the other to see them, and that it makes sense to *try* to see this or that particular aspect (see *PI* §213e).

3. In an important sense, an aspect is *undetachable* from the object – or perhaps I should say from the experience – in which it is seen. Objects of sight of the first category, Wittgenstein tells us, can be described (or otherwise represented). Can aspects not be described? Well, it would seem that in some sense they can be: I see a likeness between the two faces, and I (may) *say* that I see a likeness between them. Have I not described the aspect? The answer is that things are more complicated than that. To begin with, *what* is it exactly that I have here (purportedly) described? The faces? The way I see them? My visual experience or "impression" (*PI* §195i)? To say that I have described an aspect that I saw in the faces would be no good; partly because our aim, and Wittgenstein's, is to become clearer about what a Wittgensteinian "aspect" is, or might be, and partly because it is none too clear what "description" might mean here. These two unclarities go hand in hand: "The concept of a representation of what is seen ...", Wittgenstein writes, "is very elastic, and so *together with it* is the concept of what is seen" (§198c). In order to attain clarity here, Wittgenstein suggests, we would need to remind ourselves of "the occasion and purpose" of different forms of "description" (§221e). "It is necessary to get down to the application" (§201a), he elsewhere urges, to ask oneself "What does anyone tell me by

saying 'Now I see it as …'? What consequences has this information? What can I do with it?" (§202f).

4. It is important that Wittgenstein characterizes aspects by way of
characterizing the *experience* of *noticing* an aspect. When you
notice an aspect, he says, you suddenly see something in the object
that you have not seen before. When this happens, you know, and
in a suitable sense also *see*, that the object (the two faces) has not
changed, and yet you see it differently. "Everything has changed,
and yet nothing has changed" is one characteristic way in which the
dawning of an aspect might be expressed. An important question
to ask is whether, and if so in what sense, Wittgensteinian aspects
may be seen apart from being *noticed*, or *striking* us. In several of
his remarks, Wittgenstein suggests that aspects, to be seen, *must*
strike us – otherwise they would not be (what he calls) aspects. An
aspect, he suggests, "only dawns" and "does not remain" (*RPP I*
1021); "[it] lasts only as long as I am occupied with the object in
a particular way" (*PI* §210c).

The significance, for Wittgenstein, of aspects

Why or how Wittgenstein came to care so much about aspects is itself
an interesting question for which there are several plausible lines of
answer that are not necessarily mutually exclusive and that may even
connect with one another in interesting ways.

1. In his work Wittgenstein was trying to bring about the dawning
(coming to light, *Aufleuchten*) of "aspects of things that are most
important to us, [but which are] hidden because of their simplicity
and familiarity" (*PI* §129). He was also trying to bring about *changes*
in the ways we look at, and see, things – changes that may plausibly
be thought of as changes of aspect (§144). Seeing Wittgenstein's
peculiar mode of philosophizing in this light – seeing it under "the
aspect of aspects", if you will – may well prove rather illuminating.[2]

2. Wittgenstein was interested in the structural affinity, and possible
deeper connections, between, on the one hand, the ability to see,
not this or that *particular* aspect but aspects *as such*, and, on the
other hand, the ability to "experience the meaning" of words (*PI*
§213d). Wittgenstein's interest in this link has been taken by some
to form part of an attempt to work out the limitations of his "idea"
that "the meaning of a word is its use in the language" (§43), or
that "essence is expressed by grammar" (§371).[3]

3. The seeing of aspects is arguably fundamental to aesthetic experience, judgement and understanding. Wittgenstein notes this in various places (cf. *PI* §§202e, 202h, 205h and 206i).[4] And if we keep in mind that in other places he likens linguistic understanding to the understanding of art (cf. §527), it would seem that this line of thinking about the significance of aspect perception can be taken quite far, and be connected with both of the preceding lines of thinking.

4. Yet another line of answer takes Wittgenstein to have believed, together with Gestalt psychologists and phenomenologists, that our ability to be struck by aspects – to have aspects dawn on us – somehow reveals something fundamental about human perception, or about the human relation to the world, *as such*.[5] We shall come back to this line of answer.

5. Wittgenstein's first *sustained* investigation of aspect perception is found in the second part of *The Brown Book*. And it is interesting that Wittgenstein there comes to invoke aspects through none of the above routes, but rather as part of an attempt to characterize a particular kind of "illusion" that according to him occurs when we try to discover the essence of Φing – understanding, thinking, naming, following a rule … – by way of focusing on an instance of Φing and asking ourselves *what happens* when we Φ. How exactly the seeing of aspects helps Wittgenstein to characterize the resultant illusion is too long a story to be told here.[6]

All of the above lines of answer presuppose that it is *already* clear, or anyway that it was clear enough to Wittgenstein, what is meant – what *he* meant – by "aspects" and by "seeing an aspect". Part of what I hope to show in the remainder of this chapter is that it is hard to attain clarity with respect to the concept of "aspect" or "seeing an aspect", and that, therefore, this concept has an *intrinsic* philosophical interest – an interest that does not derive from any *general lesson* that might be drawn from the seeing of aspects about perception, or language, or art, or philosophy, or anything else.

The philosophical difficulty of aspects

Having characterized the concept of "noticing an aspect", Wittgenstein says that he is interested, not in the causes of this (type of) experience, but in "the concept [of noticing an aspect] and its place among the concepts of experience" (*PI* §193e). That becoming clearer about *that* could have turned out to be such an enormous and elusive task, is itself philosophically (and not merely biographically) interesting. One thing we find, in thinking about seeing aspects, is that our concept of "seeing" is "tangled" (§200a); and in the course of trying to disentangle its tangles we further find that "there are here hugely many interrelated phenomena and possible concepts" (§199d). Often, perhaps even typically, we ourselves create (further) philosophical entanglements when we try to force our concepts into simplistic moulds – for example, into a simplistic picture of what seeing must be, and (hence) of what "seeing" must mean: "We find certain things about seeing puzzling, because we do not find the whole business of seeing puzzling enough" (§212f; see also §§200e, 200f).

The complexity of "seeing" and of "seeing an aspect" shows itself, first of all, in the variety of cases that, given our initial characterization above, may be thought of as falling under "seeing an aspect": seeing the likeness between two faces; seeing an ambiguous figure such as the famous Necker cube as oriented one way or another in space; seeing the famous duck–rabbit as a duck or as a rabbit; seeing a triangle – either drawn or "material" – as pointing in this or that direction, or as hanging from it apex, or as having fallen over … (*PI* §200c); seeing a sphere in a picture as floating in the air (§201e); there is the aspect we may be said to see when something strikes us in a picture of a running horse and we exclaim "It's running!" (*RPP I* 874); hearing a piece of music as a variation on another, or as plaintive (*PI* §§209f, 209g), or hearing a bar as an introduction (§202h); there is the experience in which "everything strikes us as unreal" (*RPP I* 125–6).

Wittgenstein considers many other types of cases, as well as various more or less similar or related phenomena. The reader is invited to think of some examples of his or her own. In his remarks on aspects, as elsewhere, one of Wittgenstein's chief aims is to "teach us differences" (cf. *PI* §§207b–h). Anyone who wishes to speak of *the* seeing of aspects, and to draw *general* conclusions about human perception as such from the seeing of aspects, had better mind these differences. There are two related differences that I wish to point out in particular. The first difference is that between, on the one hand, being struck by an aspect in the course of everyday experience and, on the other hand, seeing an aspect in an object to which we attend in the artificial context of "doing philosophy (or psychology or what have you)" and which is therefore cut off from what phenomenologists call "our perceptual field". The second is the difference between, on the one hand, being struck by an aspect in an "ambiguous" object, in which different aspects compete with each other, as it were, and, on the other hand, being struck by an aspect – such as the likeness between two faces – that has *not* replaced, or eclipsed, some other aspect.

Another way in which the complexity of Wittgenstein's subject shows is in all of the *other* "concepts of experience" that come up in his remarks on aspects – the concepts among which he wishes to place the concept of "noticing an aspect": "seeing" (and, or versus, *"seeing"*), "seeing a property of the object" (as opposed to "seeing an aspect"), "being struck", "noticing", "interpreting", "knowing (merely knowing) what one sees", "not knowing what (or who) one sees", "seeing something as something", "treating something as something (*alsbehandeln*)", "regarding something as something (*alsbetrachten*)", "taking something as (or for) something (*fürhalten*)", "conceiving (*auffassen*) something in one way or another" (as opposed to *seeing* it as this or that), "having what one sees come alive for one", "seeing something three-dimensionally", "being conscious (aware) (*Bewußtsein*) (of something)", "looking without being aware (of something)", "thinking (of what one sees/looks at)", "recognizing", "seeing something without recognizing it", "having something one sees be, or feel, familiar (or unfamiliar) to one", "imagining", "feeling" (as in "one *feels* the softness of the depicted material" or in *"feeling* the ending of a church mode as ending"), "reading" (as in "reading timidity into a face"), "knowing one's way about" (in a drawing, say), "concerning oneself with what one sees", "paying attention", "being blind to an expression", and so on. And consider further that the criteria that inform the application of each one of these concepts are themselves complex and context dependent. It is not obvious that one ought to lose one's appetite for a general theory of perception upon consideration of the richness, complexity and context sensitivity of our concepts of experience. It does seem to me rather difficult, however, to consider the richness, complexity and context sensitivity of our concepts of experience seriously and not become deeply dissatisfied with at least many of the (purportedly) comprehensive, unified and complete theories of perception (or experience) that Western philosophy has so far produced. Wittgenstein, at any rate, was highly suspicious of such theories.

Let us move closer and consider one particular area of difficulty. This will also give us an opportunity to get a sense of how Wittgenstein works. It is tempting to suppose, when an aspect strikes us and we *see* some thing differently, that before the new aspect dawned we had been seeing the thing all along under some other aspect. It is tempting, in other words, to suppose that there is, that there *must* be, some continuous version to the seeing of aspects. For surely, we *were seeing* the object before the new aspect dawned; so it must have been under *some different* aspect. This insistence will be further encouraged by the choice of the duck–rabbit, and other ambiguous and artificially encountered figures, as one's paradigmatic examples of aspect seeing. For in the case of those figures there seems to be an obvious candidate for what the other, preceding, aspect was.

Think, however, of being struck by the likeness between two faces, for example, and I think you will find less appealing the idea that the aspect that dawns always replaces some other aspect that was seen continuously. For what might be the aspect that the likeness between the faces allegedly replaced? And when we come to hear a bar as an introduction, what might be the aspect under which we were hearing the bar before?

Even with ambiguous objects it is not at all clear in what sense the "old" aspect was *seen* before the new aspect struck us. The problem, in other words, is not that it is *wrong* to suppose that there must be a continuous seeing of aspects, but that it is not yet clear what exactly one might be supposing in supposing this. And since *this* is the problem, it may help to ask ourselves, with Wittgenstein, whether the fact that I have just been struck by an aspect and now see the object in a way I have not seen it before "prove[s] that I in fact *saw* it as something definite" (*PI* §204f); or to consider his suggestion that while there is no doubt about the possible aptness of the "never" in "I've never seen this in that way before", the aptness of "always" in "I have *always* seen this like that" is not equally certain (see *RPP I* 512); or that when we say "I've always seen it in this way" what we really mean to say is "I have always *conceived* (*aufgefaßt*) it *this* way, and *this* change of aspect has never taken place" (*RPP I* 524); or that when you say "I have always seen it with *this* face", you still have to say *what* face, "and that as soon as you add *that*, it's no longer as if you had *always* done it" (*RPP I* 526); or that to say of a real face, or of a face in a picture, "I've *always* seen it as a face" would be queer, whereas "It has always been a face to me, and I have never seen it *as something else*" would not be (see *RPP I* 532); or that when we see an aspect we are thinking of it (*PI* §197c), or occupied with it (*LWPP II* 14), and that therefore "If someone were to tell me that he had seen the figure for half an hour without a break as a reversed F, I'd have to suppose that he had kept on *thinking* of this interpretation, that he had *occupied* himself with it" (*RPP I* 1020); or that "If there were no change of aspect then there would only be a *way of taking* (*Auffaßung*), and no such thing as *seeing* this or that" (*RPP II* 436).

Beyond helping us see that, in insisting on what *must* be true of human perception given that aspects sometimes dawn on us, we have not so much as succeeded in insisting on anything clear, is there some other, more general lesson to be drawn from the above series of remarks? Well, there is the implied claim that we do not know in advance – part of our problem is precisely that we *think* we may know in advance – what we will find when we set out to investigate our concepts by asking ourselves what we might say in this or that situation and what we might reasonably be taken to mean if we said this or that. And this means that the structure of the region of human experience that these words are used to articulate, though in a sense familiar, is something that we do not yet clearly see. "Let the use *teach* you the meaning", Wittgenstein urges, as he similarly urges us in many other places, "Don't think that you knew in advance what [a particular word or expression] means!" (*PI* §212e). This, as we just witnessed, is *not* part of Wittgenstein's contribution to a theory of meaning; rather, it is an encouragement to see differently what lies at the root of our philosophical difficulties, and to change accordingly the way in which we think of, and seek, philosophical satisfaction.

Placing Wittgensteinian "aspects"

"But what about (our concept of) seeing", one might here protest; "is there some general lesson about *it* in the above series of remarks?" Well, here is the sketch of a possible lesson: seeing, in the particular sense in which Wittgensteinian aspects are seen, is to be distinguished both from *habitual*, "unthinking", ways of regarding, treating, or relating to things, and from certain *cognitive* (propositional) attitudes that we might adopt toward things, on the other hand. "See", or even "see as", *may* be used in all three areas of experience, but what would normally be meant by it in each area would be different in important respects from what it would mean in the other two areas. Thus I might say of my little sister, "I guess I always saw her as my little sister, and this is why it never occurred to me to turn to her for help in this matter". I would be using "see as" in order to describe my attitude towards my sister, but not an aspect under which I was seeing her. Of course, one *could* insist that I was seeing her under the aspect of "little sister", but one is only likely to confuse oneself and others in thus insisting, since both "aspect" and "seeing" would mean something different here from what they mean when Wittgenstein speaks of the seeing of aspects. And I might also say, "I see the situation in the Middle East as hopeless", and thereby simply express my opinion on the situation, not an aspect under which I am seeing it.

"Seeing", I am suggesting, in the sense in which Wittgensteinian aspects are seen, is to be distinguished from "regarding" or "treating"

– in either the latter's "habitual" sense or in its "cognitive" sense. The former is, while the latter is not, grammatically, "a state" (*RPP II* §43; cf. *PI* §212d): like other states, such as, say, paying attention to something, the seeing of an aspect has a determinate and, normally, limited duration, and it can be interrupted. The seeing of an aspect is *an experience*. In the expression of the dawning of an aspect, the same form of words that in *other* contexts might have been used to say how the person is treating or regarding the thing is being used to give voice to an experiential state: "The expression of the aspect is the expression of a way of taking [*Auffaßung*] (hence, of a way-of-dealing-with [*Behandlungsweise*], of a technique); but *used* as description of a state" (*RPP I* 1025).

Phenomenology, and possible limitations of Wittgenstein's approach

It is easy to find oneself dissatisfied with Wittgenstein. Are there not broader and deeper lessons that may be drawn from the fact that aspects may sometimes dawn on us – lessons that he stubbornly, some might even feel perversely, refuses to draw?

From our ability to see ambiguous figures one way or another, the Gestalt psychologists, for example, drew the conclusion that human perception as such is "holistic", in the sense that each thing perceived acquires its particular identity or "significance" only in relation to the rest of our perceptual "field" – just as the ears of the rabbit aspect of the duck–rabbit would not be ears, apart from being part of the rabbit-aspect – and in turn contributes to shaping the field as a whole.

Phenomenologists have gone further than that and insisted that experiences such as the dawning of aspects show that we have a "pre-objective" or "pre-reflective" relation to the world that is more "primordial" than the cognitive relation of knowing or believing, but that still has its own intelligence or "intentionality" – it is not *merely* animal, and is not reducible to physiology. Consider the duck–rabbit. I might know (believe, think, guess …) that it may represent – may serve as a drawing of – a duck, and *at the same time* also know that it may represent a rabbit; my having one so-called propositional attitude towards the drawing does not compete with, or eclipse, my having the other. But I can *see* only one aspect at a time, and it is very hard to look at the duck–rabbit and not see either a duck or a rabbit.[7] This suggests that it is possible, and perhaps also normal, for us to stand towards objects in a perceptual relation that is not (yet) *cognitive* – not a matter of judging, or making up one's mind, as it were – but that may still be assessed in terms of *appropriateness*.

One could even go a step further, following the work of Maurice Merleau-Ponty, and argue that our ability to see aspects shows that we are neither Cartesian (nor, for that matter, Kantian) egos or minds – altogether outside of the world, observing and intellectually organizing it as if it were a mere "spectacle" (Merleau-Ponty 1962: 52) – nor mere machines that may fully be characterized and explained by the mathematical sciences. Rather, this line of thought continues, we are normally always already engaged with a world that *matters* to us in various specific ways; we always find ourselves in this or that *meaningful situation* (*ibid*.: 79). The things of our world, as we "pre-reflectively" experience them, have no properties, but rather have "style", "physiognomy", "significance" – their own particular way, or potential ways, of mattering. Our "lived", "phenomenal", body is not a mere machine, but rather is a "point of view upon the world", "our means of communicating with it" (*ibid*.: 70); it "surges towards things" and takes hold of them (*ibid*.: 92). Our *gaze*, which is part of our phenomenal body, is "a natural instrument analogous to the blind man's stick": "It gets more or less from things according to the way in which it questions them" (*ibid*.: 153). It is with our gaze as an extension of our body that we quite literally *make* the ambiguous figures look one way or the other – which in turn is made possible precisely by the fact that we encounter them in an "artificial" context, in which they do not "belong to a field" (*ibid*.: 216), but rather are "cut off" from it (*ibid*.: 279, 281). To see the triangle as pointing to the right, for example, is to see it as *directing us to turn right*; to see it as having fallen over is to see it as, say, *needing to be put back up*; to see it as a triangular hole is to see it as something *we could peer through*. And we can do all this, precisely because our perception is not separable from our bodily orientation and potential engagement with things.

There are many remarks of Wittgenstein's that could plausibly be taken to support this type of analysis, which Merleau-Ponty does not hesitate to call "theory". And yet, as I said, Wittgenstein methodically resists the temptation to turn his findings into a theory. He insists on remaining at the level of what we would or might or could *say* – what *he* would or might say, or is inclined to say – and what the *significance* might be of saying this or that. That basic aspects of our experience nonetheless come to light in this way is arguably not surprising, since the concepts Wittgenstein investigates have their natural home not in scientific, objective, reflection, but in the hustle and bustle of everyday existence and experience.

Now, consider a passage like the following:

Look at a long familiar piece of furniture in its old place in your room. *You would like to say*: "It is part of an organism". Or "Take it outside, and it is no longer at all the same as it was", and similar things. And naturally one isn't thinking of any causal dependence of one part on the rest. Rather it is like this: ... [I]f I tried taking it quite out of its present context, *I should say* that it had ceased to exist and another had got into its place.

One might even feel like this: "Everything is part and parcel of everything else" ... Displace a piece and it is no longer what it was ... *And what is anyone saying, who says this?*

(*RPP I* 339, emphases altered)

Clearly, this remark has interesting connections to the phenomenologist's account sketched above. Also clearly, however, no general theory of perception is being offered here, but only an examination of things one might say or be inclined to say or feel like saying, and of how they are to be understood. It seems to me that an interesting methodological question would be this: What, if anything, might be lost, and what, if anything, is gained, by remaining, with Wittgenstein, on the level of what might be called *linguistic* phenomenology,[8] and refusing in this way to turn one's reflection into a theory?

Conclusion

The seeing of Wittgensteinian aspects may be found philosophically interesting in various ways. It arguably plays an important role in aesthetics, and in other related areas of human experience and discourse. It may be thought to reveal something important, perhaps even fundamental, about human perception, and about our acquisition and employment of language. It may also be found to be intrinsically interesting: just coming to see the phenomenon aright may prove to be difficult. And *that*, in turn, could reveal something important about philosophy, and in particular about the nature of philosophical difficulty. Then there are *Wittgenstein's remarks* on aspect perception. In them, I suggested, Wittgenstein's philosophical *approach* comes out quite vividly. For anyone interested in familiarizing themselves with that approach, and in assessing its possible advantages and limitations, the remarks on aspects may prove particularly helpful.

Notes

1. The edition referred to in this chapter is *Philosophical Investigations* (2001a).
2. This way of thinking of the significance of aspects to Wittgenstein was first proposed by Debra Aidun (1982), explored later at much greater length by Judith Genova (1995), and received a quite insightful and contemporary twist in Steven Affeldt's "On the Difficulty of Seeing Aspects and the 'Therapeutic' Reading of Wittgenstein" (forthcoming).
3. In line with Rush Rhees's preface to *The Blue and Brown Books* (1965).
4. This issue is explored in Roger Scruton's *Art and Imagination: A Study in the Philosophy of Mind* (1974).
5. This line of thinking is pursued by Stephen Mulhall (1990; 2001: 153–82). See also Johnston (1994).
6. See my "Seeing Aspects and Philosophical Difficulty" (forthcoming).
7. Note that I do not say "*see it as* a duck or a rabbit"!
8. The term "linguistic philosophy" is borrowed from Austin (1979: 182).

Further reading

Tractatus, 5.6–5.641, 6.37–7.

ELEVEN

Knowing that the standard metre is one metre long

Heather Gert

In *Philosophical Investigations*, we find the following statement: "There is *one* thing of which one can say neither that it is one metre long, nor that it is not one metre long, and that is the standard metre in Paris" (§50).[1] There has been a fair amount of debate about the claim stated by this sentence. Some have argued that it is true, others that it is false.[2] But one thing that has generally been taken for granted – many will say, one thing that is obvious – is that the sentence expresses a claim Wittgenstein believes. He is rejecting the idea that it is possible to say, of the standard metre, that it is a metre long. In what follows I shall try to explain the sort of thing many philosophers have in mind when they discuss that sentence. But I shall also explain why I think they are mistaken. The sentence is certainly in *Philosophical Investigations*. But like many other sentences in that book, it expresses an idea to which Wittgenstein takes his interlocutor to be committed, rather than Wittgenstein's own view.

I

To see how Wittgenstein intended his standard-metre statement to be understood, we need to know at least a little bit about the theory he is using the example to criticize. Everyone agrees that the interlocutor he has in mind is some version of his own earlier self: what we might call a *Tractarian* interlocutor. It will also be useful to have a bit more of *Philosophical Investigations* §50 before us. First, here is more of the passage:

What does it mean to say that we can attribute neither being nor non-being to elements? ...

One would, however, like to say: existence cannot be attributed to an element, for if it did not *exist*, one could not even name it and so one could say nothing of it at all. – But let us consider an analogous case. There is *one* thing of which one can say neither that it is one metre long, nor that it is not one metre long, and that is the standard metre in Paris. – But this is, of course, not to ascribe any extraordinary property to it, but only to mark its peculiar role in the language-game of measuring with a metre-rule. ...

Interpreters all agree that what is being criticized here is the *Tractarian* theory of simples or elements. According to that view, there is an intimate connection between language and the world. The most basic objects in the world are elements. And the most basic bits of language are names. On this view each name gets its meaning by association with a particular element, and a sentence is nothing more than an ordered series of names. That sentence is true if the relations between the names in it mirror the actual relations between the objects named. There is much more to the view, but for our purposes the only other thing that needs mentioning is that, on this view, a sentence cannot be meaningful unless its negation is meaningful as well.

The interlocutor that Wittgenstein is addressing holds the view I have just described and as a consequence believes that we cannot attribute being or non-being to elements. Here's why: on that view, a sentence has meaning only in so far as it is constructed out of meaningful names, and a name has meaning only in so far as it corresponds to an element. But then the alleged sentence "Element-S does not exist" must be patent nonsense. "Element-S" can be a meaningful term only if, so to speak, Element-S exists. And that sentence says it does not. Moreover, because a sentence is meaningful only if its negation is also meaningful, "Element-S exists" is also meaningless.

Interpreters agree that the Wittgenstein of the *Investigations* does not believe this. But, many will say, he believes something closely related. The usual interpretation of §50 goes something like this:[3] It is impossible to describe the standard metre as being a metre long because the claim that an object is a metre long is really just the claim that it is the same length as *this* stick; perhaps that the end points of the object match up with the end points of the stick. It is impossible to take an object (for instance, the standard metre stick) and match it up against itself to see that its end points match its own end points. That just does not make sense. So the reason that we cannot say that the standard metre is a metre long is not because there is anything special about the stick itself. It is simply a by-product of the role the stick plays in the language-game of talking about things being a metre long. If we were playing a different language-game, and perhaps even if we just changed things around and let something else play that role in this game, then it would be possible to say how long *that stick* is, and perhaps even to say that it was a metre long. Similarly, so this interpretation goes, Wittgenstein agrees with his interlocutor that (there is a sense in which) it is impossible to say of an element that it exists. But, as with the standard metre, this is not because there is anything special about the object. Actually, being an element is nothing more than playing a particular kind of role in a given language-game – more or less the role of the most basic thing mentioned there. So its existence is taken for granted, so to speak, in that language-game. But that very object can be talked about in other language-games, and in those other language-games it would be possible to say of *it* that it exists, or that it does not.

As noted, some philosophers who accept something like this as a correct account of what Wittgenstein is saying about the standard metre also believe the claim is true, while many do not. Nonetheless, there is broad consensus that it does not *seem* true. That is, almost all agree that, on first consideration, it seems natural and true to say that the standard metre is one metre long. Saul Kripke begins his discussion of the example with a short proof that is supposed to show this: "If the stick is a stick, for example, 39.37 inches long (I assume we have some different standard for inches), why isn't it one meter long? Anyway, let's suppose that [Wittgenstein] is wrong, and that the stick is one meter long" (Kripke 1980: 54). Nathan Salmon is slightly more sympathetic in his article , "How to Measure the Standard Metre", but he introduces his discussion of the contrast between Kripke's and Wittgenstein's analyses of the situation by noting that "It must be admitted that Kripke has more plausibility on his side than Wittgenstein does. ... Frankly, I suspect Wittgenstein is ultimately completely wrong regarding the Standard Metre" (1988: 195). Eric Loomis, an interpreter who really is sympathetic to what he takes to be Wittgenstein's claim, writes: "So is the expression 'The standard meter in Paris is one meter long' meaningful at all? To deny that it is certainly seems counter-intuitive, if not false" (1999: 303). Even Robert Fogelin, who defends as straight a reading of Wittgenstein's claim as anyone, begins his explanation about the truth of the metre statement by admitting that, " ... it may not seem obvious that we cannot say of the standard meter that it is a meter long; indeed, we may be inclined to say the opposite, that it is the only thing that *really* is one meter long" (1987: 127).

It is also worth noting that the philosophers who say that Wittgenstein's claim is true generally take him to mean something more limited than, on a first reading, the sentence seems to say. It is easy to understand the statement "There is *one* thing of which one can say neither that it is one metre long, nor that it is not one metre long, and that is the standard metre in Paris" as the claim that, come what may, it would never make any sense to say that *this* stick (the one that is, in fact, the standard metre) is a metre long. But, as my account above suggests, sympathetic interpreters almost always agree that if that stick stops being the standard, and something else becomes the standard instead, it can be measured. And they agree that when this happens, the stick is going to be a metre long unless its length changed in the meantime. For instance, this seems to be what Robert Fogelin has in mind when he writes that "we can always remove something from its position as standard and measure it against some other standard" (1987: 128). And Gordon Baker and Peter Hacker make the same point in the first volume of their analytical commentary on *Philosophical Investigations* (Baker & Hacker 1980: 292). Thus, even the philosophers who believe that Wittgenstein's statement about the standard metre is true usually agree with less sympathetic interpreters that it is false on the most superficial reading. But sympathetic interpreters believe that something like the story I gave above takes better account of Wittgenstein's views more broadly. And understood that way, they say, the statement is true.

II

As I have noted, the purpose of this chapter is to show that the metre statement is not true, and that Wittgenstein does not think it is. Moreover, for Wittgenstein's purposes it is not only important that the statement is false, it is important that it is obviously false. He is using this example to show his interlocutor what is wrong with her idea that it is impossible to say of any particular element that it exists. He wants her to see that if she is committed to this, then she is also committed to the claim that we cannot say that the standard metre is one metre long. But the standard metre obviously is one metre long, so the interlocutor must be making a mistake. Thus the metre statement serves Wittgenstein's purpose only if his interlocutor can easily see that it is false.

I shall begin with some reasons for thinking it is false. Then I shall go on to defend my claim that this was Wittgenstein's view as well.

We have already seen one reason for rejecting the idea that you cannot say that the standard metre is one metre long. Kripke notes that there is nothing keeping us from using a different standard – a standard for a different unit of measurement – to measure it. So, as Kripke says, the standard metre stick is surely 39.37 inches long. He does not think anyone would want to debate that, and I expect he is right. But others would, and have, denied that it is possible to get from here to the fact that the stick is *one metre* long (Luckhardt 1977: 84; Pollock 2004: 150–51). This is because you cannot determine that the standard metre stick is one metre long simply by measuring it with a yardstick. Measuring it with a yardstick is helpful for this purpose only if we already know how to convert between inches and metres. But that is something we can know only by making use of the standard metre. In order to know how to convert from inches to metres we would need to compare some physical thing – the standard inch, I suppose – to the standard metre stick. The conversion is then determined by how many inches long the standard metre is. So when we say that the standard metre is a metre long because it is 39.37 inches long and 39.37 inches is one metre, all we are really saying is that the standard metre stick is the same number of inches long as the standard metre stick.

So we should not confuse the statement in *Philosophical Investigations* §50 with the claim that there is one thing that cannot *be measured and thereby found to be*, or not to be, one metre long. That is true, at least in so far as the person doing the measuring already accepts that what he is measuring as the standard metre. If a person holds one hardware-store metre stick up against another, and they do not match precisely, he has no way of knowing which (if either) is the accurate measure. By contrast, if he (knowingly) holds a hardware-store metre stick up to the standard metre stick, there is no question which is accurate. If there is a mismatch, it is the standard that is correct; the other stick is a little long, or a little short, of being one metre simply in virtue of being a little longer than, or a little shorter than, the standard metre stick. For this reason neither can he get any additional information about the length of the standard metre if it and the hardware-store metre stick are the same size. But from the fact that you cannot discover by measuring this stick – which you know to be the standard metre – that it is one metre long, it does not follow that you cannot meaningfully state that it is.

Here is a better way of showing that it is possible to sensibly say that the standard metre is a metre long. Suppose Sally came across the standard metre bar, and – not knowing what she had in front of her – proceeded to measure it with the handy metre stick she brought with her from her local hardware store. (Perhaps Sally, a typical mono-lingual American, cannot read the tag that says it is the standard metre.) If the

141

store where she got her stick is selling well-calibrated metre sticks, Sally will discover, of this thing that is in fact the standard metre, that it is a metre long. And if the spirit moves her, she might even say, speaking of what in fact *is* the standard metre, "This stick is one meter long." So even though Sally does not know exactly what she is doing, she is saying of the standard metre that it is one metre long. Scenarios of this kind are clearly possible.

This does not yet show that someone who knows that the stick he is talking about is the standard metre can say that it is one metre long. But it still seems to pose a problem for someone who wants to hold that the statement from §50 is true. There is absolutely no doubt that someone like Sally could exist, and could take herself to be meaningfully saying that this stick (which unbeknownst to her is the standard metre) is a metre long. As far as Sally can tell, her claim would be perfectly meaningful in exactly the same way as all her other claims about things being a metre long. Someone might object that, unfortunately for Sally, her sense that her claim is meaningful has no more power to make it meaningful than her sense that it is true has the power to make it true. Wittgenstein himself makes a similar point with his example of the (alleged) claim that it is 5 o'clock on the sun (*PI* §350). A person might *think* it makes sense to say that such-and-such occurred when it was 5 o'clock on the sun, but it does not yet make sense. Until a new convention is established that gives claims about times on the sun a use, it is meaningless.[4]

In Sally's case, however, we have more than her sense of the claim's meaningfulness. She can treat the stick she has measured as if it were a metre long; and unlike the 5 o'clock on the sun case no new convention is needed for that. For instance, if she has been looking for a metre-long metal stick to use in a construction project, she can use this one. It can play the role, for her and for others, of a stick that is one metre long. I mean, it can play the same non-standard role that any old metre-long stick plays in virtue of being one metre long.

Then again, perhaps philosophers such as Fogelin, and Hacker and Baker would be happy to agree that Sally can say, of the standard metre, that it is a metre long – as long as she does not know that it is the standard.[5] I have already mentioned that they agree that *that stick* can be described as one metre long if something else takes on the role of metre standard. Maybe they would be willing to grant that the fact that Sally is ignorant of the stick's status is functionally equivalent to saying that, for her, it no longer has that status. So perhaps we should return to the question of whether someone can *knowingly* say of the standard metre that it is a metre long.

Recall, however, that according to the usual interpretation the problem was supposed to be that the term "metre" gets its meaning, in some important sense, from its association with this very stick. Not from mere association, of course, but association with this stick *in its role* as metre standard; as the thing against which members of this language community must measure an object in order to determine that it is a metre long.[6] If that is so, if that is how "metre" gets its meaning, then it is so regardless of what Sally knows about the stick in front of her. Thus it is difficult to see how her ignorance could make any difference to whether her utterance is meaningful. If Sally, a generally competent English speaker, utters the sentence "Six is the square root of thirty-six", what she says is true even if she does not know what a square root is. The words she utters mean the same thing whether she knows it or not. If Sally's utterance about the metre stick is nonsense when she knows what she is saying – when she knows that things are said to be a metre long in virtue of matching *this* stick – it should also be nonsense when she does not know that *this* is the stick things must match in order to be a metre long. And conversely, if Sally's words make sense when she is ignorant, that is good reason to suppose they would make sense even if she were not ignorant.

So, suppose that Sally's friend Mabel needs something one metre long to temporarily prop up her piano. And suppose that in this scenario Sally not only sees the standard, she also knows how to read French. Thus in this version of the story, unlike the original one, Sally knows the stick she is holding is the standard metre. She can still give it to Mabel *and tell her that it is a metre long*. And surely the information Sally conveys when she says this is that the stick is a metre long; that, among other things, it is the right size to prop up Mabel's piano. We can also stipulate that when Sally says this she does so with the full intention of returning the stick to the authorities so it can be the standard, and even, if need be, of using the stick as the standard while it is propping up Mabel's piano.

All sorts of things can affect whether a given object is, or can be said to be, one metre long. But the information and mindset of a speaker is not one of them. Granted there are not many circumstances under which someone who knows that a particular stick is the standard metre will have any reason to mention that it is a metre long. But if she can say this about the standard metre when she does not know that it is the standard, she can say it about the standard when she knows that it is.

So, along with most people on the street, I think it is possible to say that the standard metre is one metre long. Why should we believe that is what Wittgenstein thinks? Let us look again at the original statement:

There is *one* thing of which one can say neither that it is one metre long, nor that it is not one metre long, and that is the standard metre in Paris.

First, notice that Wittgenstein does not write: "Here is something you cannot say", or "Here is one sentence you cannot meaningfully utter", or anything along these lines. Instead, he writes: "There is *one* thing of which one cannot say …" ("Man kann von *einem* Ding nicht aussagen …"). In saying this, he appears to be noting that there is a certain object, and to be claiming that something cannot be said *about it*. This does not look like a way of saying that a particular sentence – "The standard metre is a metre long" – cannot be meaningfully uttered, or even that a certain claim cannot be made of a particular object *under one description* of that object. These are both things that Wittgenstein could have indicated clearly, in sentences no more complicated than the one he used. But he did not choose to. Why not?

Here is one reason: As I noted at the beginning of this chapter, Wittgenstein is talking about what can be said about a specific object – the standard metre stick – because his interlocutor was talking about what could, or could not, be said about specific objects – elements. Everyone agrees that Wittgenstein is drawing an analogy between the metre statement and another statement about *Tractarian* elements. He explicitly says as much. Wittgenstein's interlocutor claims that it is impossible to say that elements exist, or that they do not exist. And she takes herself to be saying this about particular objects, not simply saying that certain sentences cannot be meaningfully uttered, or that these objects cannot be said to exist under a specific description. (They cannot be described at all, on the interlocutor's view. So she certainly is not saying that a particular claim cannot be made about them under a particular description.) Of course, whether the interlocutor is right about elements is another matter. But she means to be saying something about specific objects, and she is the person Wittgenstein is addressing. So if the statement in §50 is intended as analogous to the interlocutor's claim, as it explicitly is, we should expect it too to be a claim about what can be said about particular objects – or about one particular object. And we should not expect the statement to be endorsed by Wittgenstein. My point, exactly.

Given the interlocutor's ideas about language and the world, described in Section I above, one way to address her claim that it is impossible to say that elements exist would be to begin with a demonstration of the fact that a sentence can be meaningful even when its negation is not. Another would be to show that, despite appearances, the negation of the sentence the interlocutor is interested in is meaning-ful: elements can be said not to exist. But neither of these is the method Wittgenstein is using here. Rather, he begins with examples intended to make his readers, and the interlocutor, question her conclusion: it *is* possible to say that elements exist – because a particular statement that is analogous to it is *obviously* meaningful and true. The interlocutor's conclusion itself shows that her argument is mistaken.

After mentioning the standard metre, as well as an imagined standard patch of sepia – objects that play a role in language something like the one *Tractarian* elements are supposed to play – §50 ends with a wave in the direction of explaining why one might *mistakenly* have thought that it was impossible to say that elements do not exist.

> We can put it like this: This [sepia] standard is an instrument of the language used in ascriptions of colour. In this language-game it is not something that is represented, but is a means of represen-tation. – And just this goes for an element in language-game (48) when we name it by uttering the word "R": this gives this object a role in our language-game; it is now a *means* of representation. And to say "If it did not *exist*, it could have no name" is to say as much and as little as: if this thing did not exist, we could not use it in our language-game.

In a world where a particular element (call it "Element-E") did not exist, it is indeed true that its name would be unavailable for use in the sentence "Element-E does not exist." In *that* world it would be impos-sible to express the proposition "Element-E does not exist." But, by hypothesis, we are not in that world. Element-E does exist, and we can use its name – even to describe a situation in which it does not. Similarly, we would not be able to use "metre" in a world in which the metre stick failed to play the role it actually plays – one in which it does not exist, for example. But that is beside the point. In our language-game the standard metre stick actually plays that role, so we can use the word that gains its meaning from association with it – the word "metre" – to describe the stick. And using that word, we can make the claim that the standard metre is one metre long – as well as say meaningfully, but falsely, that the standard metre is not one metre long.

Finally, it is important to bear in mind that the standard-metre ex-ample is found immediately after – and in the middle of the discus-sion about – another example intended to help us understand how the *Tractatus* picture of elements went wrong. This is the example that Wittgenstein is referring to when he talks about language-game (48) – a language-game that he introduces in *Philosophical Investigations* §48. This simple language-game is designed to fit the *Tractatus* picture of language well, as it is possible for a language to fit that picture. Thus the only objects in language-game (48) are monocoloured red, black, green and white squares of a uniform size, and the larger squares that can be built out of them. The only words – names – refer to the individual coloured squares, and a person must learn these names by seeing which squares they label; he must learn by ostension. The only sentences are strings of those names, read in such a way that they "describe" the larger squares.

According to the *Tractatus* picture of language, it is impossible to describe elements; it is possible only to *name* them. So if Wittgenstein really manages to capture that picture, it should turn out to be impossible to describe the unit squares from within language-game (48). And Wittgenstein acknowledges that – within that language-game – any attempt to describe an element will *look like* naming it: "when in a limiting case a complex consists of only *one* square, its description is simply the name of the coloured square" (§49). It would be a mistake, however, to conclude that the unit squares are not being described. It is not really true that some signs are names, while others are descriptions. Instead, whether a sign names or describes in a particular instance depends on what the speaker is doing with it.

> If A has to describe complexes of coloured squares to B and he uses the word "R" *alone*, we shall be able to say that the word is a description – a proposition. But if he is memorizing the words and their meanings, or if he is teaching someone else the use of the words and uttering them in the course of ostensive teaching, we shall not say that they are propositions. In this situation the word "R", for instance, is not a description; it *names* an element – but it would be queer to make that a reason for saying that an element can *only* be named! (*Ibid.*)

A little further on in §49 he writes:

> Naming is so far not a move in the language-game – any more than putting a piece in its place on the board is a move in chess. We may say: *nothing* has so far been done, when a thing has been named. It has not even *got* a name except in the language-game.

So, in §§48 and 49 Wittgenstein is demonstrating his view that *within a particular language-game* (i) a sign is a name in so far as, for instance, it is taught by directing a student's attention to the object it names; (ii) these signs, which are names, can also be used as descriptions; and (iii) a sign that is a name can be used to describe the very thing that, by means of ostension, is used to teach its meaning.

With this in mind, let us return to §50. A few pages back I quoted the third paragraph of this section, where he talks about the standard patch of sepia. That patch is introduced in the second paragraph, where he writes:

> – Let us imagine samples of colour being preserved in Paris like the standard metre. We define: "sepia" means the colour of the standard sepia which is there kept hermetically sealed. Then it will make no sense to say of this sample either that it is of this colour or that it is not.

It is clear from this passage that Wittgenstein wants us to think of the standard patch of sepia as playing exactly the same kind of role as the standard metre. Whatever points he makes about the patch of sepia, surely he means us to apply these to the metre stick as well.

Looking back at the third paragraph of §50, quoted on page 145 above, we find the following claim about the standard patch of sepia: "In this language-game it is not something that is represented, but is a means of representation. – And just this goes for an element in language-game (48)". Thus we see that we are to apply the lessons from Wittgenstein's discussion of language-game (48) to the standard patch of sepia – and to the standard metre as well. Was the lesson of language-game (48) that it is impossible to describe elements? Well, Wittgenstein would agree that, from within language-game (48) there is no way to give an account of what a person is doing when she describes unit squares – or when she describes complex square, for that matter. Nonetheless, Wittgenstein tells us that people in that language-game do describe elements. This is the point of the claim, in §49, that: "If A has to describe complexes of coloured squares to B and he uses the word 'R' *alone*, we shall be able to say that the word is a description – a proposition." Thus, if what Wittgenstein is saying about the standard sepia in this passage – and thus also about the standard metre – is to accord with what he says about the elements of language-game (48), he cannot be saying that it is impossible to describe these standards using the terms they are used to introduce.

To summarize this last bit: (i) Wittgenstein demonstrates that the elements of language-game (48) can be described using the names that they were used to teach; (ii) in §50, Wittgenstein identifies the standard patch of sepia with the elements in language-game (48); (iii) therefore Wittgenstein also believes that "sepia" can be used to describe the object that was used to give that name meaning – it can be used to describe the standard patch of sepia; (iv) in §50, Wittgenstein mentions both the standard metre stick and a standard patch of sepia, and clearly believes that what he says about one is true about the other as well; (v) therefore he believes that the word "metre" can be used to describe the standard metre stick – and in particular that the standard metre can truly be said to be one metre long.

Philosophical Investigations §50, like many passages in that book, is very puzzling. Many philosophers have attempted to interpret it, and they have offered many ways of understanding it. Almost all, however, have assumed that Wittgenstein believes the statement he introduces as analogous to his interlocutor's admittedly confused claim. But the best reading of that passage recognizes that this is not so. Even Wittgenstein knows that the standard metre is one metre long.

Notes

1. The edition referred to in this chapter is *Philosophical Investigations* (1958).
2. Among those who hold it to be true are: Fogelin (1987) and Baker & Hacker (1980). Among those who believe it is false are Kripke (1980) and Salmon (1988).
3. For a more complete account see Fogelin (1987: 122–30).
4. Our way of measuring time on earth depends on one's relation to the sun. It is noon when the sun is directly overhead. It is also worth recalling that the claim that it is 5 o'clock on earth does not make sense either. When it is 5 o'clock here, it is 6 o'clock in the next time zone, and so on.
5. In fact, I doubt that they would accept this. But let us just suppose.
6. The measuring does not have to be direct. Objects can be measured against objects that have been measured against the standard metre and found to be the same length. And so on.

TWELVE

Therapy

Rupert Read and Phil Hutchinson

In a number of remarks, dating back to the early 1930s, Wittgenstein drew an explicit analogy between his methods of philosophical enquiry and psychotherapy. So, alongside the famous remark from *Philosophical Investigations* directly on this (see below), we have other remarks from the *Big Typescript* and from his dictations to Friedrich Waismann for Moritz Schlick. These are those places where Wittgenstein explicitly coins the term by way of elucidating his method. Here are some samples of his explicit references to therapy:

> Our method resembles psychoanalysis in a certain sense. To use its way of putting things, we could say that a simile at work in the unconscious is made harmless by being articulated. And this comparison with analysis can be developed even further. (And this analogy is certainly no coincidence.)
> (Diktat für Schlick 28, in Baker 2003: 69e–71e)

> One of the most important tasks is to express all false thought processes so characteristically that the reader says, "Yes, that's exactly the way I meant it". To make a tracing of the physiognomy of every error.
> Indeed we can only convict someone else of a mistake if he acknowledges that this really is the expression of his feeling. //
> … . if he (really) acknowledges this expression as the correct expression of his feeling.
> For only if he acknowledges it as such, is it the correct expression. (Psychoanalysis.)

What the other person acknowledges is the analogy I am proposing to him as the source of his thought.

(BT §410, in *PO* 165)[1]

It is not our aim to refine or complete the system of rules for the
use of our words in unheard-of ways.

For the clarity that we are aiming at is not *complete* clarity.
But this simply means that the philosophical problems should
completely disappear.

The real discovery is the one that makes me capable of stop-
ping doing philosophy when I want to. – – The one that gives
philosophy peace, so that it is no longer tormented by questions
which bring *itself* in question. – – Instead, we now demonstrate
a method, by examples; and the series of examples can be broken
off. – – Problems are solved (difficulties eliminated), not a *single*
problem.

There is not *a* philosophical method, though there are indeed
methods, like different therapies. *(PI* §133)

The philosopher's treatment of a question is like the treatment
of an illness. *(PI* §255)

In addition to these explicit references to therapy, there are, of course,
many remarks where Wittgenstein talks the language of therapy, as it
were (and many more still where that language can be profitably applied
as a hermeneutic device by one puzzled by his texts). For example,
he talks of the centrality of gaining consent from one's interlocutor
as to what they take themselves to mean by their locution (see below
for a full discussion of this key point); he talks of relieving or being
subject to mental torment and disquiets *(PI* §111), cravings *(BB* 17)
revulsions *(BB* 15), angst *(BB* 27), irresistible temptations *(BB* 18) and
so on. Wittgensteinian philosophy is a quest to find a genuinely effective way of undoing the suffering of minds in torment.[2] The analogy
with therapy is with "our method" of philosophy; it is not claimed to
be with philosophy, *per se.* "Our method", the therapeutic method,
is concerned with bringing to consciousness similes or pictures that
have hitherto lain in the unconscious, constraining one's thought (and,
maybe, leading one to believe one needed to produce that theory, to
do that bit of metaphysics). Similar to Freudian psychoanalysis (for
more on which see below), the very act of the bringing of the simile
or picture to consciousness, of articulating it and acknowledging it
as a simile or as a non-obligatory picture (aspect of things), breaks

its thought-constraining grip. (And then the real challenge begins: of not backsliding into being reconstrained at future "opportunities" for doing so ... The price of philosophical liberty is eternal vigilance. This is why Wittgenstein sometimes remarked that we would never come to the end of our job, in philosophy [see especially Z §447]. If one takes the analogy with therapy seriously, one will not mis-cast Wittgenstein crudely as an end-of-philosophy philosopher [cf. Z §382; PO 185–6].)

The analogy is with psychotherapy as a practice, not psychoanalysis as a theory of mind. Wittgenstein was scornful of Freud's scientific pretensions, thinking his theory of mind to be myth (albeit a deep, powerful and creative myth): a myth dangerously unaware of its nature *as* myth. The purpose of practising philosophy as therapy is to achieve freedom of thought, clarity about what we mean by our employment of words on actual and possible occasions, and justice in our takings of the world.

Wittgenstein is, therefore, attempting to break us (and himself) free of the impulse to metaphysics. To talk of "breaking us free" of impulse is already to talk therapeutically. How is that therapy pursued? Well, one finds it pursued in a number of ways, for there are methods not *a* method. However, there is a shift between Wittgenstein's writing in the early 1930s and his later work in *Philosophical Investigations*. The shift is in the way he practises his therapy. In *Investigations* Wittgenstein pursues the therapeutic task by engaging us in "dialogues" with a diverse and dialectically structured range of philosophical impulses. These impulses are presented as the voice of Wittgenstein's imaginary interlocutor(s) in *Investigations*. Through these voices, Wittgenstein presents us with different aspects of our language use, customs and practices with the intention of facilitating our freeing *ourselves* from the grip of a particular, entrenched, simile, picture or its lure. This then frees us of the thought-restricting tendencies (mental cramps) fostered by our being held in thrall to a particular picture to the exclusion of other equally viable ones.

In contrast to the dialogical and dialectical nature of *Philosophical Investigations,* in what is sometimes termed as his middle period Wittgenstein often deployed slogans, particular turns of phrase (attempts at finding liberating words[3]), to therapeutic ends. The move from the "middle period" to *Investigations* can be very roughly summed up as being from combating prejudice through carefully chosen slogans to facilitating the dawning realization that one is in the grip of a picture or simile – which led one to prejudicial views – through engagement in imaginary scenarios. Both of these approaches can be covered by the label "therapy". The latter is more effective, working with the will rather than against it. This can be seen in the move from his coining of the slogan "thinking is operating with signs" in the early 1930s, to his presenting the reader with the "trip to the [world's weirdest] 'grocer'" and other scenarios in *Investigations*. (See Chapter 7, "Thinking".)

This is an important point to bear in mind, one often overlooked even by those most sensitive to Wittgenstein's therapeutic endeavours. To present Wittgenstein as fundamentally in the business of *combating* prejudice, as does Katherine Morris (2007), might, we suggest, be a little misleading. For while Wittgenstein is, throughout his philosophical life, in the business of *absenting* prejudice from the mind of the philosopher, to talk of *"combating"* is to risk seeming as if one has failed to be sensitive enough to the way Wittgenstein pursues his therapeutic objectives, at least from about the *Philosophical Investigations* on. This point might seem to be of minor significance; we submit that it is pretty important. To talk of "combating" suggests a conflict situation, one initiated by the philosopher practising therapy. This does, in a way, capture what Wittgenstein is up to in his "middle" period, when he employs slogans designed to jolt his readers or interlocutors out of their settled, prejudicial way of thinking about some thing (such as, for example, that the meaning of a word is projected onto the word by a mental act[4]). It does not capture very well what Wittgenstein is up to in *Philosophical Investigations*, when he constructs imaginary scenarios in which his readers and interlocutors become immersed, and of which their attempts to make sense lead to a reorientation of their thoughts.[5] This latter way of practising therapy is expressly designed to avoid conflict (confrontation), rather trying to work with the will of the reader or interlocutor and not to meet that will with equal force of will.

We are inclined to be charitable here. One might say that this does not present a problem; that the concept of combat can encompass the non-confrontational methods we are submitting are in evidence in *Philosophical Investigations* and elsewhere in Wittgenstein's work from (roughly) the late 1930s and the 1940s. Why? Because it is *prejudices* that are being combated in Wittgensteinian philosophy, not people.[6] And prejudices can be "combated", at the very least in a metaphorical sense, by a variety of means, including by Wittgenstein's subtle methods of deluding his readers into the truth. So: here "combat" covers *both* the more confrontational attempts at therapy, in the use of slogans designed to jolt readers or interlocutors out of their entrenched way of thinking, from (roughly) the early 1930s; *and* the more facilitatory attempts at therapy, in the invitation to immerse oneself in scenarios that serve to reorientate one's thoughts. To coin a combat-sport analogy: boxing and aikido are both combat sports, but while the former is by and large primarily and straightforwardly about fighting, about confronting one's opponent's force with force (and skill), the latter is by and large about using (working with) one's opponent's force and momentum so as to render them no longer a threat. In Wittgenstein's most mature practice of therapy, one practises a subtle form aikido or jujitsu upon oneself / one's interlocutor, and largely gives up any effort to *fight*.

The point we wish to make, here, is not one of terminology: whether one "can" or "cannot" employ the term "combat" to describe what Wittgenstein does in practising therapy. We strive for clarity. Therapy is about freeing someone from what might be termed pathologies of mind.[7] It can be achieved in many ways. Wittgenstein explored these ways, and settled eventually on the one(s) he thought best.

Now, what is it about philosophical problems that makes them suited to treatment by therapy rather than by argument as traditionally conceived? Well, as we have noted elsewhere (see e.g. Hutchinson 2007), philosophical problems, on Wittgenstein's understanding, do not cause mental disturbances, but rather we see philosophical problems *as* mental disturbances – we feel them deeply. This is related to Wittgenstein's claim that the problems of philosophy are problems of the will, not of the intellect;[8] our inability to acknowledge other pictures of how things might be stems from certain pathologies. Put another way, Wittgenstein saw philosophical problems as (took them to be) existential problems; thus their treatment was to take the form of therapeutic treatment of the person and that person's mode of engagement with the world: his or her mode of being in the world. That is, it is not to take the form of dealing with the problem in abstraction from the person whose behaviour manifests it.

And (and this point is critical), it is the person in question who is the ultimate authority for the successful resolution of the problem. As already hinted above, this is the very core of Wittgenstein's promotion of the therapeutic analogy for philosophy:

> We can only convict another person of a mistake … if he (really) acknowledges this expression as the correct expression of his feeling. // For only if he acknowledges it as such, *is* it the correct expression. (Psychoanalysis.) (*BT* §410)[9]

> [O]ne can only determine the grammar of a language with the consent of a speaker, but not the orbit of the stars with the consent of the stars. The rule for a sign, then, is the rule which the speaker *commits himself* to. (Baker 2003: 105)[10]

One commits oneself to something by standing by it, on reflection: your words do not speak for you. It is *you* who speak, and it is fatally bad faith to hope or pretend otherwise. One can concede the point most famously made by poststructuralists, that the meaning of an utterance is not *determined* by the utterer (issues of structure, context and occasion-sensitivity – to coin Travis's term – can all play a role).[11] However, when one is asked to take responsibility for one's utterances, then one, following reflection and clarification, is asked to consent to the meaning of those words as being expressive of the thought one was seeking to express in the utterance in question. In this sense, one is ineluctably responsible for and committed to the words one speaks.

Here is the central reason for the disanalogy between philosophy and science. That disanalogy can only be taken seriously by Wittgensteinians who genuinely embrace some version of the therapeutic conception of philosophy: an emphasis on use, or "ordinary language", without a central place for the consent/acknowledgement of the speaker, fails to generate a genuinely non-scientistic conception of philosophic method.[12]

The analogy with therapy, then, demands to be taken seriously, as a key to Wittgenstein's later philosophical methods. But what of early Wittgenstein? Presumably, early Wittgenstein can be contrasted on this score with later. Was early Wittgenstein not a builder of theories, even if he declared those theories to be unsayable or ultimately self-refuting?

We do not believe so. The current generation of Wittgenstein scholarship has witnessed the rise to prominence of a loose "school" of thinkers[13] who take Wittgenstein's self-appointed task *from the* Tractatus *onward, inclusive,* to be one of overcoming our tendencies to metaphysics through delicate attention to our inchoate desire to speak "outside 'the limits' of language".

We submit that the difference between the *Tractatus* and the later work is not a difference between a non-therapeutic and a therapeutic conception of philosophy: rather, it is the difference between less and more effective methods, less and more effective therapies. Just as Wittgenstein moved beyond the subtle, carefully chosen sloganeering of the early 1930s to the subtle engagement with imaginary scenarios[14] of his fully mature work, so he had earlier moved beyond the attempt to do therapy as one gigantic exercise in overcoming (the *Tractatus*) to a much more engaged and variegated approach (in the early 1930s). (Though there is at least one important respect in which the *Tractatus* is *more* therapeutically engaged and honed than most of what Wittgenstein wrote for the next fifteen years or so: its masterfully deliberate enticement of its reader deep into nonsense, an enticement echoed and explored retail in the *Philosophical Investigations*.) Wittgenstein, we suggest, came to see that the *Tractatus* had not got its hands dirty enough in the immense variegation of ordinary language, and had not been user-friendly enough to engage the reader in the therapeutic dance that now (from the early 1930s onward) he made explicit, and practised with increasing sophistication in the last decade or so of his life.

What is the justification for attributing such a conception of philosophy to early Wittgenstein too? Here is how it was put in the "Introduction" to *The New Wittgenstein*:

> [The authors in this collection] agree in suggesting that Wittgenstein's aim in philosophy is ... a *therapeutic* one. These papers have in common an understanding of Wittgenstein as aspiring, not to advance metaphysical theories, but rather to help us work ourselves out of confusion we become entangled in when philosophising. More specifically, they agree in representing him as tracing the sources of our philosophical confusions to our tendency, in the midst of philosophising, to think that we need to survey language from an external point of view. They invite us to understand him as wishing to get us to see that our need to grasp the essence of thought and language will be met – not, as we are inclined to think in philosophy, by metaphysical theories expounded from such a point of view, but – by attention to our everyday forms of expression and to the world those forms of expression serve to reveal.   (Crary & Read 2000: 1)[15]

The *locus classicus* here is Cora Diamond's paper "Throwing away the ladder", which among other things presses the case for the *Tractatus* to be read as asking its reader to overcome the temptation to hang on to any of its *Sätze*. If one wants to understand fully the "therapeutic" reading of early Wittgenstein, one can do no better than to begin by reading that paper, and by reflecting upon the wording of the *Tractatus* 6.54.

But there is also a less well-known passage, from Wittgenstein's explicitly therapeutic writings of the early 1930s, that provides a particularly fascinating bridge back to the *Tractatus*, on the therapeutic reading of that work, and offers a key clue to a continuity present in Wittgenstein's thinking throughout, so far for instance as his use of "nonsense" as a term of criticism is concerned:

> [T]he uneasiness which one feels with the expression: "The rose is identical with red" could make somebody conclude that something is wrong with this expression, which, in turn, means that it somehow does not agree with reality, hence that it is an

incorrectly formed expression and that sometimes reality guides grammar. Then one would say: the rose is really not identical with red at all. However, in fact this only means the following: I do not employ the words "rose" and "red" in such a way that they can be substituted for each other, and therefore I do not use the expression "identical" here. The difficulty I run into here, that is the uneasiness, does not result from a non-agreement of the grammatical rules with reality, but from the non-agreement of two grammatical rules which I would like to use alternately. The philosopher does not look at reality and ask himself: is the rose identical with red? What is warring inside the philosopher are two grammatical rules. The conflict that arises in him is of the same kind as one's looking at an object in two different ways and then trying to see it in both ways simultaneously. The phenomenon is that of *irresolution*.   (Baker 2003: 235)

This passage is so remarkable (although it is by no means the only such passage in Wittgenstein's *Nachlass*) because it culminates in explicitly indexing the very word that has come to be most closely associated with the therapeutic reading of the *Tractatus*: the word *resolute*. The most common appellation now for the "therapeutic" reading of the *Tractatus* is *the resolute reading*. And this passage from Wittgenstein's "middle" period explicitly places centrally in his method the phenomenon of irresolution, and (by implication) the opposing phenomenon, of resoluteness/resolution.

Wittgenstein's aim, in his therapy, is to enable one no longer to equivocate, in philosophy, and no longer to suffer from the conflicting desires that one is inclined to equivocate between. No longer to have words or phrases or concepts "flicker" before one's mind's eye, such that one cannot decide what one wants to mean by one's words.[16] No longer to be hovering between different possible resolutions, different possible commitments that one could make – that one *needs* to make only one of, at a time – between desires to mean.

Once one commits, then the philosophical problem ebbs away. One is no longer pulled in two directions at once, pulled ("compelled") to endorse a picture that clashes with something else that one feels (perhaps rightly, perhaps not) unable to give up.

We might then describe Wittgenstein's entire career thus: as a sequence of (on balance) deepening experiments in how to conduct philosophy such that it is actually therapeutically effective. In a manner that standard allegedly Wittgensteinian methods ("ordinary-language philosophy", philosophy as linguistic topography, philosophy as "grammatical analysis" – laying down what is grammatical and what is not, etc.) are not effective.

One *can* of course choose not to accept Wittgenstein's invitation to philosophical therapy. One can stay "safe" by being a metaphysician or a word-policeman. But this is a very poor – a strikingly unsafe – "safety" – an *illusion* of safety.[17] It is a "safety" that deprives one of all that Wittgenstein can offer. And here it is important to realize that Wittgenstein knew full well that people would resist what he had to offer: that is a key reason why the *Tractatus* and the *Philosophical Investigations* have the form that they do. Both are designed, in different ways, to dump the reader *in media res* into philosophy, and deceive them into the truth by offering an apparent way out that dissolves upon one. In the *Tractatus*, one is thrown into the deep end of what appears to be a metaphysics, and inhabits its attractions, and then one gradually emerges from and throws off that metaphysics and its associated theoretical attractions. In *Philosophical Investigations*, one is dropped into an attractive way of thinking about language by means of a quote from someone else; one believes one is overcoming those attractions by developing something like a theory of "language-games" or of "use"; and then one overcomes the attraction of that, too, as one starts to see that the apparent solution was only an illusion of a solution.

"At the end" of either book, one has to stand and speak for oneself. Wittgenstein never does one the "favour" of thinking *for* you. If you want to be healed, in philosophy, then you must be your own physician. It is thyself that can help – for there is no analogue, in this therapy, to drugs or surgery. *You have to want to get well.* And you have to be prepared to struggle, to achieve such wellness ongoingly. That is why philosophy is hard work, and why it requires, as Wittgenstein remarked on more than one occasion, courage ... [18]

Notes

1. Editions referred to in this chapter are *Philosophical Investigations* (2001a), *The Blue and Brown Books* (1965), *Philosophical Occasions* (1958) and *Zettel* (1967).
2. Though cf. *On Certainty* §37; sometimes, of course, the problem is that one's interlocutor *does not* feel tormented, because they have not *yet* noticed how different areas of their practice or different desires that they have are incompatible.
3. "In this matter it is always as follows. Everything we do consists in trying to find the liberating word. In grammar you cannot discover anything. There are no surprises. When formulating a rule we always have the feeling: That is something you have known all along" (Waismann 1979: 77).

4. So in the early 1930s Wittgenstein is happy to coin the slogan "meaning is use"; in later work he is more circumspect. Modal qualifiers abound in *Philosophical Investigations* (see Hutchinson & Read 2008). Wittgenstein in his full maturity wanted to guard against the slogans ossifying and themselves becoming thought-constraining pictures.

5. This is not to suggest that he does not talk directly about things such as meaning and thinking and so on in *Philosophical Investigations*. It is just that he does not employ slogans to therapeutic effect. He moves from "Meaning is Use" to the very delicately worded §43: "In a large class of cases – though not for all – in which we employ the word meaning, it can be defined thus: the meaning of a word is its use in the language." One might see this latter locution on the subject of meaning as suggestive (and: of a practice that we can engage in) rather than sloganeering.

6. In our forthcoming monograph on Wittgenstein, we investigate this issue more deeply, because of course it is not quite that simple: people's prejudices can appear to them to be constitutive of their very identity.

7. Though this "pathologizing" move of ours is of course not an othering move: "Language contains the same traps *for everyone*; the immense network of well-kept//passable//false paths" (Typescript 213, 90; emphasis added). Moreover, much of one's task in philosophy involves "putting up signs which help one get by the dangerous places [in language]" (*ibid.*) – in that respect, our task is more like a "*prevention*" of (relapse into?) otherwise potentially chronic illnesses of the intellect.

8. See the opening of the chapter on philosophy in *The Big Typescript*.

9. There are a number of ways in which one can fruitfully follow up the analogy that Wittgenstein drew quite explicitly between his practice and the proper practice of psychoanalysis. See for instance Waismann (1979: 186), and the closing sections of G. E. Moore's "Wittgenstein's Lectures in 1930–33" (1954), for the crucial point that "a psycho-analysis is successful only if the patient agrees to the explanation offered by the analyst" (*ibid.*: 108). Wittgenstein held that the same was true of philosophy. That is why he described himself as "a disciple of Freud" (see the Introduction to *LC*).

10. For amplification, compare also: "Should we record the actual use of a word, variable and irregular though it be? This would at best produce a history of the use of words. Or should we set up a particular use as a paradigm? Should we say: Only this use is legitimate, and everything else is deviant? This would be a tyrannical ruling" (Baker 2003: 227–8).

11. In this respect see Lars Hertzberg's paper, "The Sense is Where You Find It" (2001).

12. For amplification of this point, see the closing sections of our "Towards a Perspicuous Presentation of 'Perspicuous Presentation'" (Hutchinson & Read 2008), wherein we accuse "Oxford Wittgensteinians" such as Peter Hacker of being covertly committed to a scientistic vision of philosophy, in spite of this being in their own eyes the very antithesis of their project. (See also Chapter 5, "Ordinary/Everyday Language".)

13. In terms of *Tractatus* scholarship, this reading emerged officially in Cora Diamond's writings on that book, particularly her work on nonsense and the context principle (although antecedents of this "resolute" reading of the *Tractatus* can also be found in work on Tractarian objects, undertaken by Rhees, McGuiness and Goldfarb. Conant has since become the leading advocate (along with Diamond). See Crary & Read (2000).

14. Why do we keep emphasizing the *imaginariness* of the scenarios? To distance Wittgenstein from any supposed connection with the stereotype of "ordinary-language philosophy" (see Chapter 5, "Ordinary/Everyday Language"), or with a theoreticistic or sociologistic emphasis on "use".

15. Note that paying *attention* to our everyday forms of expression is not to be equated with thinking, absurdly, that a mere record of linguistic usage can *settle* philosophical questions – see above.

16. Thus the closing sentence of Witherspoon's essay in *The New Wittgenstein*: "When Wittgenstein criticizes an utterance as nonsensical, he aims to expose, not a defect in the words themselves, but a confusion in the speaker's relation to her words – a confusion that is manifested in the speaker's failure to specify a meaning for them" (2000). In passing, we should note that some practitioners of the resolute reading do not wish to employ the term "therapeutic" to describe their practice, and moreover that some of the "New Wittgensteinians" do not like the label "therapeutic" – or the label "New", either. It would perhaps be a distraction to go into this question in detail here. Suffice to say, at present, that we believe the reasons intimated in the quotation above from Crary already sketch a decent case for the use of the term "therapeutic" to describe the resolute reading – and that our quotations from the "middle" Wittgenstein only buttress that case.

17. For detail, see Read's forthcoming monograph on *The Lord of the Rings*, and the excerpt therefrom in his *Philosophy for Life* (2007b).

18. Thanks for helpful comments to colleagues at UEA, especially to Oskari Kuusela and Tamara Dobler.

Further reading

Tractatus, Preface, 4.003–4.0031, 4.111–4.121, 6.53–6.54.

THIRTEEN

Criteria

Eric Loomis

Wittgenstein introduced the notion of "criteria" in *The Blue Book*, and it appears frequently in his later writings. The notion almost always appears in the context of the illustrations of certain uses of language. These illustrations typically occur as part of an attempt to clarify or illuminate some aspect of language that has proven philosophically troublesome or contentious, and which has thus served as prod to philosophical theory construction.

Wittgenstein's *Blue Book* introduction of criteria is embedded in a discussion of our knowledge of states such as pains. A look at this discussion can help us to draw out the nature and purpose of Wittgenstein's use of the notion:

> It might be found practical to call a certain state of decay in a tooth, not accompanied by what we commonly call toothache, "unconscious toothache" and to use in such a case the expression that we have toothache, but don't know it. ... There is nothing wrong about [this use], as it is just a new terminology and can at any time be retranslated into ordinary language. On the other hand it obviously makes use of the word "to know" in a new way. If you wish to examine how this expression is used it is helpful to ask yourself "what in this case is the process of getting to know like?" "What do we call 'getting to know' or, 'finding out'?"
>
> (*BB* 23; compare *PI* §§247, 560)[1]

It is clear that we can assign a sense to the expression "unconscious toothache" in the way that Wittgenstein suggests. But he points out that this assignment of sense results in a change in the use of the expression "to know". This change is an extension of our ordinary use that must be learned. Examining how the expression "to know" is used should be connected with what we *call* "getting to know". Why? We get part of his answer in the next paragraph:

> It isn't wrong, according to our new convention, to say "I have unconscious toothache". For what more can you ask of your notation than that it should distinguish between a bad tooth which doesn't give you toothache and one which does? But the new expression misleads us by calling up pictures and analogies ... . Thus by the expression "unconscious toothache" you may either be misled into thinking that a stupendous discovery has been made, ... or else you may be extremely puzzled by the expression (the puzzlement of philosophy) and perhaps ask such a question as "How is unconscious toothache possible?" (*BB* 23)

We may be puzzled by the expression "unconscious toothache" if we treat the expression as if it reported a stupendous discovery. Rather than focus on what we count as getting to know an unconscious toothache as it is given through explanations of the expression, we might imagine the expression referring to something that we did not know was there – an ache existing perhaps, but somehow beyond the boundary of our awareness. But is this the case? Or is this impression the product of a picture formed by an analogy with other cases of things we may be unconscious of (such as, for example, a tumour)? What we began with is a "notation", an expression, that we wish to use to distinguish between a bad tooth which does not give a toothache and one that does. This is all we have been given in the explanation of the meaning of "unconscious toothache". The picture that leads to the impression of a stupendous discovery is not necessary for making this distinction. Nor was it required or presupposed by the explanation of "unconscious toothache".

From a slightly different direction, we might be puzzled ("the puzzlement of philosophy") by "unconscious toothache", and insist that it must be meaningless. Here, we do not posit something beyond awareness, but instead deny that a pain can be unconscious. But this is again confused. It is not wrong to use the phrase "unconscious toothache" as Wittgenstein is using it, namely, to distinguish between a bad tooth which does not give a toothache and one that does. This use can be transparent, and it is what we see when we look again at what we *call* an "unconscious toothache". In a particular case we might explain that we call something an "unconscious toothache" when there is a bad tooth (like *this* one, where we might here point out a bad tooth) that does not – or does not yet – hurt. Wittgenstein is indicating to us that knowing the meaning of "unconscious toothache" need not require more than what is given by such explanations.

This example, like many in Wittgenstein's work, is simple and contrived, as he well knew. He fully understood that the use of many of our expressions is not so transparent. In such cases,

> we may clear the matter up by saying: "Let's see how the word 'unconscious', 'to know', etc. etc., is used in *this* case, and how it's used in others". *How far does the analogy between these uses go?* We shall also try to construct new notations, in order to break the spell of those we are accustomed to. (*BB* 23)

The notion of a criterion is in Wittgenstein's hands part of the construction of "new notations" aimed at breaking the spell cast by pictures of what words mean or of how language ought to work. We see this in his subsequent discussion, which also introduces a further notion, that of "grammar":

> We said that it was a way of examining the grammar (the use) of the word "to know", to ask ourselves what, in the particular case we are examining, we should call "getting to know". ... But this question is really a question concerning the grammar of the word "to know", and this becomes clearer if we put it in the form: what do we *call* 'getting to know'?" It is part of the grammar of the word "chair" that *this* is what we call "to sit on a chair", and it is part of the grammar of the word "meaning" that *this* is what we call "explanation of meaning". (*Ibid.*: 23–4)

Consonant with the above-quoted remarks, Wittgenstein here ties the "grammar" of words like "chair" and "to know" to the explanations of these words (compare *PI* §§90, 371ff., 660–64). In a general way, we could understand "grammar" in Wittgenstein's use as consisting of the rules for the correct use of expressions as these are given in ordinary explanations of those expressions. Thus, for instance, we might explain a part of what "chair" means by saying that a chair is something one sits in. Here the notion of "sitting in" something would in turn either be further explained (e.g. demonstratively), or be something we may assume the hearer already understands. "Chair" means in part what it does (it has the grammar that it does) because something counts as "sitting in a chair". We might, of course, assign the word "chair" a different meaning, perhaps using it to refer to a useless collection of wood or metal. And in such a case our explanation of the meaning of "chair" would also differ. But our meaning of "chair" is tied to the practice of sitting in chairs, and an explanation of that meaning makes reference to that practice. This is a grammatical explanation: "chair" would not mean what it does except for the practice indicated by the explanation. Similarly, "meaning" would not mean what it does if there were not certain practices that count as "explanations of meaning". And likewise for "toothache":

> In the same way, to explain my criterion for another person's having toothache is to give a grammatical explanation about the word "toothache" and, in this sense, an explanation concerning the meaning of the word "toothache".
>
> When we learnt the use of the phrase "so-and-so has toothache" we were pointed out certain kinds of behavior of those who were said to have toothache. As an instance of these kinds of behavior let us take holding your cheek. ...
>
> Now one may go on and ask: "How do you know that he has got toothache when he holds his cheek?" The answer to this might be, "I say, *he* has toothache when he holds his cheek because I hold my cheek when I have toothache". But what if we went on asking: – "And why do you suppose that toothache corresponds to his holding his check just because your toothache corresponds to your holding your cheek?" You will be at a loss to answer this question, and find that here we strike rock bottom, that is where we have come down to conventions. (BB 24)

Cheek-holding is an example of the "kinds of behaviour" that are pointed out in the explanation of "toothache". This behaviour is presented as an extension of the behaviour that *I* would engage in if I had one. But, Wittgenstein suggests, I have no answer to the question of why another's toothache behaviour corresponds to mine. At this point, he says, we come down to "conventions".

There is a distinction between the convention that certain things, like cheek-holding and third-person toothache ascriptions, are connected, and the discovery that they are correlated. The former is a matter of agreement, a product not of discovery but of stipulation, or something akin to it. The latter is not a matter of agreement but of observation. Wittgenstein uses this distinction to mark out his notion of a criterion:

Let us introduce two antithetical terms in order to avoid certain elementary confusions: To the question "How do you know that so-and-so is the case?", we sometimes answer by giving "*criteria*" and sometimes by giving "*symptoms*". If medical science calls angina [tonsilitis] an inflammation caused by a particular bacillus, and we ask in a particular case "why do you say this man has got angina?" then the answer "I have found the bacillus so-and-so in his blood" gives us the criterion, or what we may call the defining criterion, of angina. If on the other hand the answer was "his throat is inflamed", this might give us a symptom of angina. I call "symptom" a phenomenon of which experience has taught us that it coincided, in some way or other, with the phenomenon which is our defining criterion. (*BB* 25)

Thus a criterion in Wittgenstein's usage has the following properties:[2]

- it connects an expression, such as "angina" or "toothache", with certain evidence, such as the presence of a bacillus, or cheek-holding (cf. also *PI* §§51, 573);
- it plays a role in answering questions such as "How do you know that so-and-so is the case?" (cf. *PI* §§182, 692);
- it may rest on "conventions" or rules (cf. *PI* §§354–5);
- it can serve in an explanation of the meaning of an expression (cf. *PI* §§190, 322, p. 212); and
- it constitutes part of the "grammar" of the expressions for which it serves (cf. *PI* §§373–7; *BB* 64).

In the context of Wittgenstein's angina example, we can say that certain evidence (a bacillus in the blood) is "criterial" for the ascription of an expression ("angina") in virtue of a convention. The convention specifies (all or part of) the grammar of "angina". In other words, it specifies (all or part of) what it is to *call* something "angina". In still other words, it is partially constitutive of the *meaning* of "angina".

Criteria are contrasted in the above discussion with "symptoms". Symptoms, Wittgenstein has told us:

- are found in experience (cf. *PI* §§354);
- coincide with the phenomenon that is given by our criterion.

The fact that symptoms are found in experience importantly distinguishes them from the conventional status of criteria. We might think here of a convention as a stipulation of a course of action, one that specifies what counts as correct action in a particular case, and hence as something normative. Thus, for example, we must, if we are said to know what "angina" (tonsilitis) means, say that someone has angina if they have an inflammation caused by *this* kind of bacillus in their blood. Conventions in this sense serve in a role akin to that of definitions. An experiential discovery, on the other hand, is not something stipulated but something found. A report of such a finding is descriptive, not normative. It says how things are (e.g. that this person's throat is inflamed). Such findings may be found to coincide, or be correlated with, certain "criterially defined" phenomena. Thus we may, having conventionally or definitionally established that "angina" is to be the inflammation caused by a particular bacillus, find in experience that the same inflammation coincides with an inflammation of the throat. In such a case, evidence of an inflamed throat might be inductive, as opposed to criterial, evidence of angina.

What then does Wittgenstein's notion of a criterion offer us? We have observed that a criterion serves to link a piece of evidence with an expression, by providing a grammatically licensed justification for claims made using that expression. Criterial evidence is the evidence that is linked in this way. Here we can distinguish the criterion itself from the criterial evidence by regarding the former as the rule or convention that connects that evidence with an expression. The notion of a criterion thus helps us to see how the relation of certain expressions to the evidence for assertions involving them can, in some cases at least, be constitutive of the meaning of those expressions.[3] More simply put, the notion can be seen as a tool for illuminating the meaning of certain expressions and exposing how they relate to non-linguistic phenomena (criterial evidence).

Wittgenstein's notion of a criterion has been subject to a variety of criticisms (see e.g. Chihara & Fodor 1965; Lycan 1971; McGinn 1998). I wish to consider one especially important and perhaps obvious objection here.

The objection states that Wittgenstein's notion of a criterion is ill equipped to handle cases that go beyond simple "defining criterion" or "one criterion" examples such as the angina example. It may well be that there are some expressions that have only a single "defining" criterion, as perhaps "angina" might. But many other expressions that Wittgenstein seems to regard as being criterially governed, such as "toothache", are very different.[4] Consider, for instance, the fact that we have no difficulty imagining someone's holding their cheek – a behaviour that Wittgenstein has said is criterial for "toothache" – but *not* having a toothache. For instance, someone might fake their pain behaviour by holding their cheek in the absence of toothache.[5] So cheek-holding does not *entail* the presence of a toothache.

The problem that this sort of example raises for criteria is that it renders troublesome the idea that cheek-holding might be constitutive of the meaning of "toothache". Since it is obvious that we can have cheek-holding without toothaches, why is cheek-holding behaviour not more akin to a symptom that someone has a toothache? And if there is no other behaviour that entails the presence of a toothache, then it appears as if there is nothing in such cases but symptoms (cf. *PI* §354). If so, then Wittgenstein's notion of a criterion loses its distinctive status in explanation and meaning-constitution. After all, if such cases are possible, then "toothache" obviously must mean something independent of cheek-holding!

One line of response to this objection on Wittgenstein's behalf has been to argue that the meaning-constitutive function of criteria is not an entailment in many cases, such as most ascriptions of pains or psychological states.[6] Rather, criteria are meaning-constituting in virtue of being "grammatically good evidence" – evidence that is conceptually or grammatically tied to certain expressions, but whose presence does not entail the truth of any statement containing those expressions. Thus cheek-holding might be said to be grammatically good evidence for a toothache because it is part of what we mean by "toothache" that cheek-holding counts as evidence of a toothache. Nonetheless, the presence of cheek-holding does not entail that a toothache is present, since to say that the evidence is grammatically good is only to say that it is "conceptually" or "necessarily good" evidence, not that it is entailing evidence. Knowing what "toothache" means may thus require knowing that cheek-holding is evidence for someone having one; this is a consequence of saying the evidence is *grammatically* good. But since there is no entailment from the evidence to any assertion, someone *can* manifest cheek-holding in the absence of a toothache, and so the objection is answered.

An alternative line of response to the above objection argues that there *is* an entailment from certain criterial evidence for a term to the truth of certain statements involving those terms.[7] On this view it is precisely the entailment that grants to the criterion its meaning-constitutive role. However, this view can allow that any given bit of evidence, including criterial evidence, may be *defeasible*, that is, that there may be further evidence such that the criterial evidence is undercut and ceases, in that instance, to serve as a reason for some statement's truth. On this view, it could be correct to say that the *undefeated* presence of a certain behaviour (like cheek-holding, in Wittgenstein's simplified case) might entail the presence of a toothache. This is the content of saying that the evidence is part of the grammar or meaning of "toothache". Yet this view can also acknowledge that any given sample of evidence may be defeated by further considerations, such as, say, the evidence that the cheek-holder is performing in a play. So in this case the above objection is blocked not by denying an entailment, but by adding the requirement that the entailing evidence be undefeated.

It is not clear, however, whether Wittgenstein himself would have endorsed either of these proposals. Indeed, it is worth recalling what he tells us he means to be doing with his notion of criteria (as at *BB* 23, quoted above). There he tells us that he is interested in constructing "new notations" for the purpose of helping us resist certain pictures or puzzlements. And he makes clear that he intends his notion of criteria to be a part of such a project, both in *The Blue Book* and in the *Investigations*:

> In practice, if you were asked which phenomenon is the defining criterion and which is a symptom, you would in most cases be unable to answer this question except by making an arbitrary decision *ad hoc*. (*BB* 25)

> It appears we don't know what ["knowledge"] means, and that therefore, perhaps, we have no right to use it. We should reply: "There is no one exact usage of the word 'knowledge'; but we can make up several such usages, which will more or less agree with the ways the word is actually used." (*BB* 27)

> And here what is in question is not symptoms but logical criteria. That these are not always sharply differentiated does not prevent them from being differentiated. Our investigation does not try to *find* the real, exact meaning of words; though we do often *give* words exact meanings in the course of our investigation.
> (*Z* §§466–7)

These and similar remarks of Wittgenstein's deserve our attention, for they frequently surround his uses of the notion of criteria (see also *PI* §354; *RPP I* 649). The notion is not introduced by him as part of a hypothesis or theory about what is behind our actual use of language. Rather, its role is one of exposing, of rendering perspicuous, certain otherwise misleading uses of language, and it does so through a "made-up usage", a "new notation", or an exact meaning that we have given to, rather than found in, certain simplified uses of ordinary words. As we have noted, the goal is the removal of pictures that might otherwise mislead us by making certain uses of language perspicuous:

> A main source of our failure to understand is that we do not *command a clear view* of the use of our words. – Our grammar is lacking in this sort of perspicuity. A perspicuous representation produces just that understanding which consists in "seeing connexions". Hence the importance of finding and inventing *intermediate cases*. (*PI* §122)

Finding and inventing intermediate cases is a project that is compatible with the recognition that terms like "toothache" are not actually used in the simplified way outlined in *The Blue Book*. The point of such examples is not so much to conjecture that certain evidence does or does not entail certain claims, as it is to give us a simplified example that grants perspicuity to certain possible uses of language. Our own use of language might then be regarded as a progressively more complex elaboration of such simplified languages, much as a city might expand out from its ancient roots (*PI* §18). From this perspective, criteria form a part of our "map" of language, rather than a part of the terrain.

Notes

1. Editions referred to in this chapter are *The Blue and Brown Books* (1965), *Philosophical Investigations* (2001a) and *Zettel* (1967).
2. I return to the notion of a "defining criterion" that is introduced in this passage below.
3. Some commentators have also argued that criteria provide an account of *certain* knowledge, and thereby form a part of a Wittgensteinian rejection of scepticism. See, for example, Malcolm (1954), Albritton (1959). This view of criteria has subsequently been heavily criticized; see, for example, Cavell (1979a).
4. Wittgenstein did not seem to think that there are criteria for the use of all expressions. For example, the expressions for family-resemblance concepts are arguably not governed by criteria.
5. Notice that the converse of this claim, that having a toothache does not entail cheek-holding, is not something that Wittgenstein needs to deny. He can, and does, grant that there can be more than one criterion for a given term, see for instance *Philosophical Investigations* §141. "Defining criteria" seems to be Wittgenstein's term for one-criterion terms.
6. See Shoemaker (1963); Kenny (1967); Lycan (1971); and Hacker (1993) for expressions of this view.
7. See Canfield (1981: 87); McDowell (1982); and Loomis (2007), for expressions of this view.

FOURTEEN

Grammatical investigations

Roderick T. Long and Kelly Dean Jolley

Introduction

In what follows, we first provide and develop an example of a grammatical investigation. We then provide a short account of what a grammatical investigation is and is not. The example is not intended to typify the form such an investigation may take, but rather to give one form it may take; the account, short as it is, is not meant to exhaust all that could or even needs to be said about such investigations.

A grammatical investigation

At *Zettel* §504,[1] Wittgenstein observes that "Love is not a feeling. Love is put to the test, pain not. One does not say: That was not true pain or it would not have gone off so quickly." We like to think of this remark as a cloud of soap operas reduced to a drop of grammar.

What is Wittgenstein doing here? He is investigating the grammar of "love". He is also contesting an assimilation of its grammar to the grammar of "pain". Pain, Wittgenstein implies, is a feeling. Since it is a feeling, we do not typically put it to the test. We do not challenge someone when he reports being in pain. – "Ouch! That hurts." – "No, it doesn't." We can make sense of such an exchange, but not readily as a challenge to the report of pain. We can make sense of such an exchange, say, as occurring between a father and his young son, where the father is trying to encourage his son to gain a certain kind of control over his response to pain, teaching him how to bear pain manfully. (Imagine the conversation in ancient Sparta.)

Not only do we not typically challenge reports of pain, *a fortiori* we do not put the person who makes the report to the test. – "Here, twist your arm violently like you just did and hold it; let's make sure it hurts." But we do sometimes challenge someone when he reports being in love. "I love her!" – "No, you don't; but you are noxiously infatuated with her!" And, having challenged the report of being in love, we often propose a test, put the putative love to the test: "Spend some time apart. Date other people. Think about the way you act when you are around her; you act like a petulant child because what you call 'love' is not really love. How can you love her if you are unwilling to forgo anything, sacrifice anything for her?"

We cede to others the authority to determine that, and when, and to what degree they are in pain. If we challenge them, we challenge their sincerity, not their ability accurately to report their affective state. (Sometimes folks lie about being in pain. Sometimes folks malinger.) We do not cede to others the authority to determine that, and when, and to what degree they are in love. If we challenge them, we challenge their ability accurately to determine their affective state. Some folks, we know, are just not good at determining whether or not they are in love. The young are often taken to be especially worrisome in this regard. That is why, presumably, parents often ask (beg?) a child to separate, for a time, from her supposed beloved. It is why they often encourage dating many different people. It is why they favour long(er) engagements. And so on. Each of these is a way of putting the supposed love to the test. Of course, the tests do not have to be imposed on a couple by anyone external to the couple. A person may have doubts about her own feelings, and may suggest some time apart, or dating other people, or a long(er) engagement. A person may have taken herself to be in love before but turned out to be mistaken. She may even have taken herself not to be in love before but turned out to be mistaken.

Love lasts.[2] Pain can pass in a flash. It can be here and be gone, just like that. True love does not go off quickly. Sometimes it takes years to stop it, often requiring us to leave or join a church, or to spend time in the French Foreign Legion.[3] Lasting love may last continuously even during periods when a person has no cognizance of it at all, when he is for hours or days even completely occupied by something else (as when his unit in the French Foreign Legion is shelled without interruption for days). But constant pain is like a humming in the background, a kind of (white) noise; it may become the background for other things we do or feel, but is always available to us should we choose to shift what is figure and what is background. It is expressively available in a way that love may not be. (And that is one reason why it is much harder to decide if you have fallen out of love than it is to decide whether you are still in pain.)

Given these differences, against what mistake could Wittgenstein be militating in *Zettel* §504? Well, we ask this question after we have been through a rehearsal of some of the grammar. But before that rehearsal, various superficial grammatical analogies could mislead us: (i) We talk about both feeling pain and feeling love, about the feeling of pain and the feeling of love. (We do not take Wittgenstein to have missed this in *Zettel* §504; we think he just wanted to stress one use of "feeling".) The point of §504 could be taken, in the face of these analogies, to be to show that they are just superficial analogies. Pain is a feeling – but in *that* use of "feeling", love is not a feeling; and, love is a feeling – but in *that* use of "feeling", pain is not a feeling.[4] (ii) We talk of being in pain and being in love. (iii) We talk of both pain and love as "degreed" in particular ways: pains can be slight or horrible; love is deep and can deepen (can it be shallow?).

But when we consider further the ways we talk about pain and love, we see how very much unalike they really are. We do talk of being in pain and being in love – but we fall in love, not in pain (although pain often cometh after a fall). We can fall out of love, but not out of pain. Pains can be burning, stabbing, throbbing, aching, sharp and dull. Love can be erotic, filial (and here can further be fatherly, motherly, brotherly, sisterly: it might be held that feeling a father's love is not the same as feeling a mother's love), friendly. Pain can drive us crazy, but love makes fools of us all. (Samuel Butler: "All parents are fools but especially mothers.") Love is blind, pain is sometimes blinding. We localize love in our breasts, and pains can occur there, too; but we do not localize pain there. We can manage our pains with pills, often; but we can manage our loves only with potions – or by otherwise changing who and what we are. Our pains are incidents in our biographies; our loves shape our biographies.

What is a grammatical investigation?

The statements in which grammatical investigations issue bear a close resemblance to what are often called *conceptual truths* – close enough that they seem either simply to *be* conceptual truths, or else to be Wittgenstein's proposed successor to, or replacement for, the notion of conceptual truth. As such they inherit conceptual truth's ambiguity of status: are they metaphysical statements, that is statements about the denizens of some timeless Platonic or Fregean realm of essences? Or are they merely facts about conventional language use?

Wittgenstein's grammatical investigations are so clearly not intended to be investigations of a realm of essences (at least as traditionally understood; there is no doubt a *sense* in which it is perfectly all right to describe them as investigating a realm of essences) that it is a natural and seductive mistake to take them to be investigations of language use instead (as indeed the term "grammatical" seems to invite; and again there is no doubt a *sense* in which describing them as investigations of language use is quite proper).

Take for example the "grammatical remark" that I can be mistaken about whether *you are* in pain but cannot be mistaken about whether *I am* in pain. On a Cartesian understanding, this statement captures a fact about the metaphysical nature of pain; pain is just self-illuminating, and that is that. When Wittgenstein criticizes the Cartesian understanding, it is easy to read him as saying something like this:

> The problem with the Cartesian approach is that it treats our ability to be wrong about others' pain but not our own as a kind of *discovery*. But there is no fact to be "discovered" here apart from our linguistic conventions; the meanings of linguistic expression are determined by the rules for their use, and those rules are of course conventional. According to the rules of our language, a sentence like "she's in pain" may be answered with "how do you know?" while a sentence like "I'm in pain" may not. But that is an entirely contingent historical matter; we could have other rules. Just as it is the conventional rules of chess that determine which moves are permissible and which are not – so that moving a bishop diagonally is a permissible move but moving a rook diagonally is not – so it is the conventional rules of language that determine that challenging one's knowledge of another's pain is a meaningful move while challenging one's knowledge of one's own pain is not. Thus the supposed incorrigibility of self-awareness is no deep fact about the metaphysical essence of consciousness; it is simply an artefact of our linguistic conventions. And so such incorrigibility has no necessity to it; just as we could alter the rules of chess to allow a rook to be moved diagonally, so we could alter the rules of our language game to make epistemic access to our own pain corrigible, or epistemic access to others' pain incorrigible, or both, or neither. All that a grammatical investigation can tell us about is the rules of our own language.

172

What Wittgenstein actually says is so close to this that the confusion is understandable; but there is a crucial difference. Consider: is it really true that "we could alter the rules of chess to allow a rook to be moved diagonally"?

Certainly, if by "rook" one means the actual physical object that plays that role in the game. We can make up any rules we like about how to move *that*; we can play backgammon with it, or toss it over a net, or whack it with a bat. But if by "rook" one instead means something *defined in terms of the rules of chess* (the current rules, that is), then nothing counts as a rook except in so far as it is moved in accordance with those rules.

In the same way, we can devise whatever rules we like for using words like "pain", "mine" and so on, understood as *sounds or written marks* – what the Wittgenstein of the *Tractatus* would call the *signs* as opposed to the *symbols*. In other words, we can change what we mean by our words. But to say, as Wittgenstein may be imagined to say, that the incorrigibility of pain is a matter of linguistic convention is presumably to do more than state the trivial fact that it is a matter of convention that the word "pain" means something incorrigible; for it is obviously a matter of convention that it means anything at all. The stronger claim that Wittgenstein might be taken to make is that the word "pain", *meaning what it means*, is only conventionally associated with incorrigibility – so that an alteration in our linguistic conventions could bring it about that our epistemic access to our own pain is no longer incorrigible, *without changing the meaning of the word "pain"* (or the word "incorrigible", or any other of the words involved).

The real Wittgenstein agrees with our imaginary one in emphasizing that the rules of our language simply do not allow anything to *count* as a meaningful challenge to our awareness of our own pain. But the real Wittgenstein concludes that no such challenge makes *sense* (since it is in language that sense gets made). The Cartesian treats our incorrigible access to our own pain as an amazing discovery about the nature of the mind, *as though we might instead have discovered the opposite*; but the imaginary Wittgenstein makes a different version of the same mistake, treating such access as something rendered true by our linguistic conventions, *as though our conventions might have rendered it false*. And so both the Cartesian and the imaginary Wittgenstein see the incorrigibility of pain as *grounded* in something beyond itself (whether metaphysical or linguistic), something that explains it and secures it – some x such that, *but for that x*, pain would not be incorrigible. But what Wittgenstein wants us to see, what his grammatical reminders are reminding us of, is that since, given what "pain" means in our language, no sense has been assigned to expressions like "I don't know whether I'm in pain", it follows that no such x is either needed or possible; grammatical facts require no explanation or grounding, whether of a metaphysical or a linguistic sort.

Notes

1. The edition referred to in this chapter is *Zettel* (1988).
2. Love involves continuance. The moment love begins, if it is love that begins, it is sure to continue, and continue for a while. The moment pain begins, it may also end; it can be momentary, and it is not sure to continue even for a while, although it may.
3. Although less dramatic, consider the efforts of Mr Darcy to overcome his love for Elizabeth Bennet in *Pride and Prejudice*.
4. Of course, some (kinds of) pains are feelings in the way that love is a feeling, say the pain of unrequited love. The pain of unrequited love is localized where and as the feeling of love is. Other (kinds of) pains-that-are-feelings are relevantly similar to love. The grief after a death, the sweet sorrow of parting from good friends: none of these goes off quickly. Interestingly, pains-that-are-feelings are typically not challenged – or are challenged only in the sense that the sincerity of a claim to one of them is challenged. That is, they are treated somewhat like pains-that-are-not-feelings, like burning, stabbing, throbbing, sharp or dull pains. But pains-that-are-feelings do not readily sort into burning, stabbing, throbbing, sharp or dull, although they are sometimes readily described as aches. Rather, like love, they are deep and can deepen (can they be shallow?). This seems to put pains-that-are-feelings in an interesting hinterland: while they are more like love than like pains-that-are-not-feelings, they mimic some of the features of such pains; in particular we seem to cede authority over them to their claimant.

Further reading

Tractatus, 3.262–3.42.

FIFTEEN

Teaching and learning

Arata Hamawaki

Seen from a certain perspective, the expressions that we use in language can seem to be, as Wittgenstein put it, "dead" (see *PI* §454). After all, in one sense, the expressions themselves are mere marks on a piece of paper or on the blackboard, or sounds in the air. What gives those expressions "life", that is, what is it that makes those expressions bearers of meanings? I think that it is against the background of this question that Wittgenstein's preoccupation with teaching and learning a language gets its significance, but I find that it is not an easy matter saying what that significance is. In Section 2 of *Philosophical Investigations*,[1] Wittgenstein describes what he calls "a language more primitive than ours":

> The language is meant to serve for communication between builder A and an assistant B. A is building with building-stones: there are blocks, pillars, slabs and beams. B has to pass the stones, and that in the order in which A needs them. For this purpose they use a language consisting of the words "block", "pillar", "slab", "beam". A calls them out; – B brings the stone which he has learnt to bring at such-and-such a call. – Conceive this as a complete primitive language. (*PI* §1)

Can we follow Wittgenstein's instruction to us? Can we conceive of those expressions and their use of them as exhibiting a complete primitive language? What would we be conceiving? Is the use of those expressions by the builders a use of language? Do they mean something by them, or are they just sending out signals, as when a bee sends out signals that direct the rest of the colony to a nearby hive? What is the difference between saying something, and sending out signals?[2] I think that when we begin to reflect on such questions it is difficult to know how we might answer them. And this is in effect to acknowledge that we really do not have a clear idea of what we mean when we say that a certain instruction is intended to teach a child language. How are we picturing what it is that we are teaching the child, and how is the instruction we give supposed to be related to what that instruction is intended to teach? On what basis are we to say that the child has come into possession of language? A possible answer to that question would be this: we say that the child speaks when he uses expressions to say something, something that we understand. But such an answer would obviously assume what we were trying to explain. For we want to know what it is for the child to use expressions to say something, what it is for there to be something to understand in the way that he uses the expressions. Can we give a non-trivial answer to this question?

The passage from Augustine that opens *Philosophical Investigations* contains a picture of what it is that we are teaching the child when we give him instruction in a language. We are teaching him that certain words name, or refer to, or stand for, certain things. Wittgenstein writes,

> These words, it seems to me, give us a particular picture of the essence of human language. It is this: the individual words in language name objects – sentences are combinations of such names. – In this picture of language we find the roots of the following idea: Every word has a meaning. This meaning is corellated with the word. It is the object for which the word stands.   (*PI* §1)

The relation of reference, or naming, is to be set up by what Wittgenstein calls "ostensive definition" or "ostensive teaching".[3] Now if it were possible to define, or to teach, a term ostensively, then that would give us a way of explaining the difference between an empty ritual and a meaningful use of language. The latter would consist of terms that were given meaning through ostensive definition, or teaching, and the former would not. What is at stake, then, in the success or failure of ostensive teaching is whether we can understand how someone finds their way into language from a position outside it. In that sense, we could think of the child as representative of our own position: if we can understand how a child enters language, then we would have an understanding of what language is, what differentiates a meaningful use of signs from their use in an empty ritual.

Can ostensive teaching or ostensive definition do the work that it needs to do if it is to provide support to the Augustinian picture of the essence of language? In ostensive teaching we teach someone the name of an object by uttering a certain sound before an object that we are jointly attending to, one that the teacher may single out by the gesture of pointing. But Wittgenstein observes that even if teacher and pupil are attending to the same object, there are a number of different aspects of the object that the teacher could be taken to be referring to when he utters the sound he does:

> The definition of the number two, "That is called 'two'" – point-
> ing to two nuts – is perfectly exact. – But how can two be defined
> like that? The person one gives the definition to doesn't know
> what one wants to call "two"; he will suppose that "two" is the
> name given to this group of nuts ... And he might equally well
> take the name of a person, of which I give an ostensive definition,
> as that of a colour, of a race, or even of a point of the compass.
> That is to say: an ostensive definition can be variously interpreted
> in every case.   (*PI* §28)

Any object can be considered from different perspectives: depending on our interests and goals, a person can be considered as an example of a colour, a size, a shape, an ethnicity, a species, a number, or even a point of the compass. These more general concepts, you could say, lay out different possible fields of reference. For example, in order to learn by ostension what the word "sepia" means, the child will already have to have some kind of understanding of the difference between, say, a word for a number and a word for a colour. But what is that difference? How would we explain that difference?

Wittgenstein treats that difference as in part what he calls a "gram-matical" one. What he means by that is that there are certain things it makes sense to say about a colour that it does not make sense to say about a number, and vice versa. For example, it makes sense to ask how bright or how intense a colour is, but not how bright or how intense a number is. In that sense, colour terms have a certain position in our language, one that differentiates them from the position of number terms.[4] To know the difference between a colour and a number is not a matter of knowing what features are common to colour and not to numbers, and vice versa, but of knowing how to use colour terms and number terms according to their position in our language.[5] Thus an understanding of the meaning of an expression involves not just an understanding of what it "refers" to (call this the vertical dimension of meaning), but also an understanding of the ways that it can be combined with other words (call this the horizontal dimension of meaning). We are to look for the meaning of a term not only in what it "refers" to but in the place that the term has in our language as a whole. Wittgenstein writes, "So we might say: the ostensive definition explains the use – the meaning – of the word when the overall role of the word in language is clear" (*PI* §30).

The Augustinian picture could be said to fail to acknowledge the extent to which the words we learn are interlocked with each other. This point is connected to what Wittgenstein meant when he, famously, said "to imagine a language means to imagine a form of life" (*PI* §19). To see this, consider what is involved in learning the phrase "looking at something" or "to look at something". We might explain looking as something that you do when you turn your attention to something. But it is essential to looking that it is something that you can either do carefully or not (just as it belongs to reading and drawing, but not to seeing or remembering) – that is part of its "grammar". (You do not know what "looking at something" means unless you know that.) One sees this only if one sees the relation between looking and finding something out, and one in turn sees how those are related only if one sees the relation between those and missing something, or not finding something, and how all those are related to wanting to know something.[6] One can understand how to use the word "looking", that is, in what contexts it makes sense to use it, only if one grasps the point of looking, and grasping the point of looking is inseparable from knowing what counts as finding something out, and wanting to know something.[7] "Looking", together with "reading", "listening" and "drawing", project into a context in which it is combined with the words "carefully" or "uncarefully", but "seeing", "hearing", "remembering" and so on do not. To grasp why this is so, we need to understand the place that looking, reading and listening, on the one hand, and seeing, hearing and remembering, on the other, have in our form of life.[8] The idea here is that the point of these activities is not something that can be grasped independently of our grasping the interrelations of the terms that designate them in our language. Rather, the point of the activities is something that is, as it were, given in the ways in which they are interrelated. In this sense, language, as Wittgenstein conceived of it, does not just facilitate our attaining of ends that we already have independently of acquiring language. Rather, language makes possible a form of life that would not be possible without it. Our form of life is essentially embodied in our language: our form of life, you might say, is a linguistic one.[9] Thus, not only do you have to be acquainted with a form of life as a precondition of learning the meaning of a word, but learning the meaning of a word *is* to be initiated into a form of life. In this light, Augustine's description of the teaching of language as setting up a correlation between a word and the object or event, or type of object or event, that it names is a gross underdescription of just what it is that we teach the child, or rather, what the child must learn from us, even if we do not explicitly teach it to him.[10]

Augustine's picture was supposed to give us the *essence* of human language. On this picture, what is essential is the naming relation, supposedly given by ostensive definition; other aspects of language, such as the way we use a word, are depicted as derivative. For once a term is ostensively defined, its meaning would be given, and then the use of the term could be derived from its meaning. The use is something that merely accompanies the meaning, a kind of outer cloak draped over what is truly essential, which is the meaning itself. Put in such a general way, it emerges that Augustine's picture is just one of many ways of thinking of meaning, of our meaning something by an expression, for example, our meaning plus by "+", as something that *underlies* and *explains* the use that we make of the expression. Long after doubt has been cast on the adequacy of Augustine's picture itself, Wittgenstein continues to discuss the deeper and more general idea that provides its ultimate source of appeal. Thus we should not think of Wittgenstein as simply refuting views such as Augustine's but as probing them to articulate the felt need of which it is one expression.[11] The deeper picture here is that what we say and do in teaching a child the meaning of a term are mere "accompaniments" of meaning: what is essential is the state of mind that this teaching is supposed to *effect*, a state of mind from which all the examples we give in teaching are supposed to flow.[12] Why do we feel that there must be such a state of mind? Or to put the same point differently: what predicament do we think that we would face if there were no such state?

The feeling that there must be such a state is both given encouragement and thrown into crisis by Wittgenstein's presentation of "scenes of instruction"[13] in which our attempts to teach a pupil misfire in a radical and disconcerting way. It is a commonplace that any instruction we give can be misunderstood. That in itself is nothing to be alarmed about. When specific misunderstandings arise, if we are able teachers, we find ways of correcting them. But the wayward pupils with whom Wittgenstein is preoccupied exhibit a misunderstanding so basic or so radical that it is hard to know how it is possible to correct them. The silence that overcomes us when we are at wit's end with such a pupil is felt to signify not a personal failing, such as a failure of imagination, but something like a metaphysical one, as though the gulf between us is so great that nothing we can do seems in principle able to provide a bridge.[14] Here's one such example:

Now we get the pupil to continue a series (say +2) beyond 1000 – and he writes 1000, 1004, 1008, 1012. We say to him: "Look what you've done!" – He doesn't understand. We say: "You were meant to add *two*: Look how you began the series!" – He answers: "Yes, isn't it right? I thought that was how I was *meant* to do it". – Or suppose he pointed to the series and said: "But I went on in the same way". – But it would be no use to say: "But can't you see … ?" – and repeat the old examples and explanations. – In such a case we might say, perhaps: It comes natural to this person to understand our order with our explanations as *we* should understand the order: "Add 2 up to 1000, 4 up to 2000, 6 up to 3000 and so on". Such a case would present similarities with one in which a person naturally reacted to the gesture of pointing with the hand by looking in the direction of the line from finger-tip to wrist, not from wrist to finger-tip.　　　　　(*PI* §185)

The pupil was meant to continue in a certain way, but the examples I gave the pupil do not seem to dictate that he continue in one way rather than another. The examples themselves always leave open other ways of going on from them. Yet clearly, if I meant anything at all, I meant that the pupil go on in a specific way at any juncture of the continuation. My way of understanding the rule did not leave it open how the pupil is to go after he reaches 1000. But what is "my way of understanding the rule"? It seems to have the property that whatever it is, it must be significantly different from the examples I give, for those seem to leave open different continuations, and my understanding of the rule does not. But how could I articulate what my way of understanding is except by giving further examples of what I mean? Each of the examples I give may succeed in warding off this or that specific misunderstanding, but it can seem that what I mean by "+ 2" must ward off all possible misunderstandings, that it must settle how the expression is used in every possible situation. In comparison to the state of meaning itself, it looks as if the ordinary explanations and examples I give are somehow incomplete, and that only what *I* have got could give the complete explanation. But what could this state be, one that has "traversed" all the possible steps in advance? When I imagine examples such as the one given above, I seem to feel my act of meaning retreating inwards, and what I say and do when I offer instruction becoming drained of meaning, since their meaning would have to come from a mysterious inner state. So it begins to look like the examples I give can function only as evidence for what I mean: the meaning itself is something necessarily hidden, something the pupil can only guess at.[15] Wittgenstein wants us to recognize that we have no clear idea, or rather no coherent idea at all, of what such a hidden state could be: "You have no model of this superlative fact, but you are seduced into using a super-expression. (It might be called a philosophical superlative.)" (§192). The sense of being reduced to stammering in the face of the wayward pupil is pivotal. It is as if I tried to get a cat to look in a certain direction by making a pointing gesture. What I make available to the pupil seems to fall short of anything having meaning or semantic content: the examples I give seem to be nothing more than the production of marks on a piece of paper, or scratchings on a blackboard. What I produce is felt to be "dead", and the "life", the meaning, needs to be injected from the outside.

But it needs to be said that that is not the way someone who understands what is being said experiences the expressions that are being used. What is the difference? For Wittgenstein the difference is not that such a person manages to guess what I mean from the (fallible) evidence I make available to him, and the wayward pupil does not. Rather, the difference is that he knows how to use the expressions that I employ in the instructions I give him: he knows how to participate in the practice that we have with those expressions. The standard for the correct use of the expression is embodied in the practice, and I can be said to know that standard in so far as I can produce behaviour that accords with the practice. Thus in the context of the practice the examples that I use fully manifest what I mean to someone who is a party to the practice of using the expressions I employ in the examples.[16] If one is not a party to the practice, then to him, the expressions are "dead". But that does not mean that the condition of their "being alive" is that there be an inner state of meaning that "animates" them. Rather, the expressions are "alive" only in the context of the practice in which they are employed. Thus the scenes of instruction that Wittgenstein depicts, in which the examples I give to the pupil radically misfire, do not show that my meaning what I do by an expression must reside in a mysterious inner state that somehow outruns all the examples that I could give, a state from which all subsequent use of the expression could be derived, but rather they show that it is a presupposition of my behaviour displaying meaning that one have a prior familiarity with a common practice of using the expressions.[17]

Wittgenstein wants, in a way, to turn the picture of meaning as an inner state on its head. He wants us to see that it is only *in* the use or the practice that we have with certain expressions that they can be said to have meaning. He writes,

Let me ask this: what has the expression of a rule – say a sign-post – got to do with my actions? What sort of connexion is there

here? – Perhaps this one: I have been trained to react to this sign in a particular way, and now I do so react to it ... I have further indicated that a person goes by a sign-post only in so far as there exists a regular use of sign-posts, a custom.   (*PI* §198)

An apt comparison here is with an activity such as a coronation. Only in a certain context of a certain established ritual does the action of placing a crown on someone's head count as a coronation. A mental state of intending the placing of a crown on someone's head does not make the act a coronation. Similarly, merely using a symbol with the intention that it be taken to mean something does not make it the case that the use of the sign is a linguistic act. It is only if the act exemplifies a practice that it can be understood as a linguistic act. The concept of a practice is in this sense fundamental to our understanding anything as a linguistic act.[18]

I started with the question whether there is any non-trivial description of the difference between using an expression meaningfully and using it emptily, the difference between a use that is "alive" and one that is "dead". And we are seeing that for Wittgenstein, the answer can only be that there is not. He puts this by saying that we can only adduce "exterior facts" about language.[19] What he means by this is that the best that we can do is to clear away this misunderstanding or that misunderstanding, as these misunderstandings arise in everyday life. We imagine that we must be able to do more than that. We imagine that if there is anything to understand at all, then there must be something that would clear away all possible misunderstandings (cf. §87).[20] And, indeed, if there were such a thing, that would show us the difference between speaking meaningfully and uttering meaningless noises – it would explain what it is to speak a language *überhaupt*. This is the significance of the silence in the face of the wayward pupils who wend their way through the pages of the *Investigations* – all those many times our spade is turned.[21] We can give explanations only within the practices that we have, and so we can give explanations only to those who are party to our practices. And we have the practices we have only because, as it turns out, human nature is such that children can be initiated into these practices through the right kind of training. How that happens is something that could be explained in more detail. But however detailed, no such explanation would give us what we seek in philosophy, which would be an understanding of what makes it the case that someone is using an expression meaningfully. This is bound to be dissatisfying, but for Wittgenstein this dissatisfaction is one that we must learn to live with, since it is dissatisfaction with the nature of language itself.[22]

Notes

1. The edition referred to in this chapter is *Philosophical Investigations* (2001a).
2. For helpful and interesting discussions of this question in the context of *Investigations* §2, see Rhees (1970b: 71–85), and Goldfarb (2007).
3. Note that Wittgenstein himself distinguishes these, but I do not think that the distinction is relevant for the purpose of this discussion.
4. "The word 'number' in the definition does indeed shew this place; does shew the post at which we station the word" (*PI* §29).
5. We do not often command a clear view of the position of a term in the language in this sense. For Wittgenstein, this gives rise to the "grammatical" confusions that are the source of philosophical problems. For example, we confuse the grammar of "understands" with the grammar of a conscious state or process, say, "thinking of a number from one to ten". But if we are speaking of a conscious state or process, it makes sense to ask, "When did that happen?" "When did it start and when did it begin?" "How long did it last?" "Was it going all the time, even when asleep?" These questions are not obviously in place if we say that someone knows or understands something, or that someone has a capacity, like the capacity to juggle, or to ride a bike. "The grammar of the word 'knows' is evidently closely related to that of 'can', 'is able to'. But also closely related to that of 'understands'" (*PI* §150). Learning to ride a bike is something that takes place over time, not at a time. That is a grammatical statement. To say that the concept of learning to ride a bike is vague because it is not clear exactly when one has acquired that capacity evinces a grammatical confusion.
6. It makes sense to say: "I looked at him, but I didn't really see him."
7. This indicates a difference between signals and the application of a word. Signals are either useful or not in the context of a certain activity, the use of a word must also answer to queries about whether the use made sense, or was non-sense. In learning a language, you learn the difference between sense and non-sense.
8. For more examples in this vein, and a richly developed and excellent discussion of them, see Cavell (1979b: esp. 183).
9. I want to say that while creatures without language can be said to look, looking means something different when it is applied to human beings because of the role of looking in our form of life, and that role is given in the connections that the expression "looking" has with other expressions, such as, "reading", "listening" and "drawing".
10. Stanley Cavell writes, "What we learn is not just what we have studied; and what we have been taught is not just what we were intended to learn. What we have in our memories is not just what we have memorized" (1979b: 177). It is widely recognized by scholars of Wittgenstein that sharing a form of life, for example, being able to engage in certain social activities, such as building, or playing a game, is a precondition of learning a language. But I think that it is still relatively underappreciated that for Wittgenstein our form of life is essentially embodied in our language.
11. It is questionable whether Augustine's picture is even sophisticated enough to label a philosophical view. You might think of it as an orientation that many more sophisticated philosophical views share.
12. "If I am inclined to suppose that a mouse has come into being by spontaneous generation out of grey rags and dust, I shall do well to examine those rags very closely to see how a mouse may have hidden in them, how it may have got there

and so on. But if I am convinced that a mouse cannot come into being from these things, then this investigation will perhaps be superfluous" (§52). Here, the mouse would be the meaning, and the use, the grey rags and dust. For an illuminating discussion of the significance of this passage, see Diamond (1992: 39–73).

13. The expression is from Stanley Cavell.

14. You might say that such pupils represent "hyperbolic" possibilities of misunderstanding. This brings to mind Descartes' "hyperbolic doubt". It would be useful to compare the distinction between ordinary and hyperbolic possibilities here with the distinction between ordinary and hyperbolic epistemic possibilities, such as the possibility that one is dreaming as it functions in Cartesian scepticism about what we can know.

15. "'But do you really explain to the other person what you yourself understand? Don't you get him to *guess* the essential thing? You give him examples, – but he has to guess their drift, to guess your intention'. – Every explanation which I can give myself I give to him too" (§210).

16. "But if a person has not yet got the *concepts*, I shall teach him to use the words by means of *examples* and by *practice*. – And when I do this I do not communicate less to him than I know myself" (§208).

17. "Philosophy simply puts everything before us, and neither explains nor deduces anything. – Since everything lies open to view there is nothing to explain. For what is hidden, for example, is of no interest to us" (§126).

18. One thing that is shown by what I am calling "the example of the wayward pupil" is that initiation of a child into the practice of our language depends on the child's ability, and willingness, to catch on to the practices through a certain training. And this depends in turn on the child's sharing with us certain natural responses, or a sense of what is and is not natural. The child must find it natural to look in the direction in which our finger points, agree with us in our judgements about what counts as going on in the same way, find salient in a situation what we find salient there, be comforted by what we are comforted by, feel pain by what gives us pain, laugh at what we laugh at, and so on. For a bravura treatment of this point, see Cavell (1979b: 168–90).

19. "In giving explanations I already have to use language full-blown (not some sort of preparatory, provisional one); this by itself shews that I can adduce only exterior facts about language" (*PI* §120).

20. "One might say: an explanation serves to remove or to avert a misunderstanding – one, that is, that would occur but for the explanation; not every one that I can imagine … The sign-post is in order – if, under normal circumstances, it fulfills its purpose" (*PI* §87).

21. See Cavell (2005: esp. 112–14).

22. In addition to the writings by Cavell, Diamond, Goldfarb and Rhees mentioned here, I have found helpful guidance from the work of Barry Stroud and John McDowell. See, in particular, Stroud (2000) and McDowell (2009). I am grateful for discussions with Kelly Jolley on the issues discussed in this chapter.

SIXTEEN

Expression and avowal

David H. Finkelstein

But that which is in him, how can I see it? Between his experience and me there is always the expression!

Here is the picture: He sees it immediately, I only mediately. But that's not the way it is. He doesn't see something and describe it to us.   (*LWPP II* 92)

I

I am often able to say what is on, or in, my own mind, that is, what I want, believe, fear, expect, intend or hope; whether I am feeling joy or pain; whether I like the taste of this wine or find that joke funny. I seem, moreover, to manage this sort of self-ascription, or avowal, without needing to rely on the evidence that other people require in order to ascribe mental states to me. In his late work, Wittgenstein often writes about psychological self-ascriptions. Again and again he suggests that, in doing philosophy, we are liable to cling to one or another bad explanation or misleading picture of them. He aims to reorient our thinking about avowals by urging us to view them as expressions, and so to see a sincere utterance of "I am in pain" as akin to a pained wince or groan. My aim in what follows is to provide an introduction to this strand in his writing.

A good place to begin is with the quotation above – our epigraph – which was written during the final two weeks of Wittgenstein's life. In it, he sketches a "picture" that we can think of as comprising two claims. The first is that a person knows what is going on in his own mind ("that which is in him") by a kind of inwardly directed observation or perception. The second claim is that one cannot know what is going on in the mind of another person in as direct a manner as this. So: while you are able to perceive your own mental goings-on, my access to your psychology is always mediated by your behaviour. You "see" your own, for example, pains; I see only the behaviour to which your pains give rise. In this sense, your behavioural expressions of pain stand *between* me and that which they express. ("Between his experience and me there is always the expression!")

Of course, the idea is not that you literally *see* your own states of mind. (You do not use your eyes.) It is, rather, that you have a kind of access to them that is, in significant respects, akin to your visual access to what is before your eyes. Philosophers and psychologists have held a range of positions that fit this characterization. According to some – for example Bertrand Russell (1912) – while "inner sense" is in certain notable respects like the outer senses, it is nonetheless more direct and less fallible than seeing, hearing, smelling and so on ever are, or could be.[1] According to other (typically more recent and more naturalistic) theorists (see e.g. Armstrong 1968; Humphrey 1986; Lycan 1996), inner sense is just one fallible perceptual modality among others – a process that is epistemically on all fours with seeing or hearing, except that it happens to be directed inward, towards goings-on in the mind/ brain rather than outward towards the external world. As we shall see, Wittgenstein takes the whole gamut of such positions to be confused. Indeed, the whole gamut of such positions is a species of a broader genus that he would have us reject. Thus he writes: "Other people cannot be said to learn of my sensations *only* from behaviour, – for *I* cannot be said to learn of them. I *have* them" (*PI* §246).[2] Wittgenstein rejects not only views according to which I learn of my own (e.g.) sensations by some sort of inner sense, but the very idea that I learn of them *at all*.

But now, this might seem puzzling (or worse). After all, Wittgenstein would not deny that I am generally able to say when I am in pain and when I am not. Does my having this ability not entail that, somehow or other, I learn of my own sensations?

II

We can begin to address this question, along with our overall topic, by considering the following, from §244 of *Philosophical Investigations*:

[W]ords are connected with the primitive, the natural, expressions of the sensations and used in their place. A child has hurt himself and he cries; and then adults talk to him and teach him exclamations and, later, sentences. They teach the child new pain-behaviour.

"So you are saying that the word 'pain' really means crying?" – On the contrary: the verbal expression of pain replaces crying and does not describe it.

Think of this passage as suggesting a way to understand (what Wittgenstein would call) the grammar of pain self-ascriptions. What a child learns when he learns to avow his own pains is, so the thought goes, "new pain-behaviour", that is, new ways to express pains. Whereas, before, the child might express his pains by wincing or crying out, now he can also express them by saying, for example, "I bumped my toe, and it hurts!" The child learns to express his pains *by* self-ascribing them.

While *Philosophical Investigations* §244 concerns the grammar of sensations in particular, Wittgenstein elsewhere indicates that the expressive character of their deployment in the first person is a mark of psychological attributions more generally. For example, he writes:

The statement "I am expecting a bang at any moment" is an *expression* of expectation. (Z §53)

For even when I myself say "I was a little irritated about him" – – how do I know how to apply these words so precisely? Is it really so clear? Well, they are simply an expression. (*LWPP II* 70)[3]

Plan for the treatment of psychological concepts.
Psychological verbs characterized by the fact that the third person of the present is to be verified by observation, the first person not.
Sentences in the third person of the present: information. In the first person present: expression. ((Not quite right.))
The first person of the present akin to an expression.
(Z §472)

I shall leave for later *Zettel* §472's doubly parenthetical "Not quite right."[4] For now, it suffices to say that, according to Wittgenstein, we should understand a very wide range of psychological self-ascriptions – not only ascriptions of sensation, but of attitude and emotion – as akin to pained winces, desirous glances and angry door-slammings.

Clearly, what such a suggestion amounts to depends a good deal on how one chooses to address the following pair of questions: (i) in precisely which respects are psychological self-ascriptions akin to winces, smiles and door-slammings? And (ii) how should we think about winces, smiles, door-slammings and so on? What does it mean to call such behaviours *expressions*? In what remains of the present section, I shall say a little about Wittgenstein on question (ii). Later (in §IV), I shall argue against a widespread understanding of him that, I believe, goes wrong by misrepresenting his answer to question (i).

What does it mean to call something that a person does with, say, his eyes and mouth an expression? Wittgenstein writes:

> "We *see* emotion." – As opposed to what? – We do not see facial contortions and make inferences from them (like a doctor framing a diagnosis) to joy, grief, boredom. We describe a face immediately as sad, radiant, bored, even when we are unable to give any other description to the features. – Grief, one would like to say, is personified in the face. (Z §225)

We could say that for Wittgenstein, an expression is, typically, the perceptible emergence of some psychological phenomenon (or phenomena) in a creature's doings. A facial expression can make someone's state of mind immediately manifest to others. This does not, I hope, sound like a technical or idiosyncratic notion of expression. Pre-philosophically, we take it for granted that it is possible – and not at all uncommon – to see in a face, or hear in a voice, that someone else is, for example, pleased, anxious, angry, in pain or dubious about what we have just said. When we are doing philosophy, however, we are liable to conclude that this cannot really be the case – that whenever we take ourselves to see psychology in someone's face, we are in fact seeing no more than physical movements ("facial contortions") and making inferences about the hidden states and processes that might have caused them. Wittgenstein's criticisms of the ways in which we arrive at this conclusion run deep in his work, and it goes beyond the scope of the present chapter to explicate them. Any such explication would require discussion of his much-debated remarks about signs, meaning and rule-following, for he thinks that we are inclined to just the same kinds of confusion whether we are talking about the relation between signs and their semantic significance or that between behaviour and its psychological significance. For now, it will have to suffice for me to note that, according to Wittgenstein, just as we can (if we are rightly situated, know the language, etc.) see meaning in the words on a page, we can (if we have the right sensibilities, know enough about the person, etc.) see psychology expressed in someone's behaviour.

Wittgenstein's interlocutor tends to take it for granted that all we see when we look at a face are what amount to contortions – movements that are, in themselves, devoid of psychological content. For this reason, he suspects that Wittgenstein's willingness to allow that we can see psychology in a face commits him to a kind of reductive behaviourism. This interlocutor, in effect, reasons as follows: "If Wittgenstein imagines that we can see psychology in mere movements, he must hold that psychological states and processes are nothing more than behaviour; he must be 'a behaviourist in disguise'."[5] From the perspective of Wittgenstein's interlocutor, we must choose between an implausible reductive behaviourism and a position according to which we can, at best, make inferences about hidden states and processes that cause the in-themselves-psychologically-neutral movements and noises that we perceive when we look at and listen to other people. In order to understand what Wittgenstein means when he writes about expression, one needs to reject the assumption that is common to both horns of this dilemma.[6]

III

In the preceding section, I indicated that according to Wittgenstein, a very broad range of self-ascriptions should be understood as expressing the very states or events that they self-ascribe. It is important to add that he does not think *every* psychological self-ascription is such an expression. I might describe myself as angry on the basis of observing (or having it pointed out to me) that my recent behaviour towards my mother seems to be passive–aggressive. Wittgenstein would not hold that such a self-ascription was an expression of anger. He writes: "When someone says 'I hope he'll come' – is this a *report* about his state of mind, or an *expression* of his hope? – I can, for example, say it to myself. And surely I am not giving myself a report. It may be a sigh; but it need not" (PI §585).[7] It is the last sentence of this passage that I want to call to your attention. Whether or not some utterance of "I hope he'll come" should be understood as "a sigh" – that is, an expression – will, according to Wittgenstein, vary from occasion to occasion. This point is developed in the section of the *Investigations* that immediately follows the one just quoted:

> The exclamation "I'm longing to see him!" may be an act of expecting. But I can utter the same words as the result of

self-observation, and then they might mean: "So, after all that has happened, I am still longing to see him". The point is: what led up to these words?

(PI §586)

The same sentence that expresses my expectation on one occasion might, on another occasion, report a fact that I have learned via self-observation. If I know my own mental state via observation or inference, then when I self-ascribe it, I do not thereby express it. Now in such a case – one in which I characterize my own state of mind on the basis of self-observation or inference – I do not speak with what philosophers call "first-person authority".[8] There is, then, a connection between avowing one's state of mind expressively, as it were, and speaking about it authoritatively. My aim in what remains of the present section is to shed light on this connection and thereby bring Wittgenstein's suggestion that we understand avowals as expressing their subject matter into sharper focus.

I shall begin by noting two features of first-person authority. First, if you want to know what I am thinking, planning, hoping, believing, feeling and so on, I am, as a rule, the best person to ask. This is not to say that I am never wrong about my own state of mind, nor is it to deny that there are occasions when another person knows my psychological condition better than I know it myself. I might judge that I am not angry about something when, later, I come to the conclusion that, after all, I was. And a close friend might realize that I am angry before I do. Still, such cases are exceptional. Almost always, the first and best person to ask about someone's state of mind is the subject himself.

A second distinctive feature of first-person authority is that I very often seem able to speak about my own state of mind without basing what I say on any behavioural (or other) evidence. Contrast this with what it takes to speak responsibly about another person's psychological condition. Imagine I tell you that a mutual friend of ours is feeling sad, or that she loves a particular movie, or that she wants to visit Spain. You might simply accept my statement, or you might ask me how I know, or why I believe, what I have said about our friend. Whether or not you ask for grounds, if my claim is responsible, I ought to be able to provide some. I ought to be able to say, for example, "She told me that she's been saving up to buy a plane ticket to Barcelona" or "Well, she *looks* sad". Now consider a situation in which I tell you that *I* am feeling sad, or that *I* love a particular movie, or that *I* want to visit Spain. Here it would be odd, on the face of it, for you to ask me for grounds or evidence in support of my statement unless you had some quite specific reason for thinking that I might be wrong about myself.

Moreover, it does not seem as if I need to be aware of any behavioural (or other) facts that constitute evidential support in order for me to self-ascribe my mental state responsibly. I can just say, for example, "I am feeling sad", even though I have not exhibited any behaviour that would justify an attribution of sadness to me.

How does Wittgenstein's suggestion that we understand avowals as expressions enable us to better make sense of these two features of first-person authority? First, why am I the best person to ask about *my* state of mind? We might as well ask why mine is the best *face* to consider if you want to know my state of mind. If I am feeling, say, joy or anger, this is liable to be apparent, visible, in my facial expression. And, as we saw in the last section, Wittgenstein holds that the same is true of mental state self-ascriptions: they often make a person's psychological condition manifest. One reason that I am the best person to ask about my state of mind is that asking me is liable to put you in a position to hear in what I say about myself (and so to learn directly and at first hand) what I am thinking or feeling.

Let us turn to the second feature of first-person authority mentioned a moment ago. Why do I not require behavioural (or other) evidence in order to speak about my own state of mind – for example, my own amusement or pain? Well, in order for me to express a pain in my tooth *by wincing*, I do not need epistemic grounds that support the proposition that my tooth hurts. Wittgenstein's point could be put this way: If an expression of pain or amusement takes the form of a sentence about myself, instead of a wince or a laugh, it does not follow that epistemic justification is suddenly called for. If we understand an avowal as akin to a pained wince or an amused laugh, then we should not expect to find that it requires, or is based on, evidential or observational grounds.

IV

Wittgenstein's remarks about the expressive dimension of mental-state avowals have tended not to be taken very seriously by his readers. Instead we find some commentators placing great emphasis on the supposed fact that Wittgenstein's position is here open to easy refutation, while other more sympathetic readers try to minimize the significance of these unfortunate remarks. Both responses are, I suggest, due to a tradition of commentary that reads this strand in his work uncharitably. Or so I shall claim in what follows.

At the end of the preceding section, I emphasized one respect in which (what we might call) the grammar of winces is different from

that of observation reports: the former do not require epistemic justification; they are not epistemically "based on" observation, inference
or anything else. Now, another difference between the grammar of
winces and that of reports is that winces do not literally *say* anything
either true or false. (I may mislead you by wincing and cradling my
cheek when I feel no pain, but if that is all I do, then I have not *lied* to
you.) Wittgenstein's oft-repeated suggestion that we understand avowals as, or as akin to, expressions has been widely understood as showing that he is committed to a position according to which an utterance
of "I'm in pain" or "I expect an explosion" likewise says nothing either
true or false.[9] Following recent practice, I shall call this sort of position
"simple expressivism".[10] Now, simple expressivism *is* difficult to take
seriously. But, I shall argue, Wittgenstein ought not be read as a simple
expressivist.

Let us begin by trying to get in view why – or one reason why –
simple expressivism is unappealing *prima facie*. Imagine the following
scenario: my friend Tom is moving from one apartment to another
a few blocks away. Rather than hire movers, he has asked everyone
he knows to help with loading and unloading a rented truck. I have
agreed to participate, but on the day of the move, I phone him and say:
"I'm sorry. I've wrenched my back, and now it's hurting a lot. I just
don't think I can help with the move today." Tom, who knows that I
dislike lifting large objects, says: "Oh please. Your back doesn't hurt;
you just don't feel like getting off the couch." I reply: "No, Tom. I'm
telling you the truth; it hurts like hell." Given the sort of expressivism that Wittgenstein is widely thought to espouse, when I say, "I'm
telling you the truth; it hurts like hell", I seem to be either mistaken
or conceptually confused. For even if I am in awful pain, when I say,
"it hurts", I cannot, on this view, be saying something true. Moreover,
given simple expressivism, Tom and I should not be understood as
even *disagreeing*: he has made a factual claim to the effect that I am
not experiencing back pain, and I have made no claim at all. But it
seems undeniable that we *are* disagreeing. Hence the unattractiveness
of simple expressivism.

It is worth comparing this expressivism about psychological self-
ascriptions with a more familiar sort of expressivism about moral
discourse, that is, with the sort of "emotivism" championed by, for
example, A. J. Ayer (1946) or C. L. Stevenson (1944). An emotivist
holds that an utterance such as "It's wrong to eat animals" expresses
an attitude of disapproval or a preference but does not say anything
true or false. Now, there are striking similarities between this sort of
view and the simple expressivism about psychological self-ascriptions

that Wittgenstein is thought to defend,[11] but there is a crucial difference as well. Emotivists are moved by a metaphysical conviction that there are no moral facts for moral discourse to be true to. But those who read Wittgenstein as a simple expressivist about psychological self-ascriptions do not take him to be sceptical about psychological facts as such. Rather, Wittgenstein is understood to hold that only *first-personal* uses of psychological predicates yield sentences that are not truth-apt. According to the Wittgenstein that emerges on this reading, if you say that someone other than yourself is unhappy (or in pain or hoping that it will rain ...), you *do* produce a truth-evaluable assertion. This, I suggest, is one reason why the sort of expressivism that Wittgenstein is thought to espouse has proved less attractive than emotivism. Given a familiar set of metaphysical scruples, there is some plausibility in a thought that might be put as follows: "When you and I disagree about whether it is wrong to eat animals, we are *really* disagreeing in our expressed attitudes of approval and disapproval, rather than about any supposed moral facts. I am expressing disapproval of certain practices, while you are expressing approval of them." But no such diagnosis of ordinary disagreement is available to the simple expressivist about psychological avowals. According to simple expressivism, if a friend of mine describes me as "wanting to visit Colorado in the spring" and I correct her, saying, "No; it's Wyoming that I want to visit", she has made a factual claim – a statement that is either true or false – and I have not. There just does not seem to be room here to explain our apparent disagreement by appeal to anything like conflicting expressions of approval and disapproval.

Of course, even if simple expressivism is blatantly unsatisfactory, Wittgenstein might still have defended it. But what speaks against attributing the position to Wittgenstein is not merely that it is unsatisfactory. What speaks against attributing it to him is, first, the absence of any clear or compelling textual grounds for doing so and, second, the fact that reading Wittgenstein as a simple expressivist makes what he *does* say about psychological self-ascriptions substantially less interesting and persuasive. I am not claiming that Wittgenstein ever comes out and asserts that avowals *are* truth-apt. But it is one thing for a philosopher not to explicitly address a question and quite another thing to read him as if he had provided a bad answer to it.

As it happens, Wittgenstein does seem to be committed to allowing that mental-state self-ascriptions have truth-values, even if he does not address the point directly. Consider §136 of *Philosophical Investigations*. Referring to something that he had written in the *Tractatus* ("The general form of propositions is: This is how things are"; *TLP* 4.5, Ogden's translation modified), Wittgenstein writes:

At bottom, giving "This is how things are" as the general form of propositions is the same as giving the definition: a proposition is whatever can be true or false. For instead of "This is how things are" I could have said "This is true". (Or again "This is false".) But we have

'p' is true = p
'p' is false = not-p.

And to say that a proposition is whatever can be true or false amounts to saying: we call something a proposition when *in our language* we apply the calculus of truth functions to it.

Wittgenstein goes on to criticize his former self, but he does not reject what is said about "true" and "false" here. He seems to retain a thought that might be put as follows: *given* a proposition, *p*, to which we apply the calculus of truth-functions in our language-game, there is no room to deny that *p* is truth-apt. How does this bear on the question of whether Wittgenstein should be read as a simple expressivist about psychological self-ascriptions? Well, we *do* apply the calculus of truth functions to our psychological self-ascriptions. In reply to someone who has just claimed that no one in the room is experiencing any pain, I might say, "I'm in the room, and I'm in pain, *so* what you just said is false." Thus, given what he thinks about truth, Wittgenstein seems committed to allowing that mental-state avowals are truth-apt.[12]

Why has Wittgenstein so often been read as holding that psychological self-ascriptions are neither true nor false? Some commentators have failed to see any other way to make sense of the suggestion that we understand avowals as expressions. These readers have clung to an assumption that has no real foothold in Wittgenstein's writings – an assumption that might be stated as follows: "I can let another person know the state of mind that I'm in *either* by expressing it *or* by saying something true about it. But I cannot, in a single speech act, *both* express my state of mind and say, truly, that I'm in it."[13] If this assumption were correct, then simple expressivism would be entailed by the claim that mental-state avowals are expressions of that which they avow. But the assumption is false.[14] As William Alston (1967: 16) puts the point:

I can express my enthusiasm for your plan just as well by saying 'I'm very enthusiastic about your plan', as I can by saying 'What a tremendous plan!', 'Wonderful', or 'Great!' I can express disgust at X just as well by saying 'I'm disgusted', as by saying 'How revolting', or 'Ugh'. I can express approval as well by saying 'I completely approve of what you are doing' as I can by saying 'Swell' or 'Good show'. And can express annoyance as well by saying "That annoys me no end" as by saying 'Damn'.

This shows that expressing and asserting are not mutually exclusive in the way commonly supposed. [15]

Once we give up the assumption that expressing and asserting are "mutually exclusive in the way commonly supposed", readings of Wittgenstein as a simple expressivist lose much of their plausibility.

Some of Wittgenstein's readers have taken the fact that he does not like to characterize avowals as "reports" [*Berichte*] (see e.g. *PI* §585) or as "descriptions" [*Beschreibungen*][16] to suggest that he understands them as neither true nor false. But I think it makes a good deal more sense to hear his reluctance to use these words in connection with psychological avowals as indicating that he takes "report" and "description" to be closely tied to concepts like *observation* and *epistemic justification*, which, as we have seen, he thinks are out of place in this context. Here, consider the following remark from *Zettel*:

> To call the expression of a sensation a *statement* [*Behauptung*] is misleading because 'testing', 'justification', 'confirmation', 'reinforcement' of the statement are connected with the word "statement" in the language-game. (Z §549)

According to the kind of reading that I am urging against, this remark might be glossed along the following lines: "A *statement* is the sort of thing that may be true or false. In this passage, Wittgenstein is claiming that when I express a sensation by avowing it, I am not making a statement and so not saying anything either true or false." But two things should, I think, strike us about the quoted passage. First, Wittgenstein does not say that it is *wrong* to call the expression of a sensation a statement (he does not say that the expression of a sensation is *not* a statement); he says rather that it is *misleading* to call such an expression a statement. And, second, the reason why this is misleading has to do with how the word "statement" is connected in our language-game with (i) "testing", (ii) "justification", (iii) "confirmation", and (iv) "reinforcement". Notice what is conspicuously absent from this list: "truth". According to Wittgenstein, it is misleading to refer to an avowal of pain as a "statement" because we think of statements as requiring justification or confirmation – *not* because we think of statements as having truth-values.[17]

V

At the end of §I, I quoted the following from *Philosophical Investigations*: "Other people cannot be said to learn of my sensations *only* from behaviour, – for *I* cannot be said to learn of them. I *have* them" (§246). I noted that this remark might appear puzzling. If I am able to say when I am in pain and when I am not, does it not follow that somehow or other I learn when I am in pain? While we *could* decide to speak of "learning" here, for Wittgenstein this would be to invite confusion. We do not say that I need to learn that I am in pain before I can express my pain by wincing or crying out. Talk of *learning* and of *grounds* or *justification* come together in our language-game. And a way to put some of what has emerged here would be to say that, for Wittgenstein, psychological self-ascriptions are very often outside the logical space of epistemic justification. Sometimes I do need to observe, or to think about, my own behaviour in order to discover, for example, whether I am angry. But, according to Wittgenstein, I am often able to express my state of mind by avowing it, without needing to discover – to learn – anything.[18]

Notes

1. John Locke may be read as defending a view of this sort in Book II of Locke ([1690] 1975).
2. Editions referred to in this chapter are *Philosophical Investigations* (2001a) and *Zettel* (1967).
3. I have departed from the published English versions of both of these passages by translating Wittgenstein's "*Äußerung*" as "expression". (The published English translations of Wittgenstein's late writings vacillate between translating "*Äußerung*" as "expression" and as "manifestation".)
4. See note 17.
5. The phrase "behaviourist in disguise" is from *Philosophical Investigations* §307. See also the end of §244 (which I quoted at the start of §II), where Wittgenstein's interlocutor hears him as suggesting that "the word 'pain' really means crying".
6. A philosopher who is in the grip of the interlocutor's dilemma has limited resources for understanding psychological self-ascriptions. Wittgenstein represents the situation of such a philosopher in the following passage from *Zettel*: "I expect an explosion any moment. I can't give my full attention to anything else; I look in a book, but without reading. Asked why I seem distracted or tense, I say I am expecting the explosion any moment. – Now how was it: did

this sentence describe that behaviour? But then how is the process of expecting the explosion distinguished from the process of expecting some quite different event, e.g. a particular signal? And how is the expectation of one signal distinguished from the expectation of a slightly different one? Or was my behaviour only a side-effect of the real expectation, and was that a special mental process?" (§53).

Wittgenstein aims to show that if it appears to us that our only options for understanding avowals of (say) expectation are: (i) as remarks about behaviour, or (ii) as descriptions of hidden mental processes of which observable behaviour is merely a "side-effect", then (to quote the section in the *Investigations* that immediately follows the one in which Wittgenstein's interlocutor accuses him of being "a behaviourist in disguise") "the decisive movement in the conjuring trick has [already] been made" (§308).

7. I have again translated "*Äußerung*" as "expression". (See note 3.)

8. I am simplifying things a bit. It sometimes (often, I think) happens that a mental-state self-ascription is to some extent an expression of that which it self-ascribes and to some extent a report based on evidence. In such cases, we may be said to speak with a degree of first-person authority. (For more on this point, see Finkelstein 2003: 122–6.)

9. Wittgenstein is read this way by, e.g., Tomberlin (1968: 91); Hacker (1986: 298); Fogelin (1987: 197); Rosenthal (1993: 203); and Bar-On & Long (2001: 321–2).

10. Dorit Bar-On (2004) distinguishes between "Simple Expressivism", according to which avowals are understood to be expressions of their subject matter and so not truth-apt, and "Neo-Expressivism", according to which an avowal may both express its subject matter and be true.

11. And a defender of simple expressivism about psychological self-ascriptions would encounter difficulties that closely correspond to familiar problems faced by expressivists about moral discourse.

12. This paragraph is indebted to Jacobsen (1996).

13. Thus David Rosenthal writes: "I can communicate my suspicion that the door is open either by expressing my suspicion or by explicitly telling you about it ... In saying I suspect something[,] I report, rather than express, my suspicion" (Rosenthal 1993: 200).

14. Consider the remark by Rosenthal that I quoted in the last note. Once someone has sincerely asserted, "I suspect that my wife is having an affair", could he then be rightly described as "never having expressed a suspicion that his wife was having an affair"? No; one common way to express a suspicion is by *saying* that one is suspicious.

15. Alston himself holds that non-linguistic expressions such as "squeals, looks, and tones of voice do not express feelings in anything like the sense in which they are expressed by linguistic expressions [regardless of whether the latter happen to be assertions]" (Alston 1967: 17). His position thus turns out to be very different from Wittgenstein's.

16. Although see *Philosophical Investigations* §290, which shows that Wittgenstein has no real objection to our characterizing an avowal of pain as a "description", as long as we manage to bear in mind how different the language-game of describing one's own mind is from that of describing, say, one's room.

17. In §II, I quoted a passage from *Zettel* that includes these lines: "Sentences in the third person of the present: information. In the first person present: expression. ((Not quite right.)) // The first person of the present akin to an expression" (Z

§472). Given that Wittgenstein very often characterizes psychological avowals *as* expressions, why does he qualify the point here? While I cannot be entirely certain, I can suggest an answer. The two sentences that precede "Not quite right" might give the impression that Wittgenstein thinks mental-state avowals are more like cries, winces and moans than he takes them to be. It is fairly natural to read that pair of sentences as expressing a thought that could be put as follows: "If I tell you, for example, that my sister has a headache, I am offering you a bit of information, a fact. But if I say 'I have a headache', I am not stating a fact – not saying anything true – but merely, as it were, wincing with words." I believe that it is this sort of misreading of him that Wittgenstein has in mind when he worries about the pair of sentences that precede "Not quite right" in the quoted passage.

18. Thanks to Thomas Lockhart and Joshua Scodel for helpful comments on a draft of this chapter. For more about this way of reading Wittgenstein on avowals and expression, see Finkelstein (1994, 2001, 2003).

Chronology of Wittgenstein's life

1889   Born on 26 April in Vienna, Austria.

1908   Began studying engineering at Manchester; reads Russell's *Principles of Mathematics*.

1911   Visits Frege (Frege refers him to Russell); moves to Cambridge and meets Russell, attends Trinity College at Cambridge and studies with Russell.

1912   Review of P. Coffey, *The Science of Logic* for *Cambridge Review*.

1913   Dictates *Notes on Logic*; moves to Norway.

1914   Dictates notes to G. E. Moore in Norway.

1914–18   Serves in Austrian army in the First World War and is captured in October 1917; held near Monte Cassino, Italy; completes *Tractatus Logico-Philosophicus* in August 1918.

1919–28   Leaves philosophy; studies at a Vienna college for elementary school teachers; teaches elementary school; works as a gardener at a monastery; designs a house in Vienna for one of his sisters; publishes *Tractatus* in 1922.

1929   Returns to philosophy at Cambridge; publishes "Some Remarks on Logical Form", *Proceedings of the Aristotelian Society*.

1930–35   Becomes a Fellow of Trinity College. Dictates *The Blue Book* and *The Brown Book*.

1936   Lives for over a year in Norway and begins *Philosophical Investigations*.

1938–9   Returns to Cambridge and succeeds Moore as the chair in philosophy.

1940–44   Serves as a porter at Guy's Hospital in London; works in a medical lab.

1945–7   Lectures and teaches at Cambridge.

1949   Visits Norman Malcolm in America (at Cornell).

1949–50   Returns to England; lives in Oxford.

1951   Dies on 29 April in Cambridge.

1953   *Philosophical Investigations* is published.

Bibliography

Works by Wittgenstein

Wittgenstein, L. 1953. *Philosophical Investigations*. Oxford: Blackwell.

Wittgenstein, L. 1958a. *The Blue and Brown Books*. New York: Harper Torchbooks.

Wittgenstein, L. 1958b. *Philosophical Investigations*, G. E. M. Anscombe (trans.). New York: Macmillan.

Wittgenstein, L. 1958c. *Philosophical Occasions*, 3rd edn. New York: Macmillan.

Wittgenstein, L. 1960. *Preliminary Studies for the "Philosophical Investigation", Generally Known as the Blue and Brown Books*, 2nd edn. New York: Harper & Row.

Wittgenstein, L. 1965. *The Blue and Brown Books*. New York: Harper & Row.

Wittgenstein, L. 1966. *Lectures and Conversations on Aesthetics, Psychology and Religious Belief*. Berkeley, CA: University of California Press.

Wittgenstein, L. 1967. *Zettel*, G. E. M. Anscombe & G. H. von Wright (eds), P. Winch (trans.). Berkeley, CA: University of California Press.

Wittgenstein, L. 1969. *On Certainty*, G. E. M. Anscombe & G. H. von Wright (eds), G. E. M. Anscombe & D. Paul (trans.). New York: Harper & Row.

Wittgenstein, L. 1970. *Lectures and Conversations on Aesthetics, Psychology and Religious Belief*. Berkeley, CA: University of California Press.

Wittgenstein, L. [1921] 1974. *Tractatus Logico-Philosophicus*, D. F. Pears & B. F. McGuinness (trans.). New York: Routledge & Kegan Paul.

Wittgenstein, L. 1978a. *Philosophical Grammar*, A. Kenny & R. Rhees (trans.). Berkeley, CA: University of California Press.

Wittgenstein, L. 1978b. *Remarks on the Foundations of Mathematics*, G. E. M. Anscombe & G. H. von Wright (eds), G. E. M. Anscombe (trans.). Cambridge, MA: MIT Press.

Wittgenstein, L. 1980a. *Philosophical Remarks*, R. Rhees (ed.). Chicago, IL: University of Chicago Press.

Wittgenstein, L. 1980b. *Remarks on the Philosophy of Psychology, Volume I*, G. E. M. Anscombe & G. H. von Wright (eds & trans.). Chicago, IL: University of Chicago Press.

Wittgenstein, L. 1980c. *Remarks on the Philosophy of Psychology, Volume II*, G. E. M. Anscombe & G. H. von Wright (eds & trans.). Chicago, IL: University of Chicago Press.

Wittgenstein, L. 1980d. *Culture and Value*, G. H. von Wright (with H. Nyman) (ed.), P. Winch (trans.). Oxford: Blackwell.

Wittgenstein, L. 1980e. *Wittgenstein's Lectures: Cambridge, 1932–1935, From the Notes of John King and Desmond Lee*, D. Lee (ed.). Totowa, NJ: Rowman & Littlefield.

Wittgenstein, L. 1982. *Last Writings on the Philosophy of Psychology, Volume I: Preliminary Studies for Part II of Philosophical Investigations*, G. H. von Wright & H. Nyman (eds), C. G. Luckhardt & M. A. E. Aue (trans.). Chicago, IL: University of Chicago Press.

Wittgenstein, L. 1988. *Zettel*, G. E. M. Anscombe & G. H. von Wright (eds), P. Winch (trans.). Oxford: Blackwell.

Wittgenstein, L. 1989. *Wittgenstein's Lectures, Cambridge, 1930–32*, D. Lee (ed.). Chicago, IL: University of Chicago Press.

Wittgenstein, L. 1992. *Last Writings on the Philosophy of Psychology, Volume II*, H. Nyman & G. H. von Wright (eds), M. A. E. Aue & C. G. Luckhardt (trans.). Oxford: Blackwell.

Wittgenstein, L. 1993. *Philosophical Occasions, 1912–1951*, J. C. Klagge & A. Nordman (eds). Indianapolis, IN: Hackett.

Wittgenstein, L. 2001a. *Philosophical Investigations*, 3rd edn, G. E. M. Anscombe (trans.). Oxford: Blackwell.

Wittgenstein, L. 2001b. *Wittgenstein's Lectures: Cambridge, 1932–1935, From the Notes of Alice Ambrose and Margaret Macdonald*, A. Ambrose (ed.). Amherst, NY: Prometheus Books.

Wittgenstein, L. 2005. *The Big Typescript*, M. A. E. Aue & C. G. Luckhardt (trans.). Oxford: Blackwell.

Other works

Affeldt, S. forthcoming. "On the Difficulty of Seeing Aspects and the 'Therapeutic' Reading of Wittgenstein". In *Seeing Wittgenstein Anew*, W. Day & V. J. Krebs (eds), 268–89. Cambridge: Cambridge University Press.

Aidun, D. 1982. "Wittgenstein's Philosophical Method and Aspect-Seeing". *Philosophical Investigations* 5: 106–15.

Albritton, R. 1959. "On Wittgenstein's Use of the Term 'Criterion'". *Journal of Philosophy* 56: 845–57.

Alston, W. P. 1967. "Expressing". In *Philosophy in America*, M. Black (ed.), 15–34. Ithaca, NY: Cornell University Press.

Aristotle 1987. *De Anima*, H. Lawson-Tancred (ed.). Harmondsworth: Penguin.

Armstrong, D. 1968. *A Materialist Theory of Mind*. London: Routledge & Kegan Paul.

Armstrong, D. & N. Malcolm 1984. *Consciousness & Causality*. Oxford: Blackwell.

Austin, J. L. 1961. "The Meaning of a Word". In his *Philosophical Papers*, J. O. Urmson & G. J. Warnock (eds), 55–75. Oxford: Oxford University Press.

Austin, J. L. 1962. *How to Do Things with Words*. Cambridge, MA: Harvard University Press.

Austin, J. L. 1979. *Philosophical Papers*. Oxford: Oxford University Press.

Ayer, A. J. 1946. *Language, Truth, and Logic*. New York: Dover.

Bachelard, S. 1968. *A Study of Husserl's Formal and Transcendental Logic*. Evanston, IL: Northwestern University Press.

Baker, G. (ed.) 2003. *The Voices of Wittgenstein: The Vienna Circle*. London: Routledge.

Baker, G. 2004. *Wittgenstein's Method: Neglected Aspects*, K. Morris (ed.). Oxford: Blackwell.

Baker, G. P. & P. M. S. Hacker 1980. *Wittgenstein: Understanding and Meaning; Volume 1 of an Analytical Commentary on the Philosophical Investigations*. Oxford: Blackwell.

Baker, G. P. & P. M. S. Hacker 2005. *Wittgenstein: Understanding and Meaning*, rev. edn. Oxford: Blackwell.

Bambrough, R. 1961. "Universals and Family Resemblances". *Proceedings of the Aristotelian Society* 61: 207–22.

Bar-On, D. 2004. *Speaking My Mind*. Oxford: Oxford University Press.

Bar-On, D. & D. C. Long 2001. "Avowals and First-Person Privilege". *Philosophy and Phenomenological Research* 62: 311–35.

Baz, A. forthcoming a. "In Defence of Ordinary Language Philosophy".

Baz, A. forthcoming b. "Seeing Aspects and Philosophical Difficulty". In *Handbook on the Philosophy of Wittgenstein*, M. McGinn (ed.). Oxford: Oxford University Press.

Bouwsma, O. K. 1965. "The Blue Book". In his *Philosophical Essays*, 175–202. Lincoln, NE: University of Nebraska Press.

Bouwsma, O. K. 1967. "The Blue Book". In *Ludwig Wittgenstein: The Man and His Philosophy*, K. T. Fann (ed.), 148–70. Atlantic Highlands, NJ: Humanities Press.

Canfield, J. 1981. *Wittgenstein: Language and World*. Amherst, MA: University of Massachusetts Press.

Canfield, J. (ed.) 1986. *The Philosophy of Wittgenstein, vol. 7: Criteria*. New York: Garland Publishing.

Carroll, L. 1895. "What the Tortoise Said to Achilles". *Mind* 14 (April): 278–80.

Cartmill, M. 2000. "Do Horses Gallop in Their Sleep?" *Key Reporter* 66(1): 6–9.

Cavell, S. 1976a. "Aesthetic Problems of Modern Philosophy". In his *Must We Mean What We Say?*, 73–96. Cambridge: Cambridge University Press.

Cavell, S. 1976b. "The Availability of Wittgenstein's Later Philosophy". In his *Must We Mean What We Say?*, 44–72. Cambridge: Cambridge University Press.

Cavell, S. 1979a. *The Claim of Reason*. New York: Oxford University Press.

Cavell, S. 1979b. "Excursus on Wittgenstein's Vision of Language". In his *The Claim of Reason*, 168–90. New York: Oxford University Press.

Cavell, S. 1996. "Notes and Afterthoughts". In *The Cambridge Companion to Wittgenstein*, H. Sluga & D. Stern (eds), 264–5. Cambridge: Cambridge University Press.

Cavell, S. 2005. "Philosophy the Day After Tomorrow". In his *Philosophy the Day After Tomorrow*, 111–31. Cambridge, MA: Harvard University Press.

Chihara, C. & J. Fodor 1965. "Operationalism and Ordinary Language: A Critique of Wittgenstein". *American Philosophical Quarterly* 2(4): 281–95.

Collin, F. & F. Guldmann 2005. *Meaning, Use and Truth*. Aldershot: Ashgate.

Conant, J. 2005. "Stanley Cavell's Wittgenstein". *Harvard Review of Philosophy* 13(1): 50–64.

Cook, J. & R. Read 2010. "Wittgenstein and Literary Language". In *A Companion to the Philosophy of Literature*, G. Hagberg & W. Jost (eds). Oxford: Wiley-Blackwell.

Coulter, J. & W. Sharrock 2007. *Brain, Mind and Human Behavior in Contemporary Cognitive Science: Critical Assessments of the Philosophy of Psychology*. New York: Edwin Mellen Press.

Crary, A. 2002. "The Happy Truth: J. L. Austin's How To Do Things With Words". *Inquiry* 45(1) (March): 59–80.

Crary, A. & R. Read (eds) 2000. *The New Wittgenstein*. London: Routledge.

Crawshay-Williams, R. 1957. *Methods and Criteria of Reasoning*. London: Routledge & Kegan Paul.

Diamond, C. 1991. "Introduction". In her *The Realistic Spirit: Wittgenstein, Philosophy and the Mind*, 1–12. Cambridge, MA: MIT Press.

Diamond, C. 1992. "Realism and the Realistic Spirit". In *The Realistic Spirit: Wittgenstein, Philosophy and the Mind*, 39–73. Cambridge, MA: MIT Press.

Dilman, I. 1978–9. "Universals: Bambrough on Wittgenstein". *Proceedings of the Aristotelian Society* 79: 35–58.

Ewing, A. C. 1971. "The Problem of Universals". *Philosophical Quarterly* 29(84): 207–16.

Finkelstein, D. 1994. *Speaking My Mind: First-Person Authority and Conscious Mentality*. Pittsburgh, PA: University of Pittsburgh.

Finkelstein, D. 2001. "Wittgenstein's 'Plan for the Treatment of Psychological Concepts'". In *Wittgenstein in America*, T. McCarthy & S. Stidd (eds), 215–36. Oxford: Oxford University Press.

Finkelstein, D. 2003. *Expression and the Inner*. Cambridge, MA: Harvard University Press.

Fischer, E. 2005. "Austin on Sense-Data: Ordinary Language Analysis as 'Therapy'". *Grazer Philosophische Studien* 70: 67–99.

Floyd, J. 2006. "Homage to Vienna: Feyerabend on Wittgenstein (and Austin and Quine)". In *Paul Feyerabend (1924–1994): Ein Philosoph aus Wien*, K. R. Fischer & F. Stadler (eds), vol. 14, 99–152. Vienna: Institut Wiener Kreis.

Fogelin, R. J. 1987. *Wittgenstein*. London: Routledge.

Fogelin, R. J. 1995. *Wittgenstein*, 2nd edn. New York: Routledge.

Fox, C. 2006. "Wittgenstein and Myths of Meaning". Dissertation. University of Illinois at Chicago, Chicago, IL.

Frege, G, 1972. *Conceptual Notation*, T. W. Bynum (ed. & trans.). Oxford: Clarendon Press.

Frege, G. 1977. *Logical Investigations*, P. T. Geach & R. H. Stoothoff (trans.). New Haven, CT: Yale University Press.

Frege, G. 1980. *Foundations of Arithmetic*, J. L. Austin (trans.). Oxford: Blackwell.

Frege, G. 1997. *Grundgesetze*, vol. II. In *The Frege Reader*, M. Beaney (ed.). Oxford: Blackwell.

Genova, J. 1995. *Wittgenstein: A Way of Seeing*. London: Routledge.

Gert, H. 1995. "Family Resemblance and Criteria". *Synthese* 105: 177–90.

Glock, H.-J. 1989. *A Wittgenstein Dictionary*. Oxford: Blackwell.

Goldfarb, W. 1983. "I Want You to Bring Me a Slab: Remarks on the Opening Sections of the *Philosophical Investigations*". *Synthese* 56: 265–82.

Goldfarb, W. 2007. "I Want You to Bring Me a Slab: Remarks on the Opening Sections of the *Philosophical Investigations*". Reprinted in *Wittgenstein's Philosophical Investigations*, M. Williams (ed.), 17–33. Lanham, MD: Rowman & Littlefield.

Griffin, N. 1974. "Wittgenstein, Universals, and Family Resemblance". *Canadian Journal of Philosophy* 3(4): 635–51.

Griffiths, P. 1997. *What Emotions Really Are: The Problem of Psychological Categories*. Chicago, IL: University of Chicago Press.

Guetti, J. 1993."Idling Rules". *Philosophical Investigations* 16(3) (Summer): 179–97.

Hacker, P. M. S. 1986. *Insight and Illusion: Themes in the Philosophy of Wittgenstein.* Oxford: Oxford University Press.

Hacker, P. M. S. 1993. *Wittgenstein, Meaning and Mind: Volume 3 of an Analytical Commentary on the Philosophical Investigations, Part I: Essays.* Oxford: Blackwell.

Hacker, P. M. S. 1996. *Wittgenstein's Place in Twentieth Century Analytical Philosophy.* Oxford: Blackwell.

Hacker, P. M. S. 2001a. *Wittgenstein: Connections and Controversies.* Oxford: Oxford University Press.

Hacker, P. M. S. 2001b. "Philosophy". In *Wittgenstein: A Critical Reader*, H.-J. Glock (ed.), 322–47. Oxford: Blackwell.

Hallett, G. 1967. *Wittgenstein's Definition of Meaning as Use.* New York: Fordham University Press.

Hallett, G. 1977. *A Companion to Wittgenstein's "Philosophical Investigations".* Ithaca, NY: Cornell University Press.

Heidegger, M. 1968. *What is Called Thinking?* New York: Harper & Row.

Hertzberg, L. 2001. "The Sense is Where You Find It". In *Wittgenstein in America*, T. McCarthy & S. Stidd (eds), 90–103. Oxford: Oxford University Press.

Humphrey, N. 1986. *The Inner Eye.* London: Faber.

Hunter, J. F. M. 1971. "Wittgenstein on Meaning and Use". In *Essays on Wittgenstein*, E. D. Klemke (ed.), 374–93. Urbana, IL: University of Illinois Press.

Hutchinson, P. 2007. "What's the Point of Elucidation?" *Metaphilosophy* 38(5): 691–713.

Hutchinson, P. 2008. *Shame and Philosophy.* Basingstoke: Palgrave Macmillan.

Hutchinson, P. & R. Read 2008. "Towards a Perspicuous Presentation of 'Perspicuous Presentation'". *Philosophical Investigations* 31(2): 141–60.

Hylton, P. 1990. *Bertrand Russell and the Emergence of Analytic Philosophy.* Oxford: Oxford University Press.

Jacobsen, R. 1996. "Wittgenstein on Self-Knowledge and Self-Expression". *Philosophical Quarterly* 46(182): 12–30.

Johnson, A. B. 1959. "A Theory of Language". In his *A Treatise on Language*. Berkeley, CA: University of California Press.

Johnston, P. 1994. *Rethinking the Inner.* London: Routledge.

Kant, I. 1997. *Critique of Pure Reason*, P. Guyer & A. W. Wood (trans.). Cambridge: Cambridge University Press.

Kenny, A. 1967. "Criterion". In *Encyclopedia of Philosophy, Volume 2*, P. Edwards (ed.), 258–61. New York: Macmillan.

Kenny, A. 1984. *The Legacy of Wittgenstein.* Oxford: Blackwell.

Khatchadourian, H. 1958. "Common Names and 'Family Resemblance'". *Philosophy and Phenomenological Research* 18(3): 341–58.

Klagge, J. & A. Nordmann (eds) 2003. *Ludwig Wittgenstein: Public and Private Occasions.* Lanham, MD: Rowman & Littlefield.

Kripke, S. 1980. *Naming and Necessity.* Cambridge, MA: Harvard University Press.

Kripke, S. 1982. *Wittgenstein on Rules and Private Language.* Cambridge, MA: Harvard University Press.

Kuusela, O. 2008. *The Struggle Against Dogmatism.* Cambridge, MA: Harvard University Press.

Locke, J. [1690] 1975. *An Essay Concerning Human Understanding.* Oxford: Oxford University Press.

Loomis, E. 1999. "Necessity, the A Priori, and the Standard Meter". *Synthese* 121: 291–307.

Loomis, E. 2007. "Criteria and Defeasibility: When Good Evidence is not Good Enough". In *Perspicuous Presentations: Essays on Wittgenstein's Philosophy of Psychology*, D. Moyal-Sharrock (ed.), 236–57. New York: Palgrave Macmillan.

Luckhardt, C. G. 1977. "Wittgenstein: Investigations 50". *Southern Journal of Philosophy* 15 (Spring): 81–90.

Lugg, A. 2004. *Wittgenstein's "Investigations" 1–133: A Guide and Interpretation*. New York: Routledge.

Lycan, W. G. 1971. "Non-Inductive Evidence: Recent Work on Wittgenstein's 'Criteria'". *American Philosophical Quarterly* 8: 109–25.

Lycan, W. G. 1996. *Consciousness and Experience*. Cambridge, MA: Harvard University Press.

Malcolm, N. 1954. "Wittgenstein's Philosophical Investigations". *Philosophical Review* 63(4): 530–59.

Malcolm, N. 1963. *Knowledge and Certainty*. Englewood Cliffs, NJ: Prentice Hall.

Malcolm, N. 1995. "Kripke and the Standard Meter". In *Wittgensteinian Themes: Essays 1978–1989*, G. H. von Wright (ed.), 56–65. Ithaca, NY: Cornell University Press.

McCloskey, H. J. 1964. "The Philosophy of Linguistic Analysis and the Problem of Universals". *Philosophy and Phenomenological Research* 24(3): 329–38.

McDowell, J. 1982. "Criteria, Defeasibility, and Knowledge". *Proceedings of the British Academy* 68(1): 455–79.

McDowell, J. 2009. "How Not to Read *Philosophical Investigations*: Brandom's Wittgenstein". In his *The Engaged Intellect: Philosophical Essays*, 96–112. Cambridge, MA: Harvard University Press.

McGinn, M. 1998. "Criterion". In *Routledge Encyclopedia of Philosophy*, E. Craig (ed.), 711–14. New York: Routledge.

McGuinness, B. F. (ed.) 1979. *Wittgenstein and the Vienna Circle*. Oxford: Blackwell.

Merleau-Ponty, M. 1962. *Phenomenology of Perception*. London: Routledge.

Minar, E. 1995. "Feeling at Home in Language (What Makes Reading *Philosophical Investigations* Possible?)". *Synthese* 102(3): 413–52.

Monk, R. 1990. *Ludwig Wittgenstein: The Duty of Genius*. New York: Free Press.

Moore, G. E. 1954. "Wittgenstein's Lectures in 1930–33". *Mind* 63(251): 289–316.

Morris, K. 2007. "Wittgenstein's Method: Ridding People of Philosophical Prejudices". In *Wittgenstein and His Interpreters: Essays in Memory of Gordon Baker*, G. Kahane, E. Kanterian & O. Kuusela (eds), 66–87. Oxford: Blackwell.

Mulhall, S. 1990. *On Being in the World*. London: Routledge.

Mulhall, S. 2001. *Inheritance and Originality*. Oxford: Oxford University Press.

Nietzsche, F. [1885] 1978. *Thus Spoke Zarathustra*, W. Kaufmann (trans.). Harmondsworth: Penguin.

Nowell-Smith, P. H. 1962. "Contextual Implication and Ethical Theory". *Proceedings of the Aristotelian Society* Supp. vol. 36: 1–18.

Pleasants, N. 1999. *Wittgenstein and the Idea of a Critical Social Theory*. London: Routledge.

Pollock, W. J. 2004. "Wittgenstein on the Standard Metre". *Philosophical Investigations* 27(2): 148–57.

Price, H. H. 1932. *Perception*. London: Methuen.

Read, R. 2000. "Wittgenstein and Marx on 'Philosophical Language'". *Essays in Philosophy Essays in Philosophy, A Biannual Journal* 1(2). www.humboldt.edu/~essays/read.html (accessed March 2010).

Read, R. 2004. "Throwing Away 'The Bedrock'". *Proceedings of the Aristotelian Society* 105(1): 81–98.

Read, R. 2007a. *Applying Wittgenstein*. London: Continuum.

Read, R. 2007b. *Philosophy for Life*. London: Continuum.

Rhees, R. (ed.) 1965. *The Blue and Brown Books*. New York: Harper.

Rhees, R. 1970a. *Discussions of Wittgenstein*. London: Routledge & Kegan Paul.

Rhees, R. 1970b. "Wittgenstein's Builders". In his *Discussions of Wittgenstein*, 71–85. New York: Schocken Books.

Richter, D. 2004. *Historical Dictionary of Wittgenstein's Philosophy*. Lanham, MD: Scarecrow Press.

Rosenthal, D. 1993. "Thinking that One Thinks". In *Consciousness*, M. Davies & G. W. Humphreys (eds), 197–223. Oxford: Blackwell.

Russell, B. 1912. *The Problems of Philosophy*. Oxford: Oxford University Press.

Russell, B. [1917] 2004. "The Relation of Sense-Data to Physics". In his *Mysticism and Logic*, 113–41. Totowa, NJ: Barnes & Noble Books.

Russell, B. 1956. "Philosophy of Logical Atomism". In his *Logic and Knowledge*, 177–281. New York: Routledge.

Ryle, G. 1979. "Bouwsma's Wittgenstein". In his *On Thinking*. Oxford: Blackwell.

Salmon, N. 1988. "How to Measure the Standard Metre". *Proceedings of the Aristotelian Society* 88: 193–217.

Savigny, E. V. 1990. "The Last Word on *Philosophical Investigations* 43a". *Australasian Journal of Philosophy* 68(2): 241–3.

Scruton, R. 1974. *Art and Imagination: A Study in the Philosophy of Mind*. London: Methuen.

Shoemaker, S. 1963. *Self-Knowledge and Self-Identity*. Ithaca, NY: Cornell University Press.

Simon, M. 1969. "When is a Resemblance a Family Resemblance?" *Mind* 78(311): 408–16.

Sluga, H. 2006. "Family Resemblance". *Grazer Philosophische Studien* 71: 1–21.

Stern, D. 2004. *Wittgenstein's "Philosophical Investigations": An Introduction*. Cambridge: Cambridge University Press.

Stevenson, C. L. 1944. *Ethics and Language*. New Haven, CT: Yale University Press.

Stroud, B. 2000. "Mind, Meaning, Practice". In his *Meaning, Understanding, and Practice*, 170–93. New York: Oxford University Press.

Teichman, J. 1969. "Universals and Common Properties". *Analysis* 29(5): 162–5.

Tomberlin, J. E. 1968. "The Expression Theory of Avowals". *Philosophy and Phenomenological Research* 29(1): 91–6.

Travis, C. 1989. *The Uses of Sense: Wittgenstein's Philosophy of Language*. New York: Oxford University Press.

Uschanov, T. P. 2001. "The Strange Death of Ordinary Language Philosophy". www.helsinki.fi/~tuschano/writings/strange/ (accessed March 2010).

von Wright, G. H. 1982. *Wittgenstein*. Oxford: Blackwell.

Waismann, F. 1979. *Ludwig Wittgenstein and the Vienna Circle*. Oxford: Blackwell.

Weitz, M. 1956. "The Role of Theory in Aesthetics". *Journal of Aesthetics and Art Criticism* 15(1): 27–35.

Wennerberg, H. 1967. "The Concept of Family Resemblance in Wittgenstein's Later Philosophy". *Theoria* 33: 107–32.

Wilson, B. 1998. *Wittgenstein's "Philosophical Investigations": A Guide*. Edinburgh: Edinburgh University Press.

Witherspoon, E. 2000. "Conceptions of Nonsense in Carnap and Wittgenstein". In *The New Wittgenstein*, A. Crary & R. Read (eds), 315–70. London: Routledge.

Wright, C. 1982. "Anti-realist Semantics: The Role of Criteria". In *Idealism Past and Present*, G. Vesey (ed.), 225–48. Cambridge: Cambridge University Press.

Index